Praise for

GET A FINANCIAL LIFE

"Kobliner's done it again! *Get a Financial Life* gives clear and straightforward advice on how to manage your money—even in a financial meltdown. A must-read for twenty- and thirty-somethings who want to be fiscally smart and financially secure."
— Soledad O'Brien, anchor, CNN

"Beth Kobliner's book provides a much-needed and sensible guide."
— Paul A. Volcker, former chairman, Federal Reserve Board

"One of the best guides to help young people get a handle on money matters."
— Burton G. Malkiel, Chemical Bank Chairman's Professor
of Economics, Princeton University; author,
A Random Walk Down Wall Street

"If the financial crisis seems frightening to a grizzled Wall Street vet like me, I can only imagine the panic of people in their twenties and thirties, who have never seen a severe recession and are trying to save money while also paying for school, getting married, or starting a family. Stop worrying and start reading Beth Kobliner's *Get a Financial Life,* the best book to help you understand your money in the toughest financial market since the Great Depression. She's got it all: from what Wall Street's meltdown means to you, to how to keep your savings safe, to getting the best bang for the insurance and student-loan bucks. Stop dreading your finances and get informed!"
— Jim Cramer, *Mad Money*, CNBC

"A highly readable and substantial guide to the grown-up worlds of money and business. Backed up by bibliographies, source lists, and useful phone numbers, this book could be tucked into one of those ubiquitous backpacks to guide novices through the thickets of apartment rentals, mortgage applications, taxes, and more. Its strength is in explaining both the principles and the practicalities involved in each chunk of the landscape."
— *The New York Times*

"*Get A Financial Life* gives you the essential information you need to get your finances in order as you're starting your career. The rest is up to you. Educate yourself, get motivated, and get your finances in shape now by reading this book."

—Sharon Epperson, personal finance correspondent, CNBC; author of *The Big Payoff*

"Smart, thorough—a tremendously useful guide to all the essentials of sound personal finance."

—Eric Gelman, *Fortune*

"A daring book . . . A life's worth of smart financial advice."

—*Newsweek*

"With numerous insights, this fine book demonstrates that, through discipline and enterprise, anyone can win their financial independence."

—Tom Gardner, cofounder of The Motley Fool

"Beth Kobliner is telling you it's time to smell the latte. In *Get a Financial Life,* Kobliner serves a rich, smooth brew of common sense on everything from paying off your student loans to saving for (gasp) your future. The advice is thoughtful, precise, and up-to-date. But the simple, step-by-step explanations make getting a financial life easier than steaming the perfect froth on a cappuccino."

—Saul Hansell, *The New York Times*

"Shaw said youth is wasted on the young. I suspect the Kobliner financial wisdoms will work out well at all our ages."

—Paul A. Samuelson, Institute Professor Emeritus, MIT; Nobel laureate in economics

"An eminently digestible resource. Buying this book right now is probably one of the best—and cheapest—investments."

—*Time Out New York*

"Beth Kobliner has written one of the best personal finance books currently available. *Get a Financial Life* is 'must' reading for young adults—and has a lot of solid information for the forty-and-over crowd as well."

—*The Midwest Book Review*

"If getting a financial life is terrifying, Kobliner eases readers into it gently. . . . Financial books generally aren't light reading, but this one is easily digestible."

—*Kiplinger's*

GET A
FINANCIAL
LIFE

PERSONAL FINANCE IN YOUR TWENTIES AND THIRTIES

BETH KOBLINER

A FIRESIDE BOOK

Published by Simon & Schuster

New York   London   Toronto

Sydney

FIRESIDE
A Division of Simon & Schuster, Inc.
1230 Avenue of the Americas
New York, NY 10020

This Fireside trade paperback edition March 2009

FIRESIDE and colophon are registered trademarks of Simon & Schuster, Inc.

For information about special discounts for bulk purchases, please contact Simon & Schuster Special Sales at 1-800-456-6798 or business@simonandschuster.com.

Designed by Claudia Martinez

Manufactured in the United States of America

10 9 8 7

Library of Congress Cataloging-in-Publication Data

Kobliner, Beth
Get a financial life : personal finance in your twenties and thirties /
Beth Kobliner.—3rd ed.
     p.   cm.
"A Fireside book."
Includes bibliographical references and index.
1. Finance, personal.   2. Young adults—Finance, Personal.   I. Title.
HG179.K59   2009
332.0240084'2—dc22   2008046645

ISBN-13: 978-0-7432-6436-5
ISBN-10:   0-7432-6436-3

To my parents, Harold and Shirley Kobliner,
who taught me how to handle money,
and to Sylvia Porter,
who gave me the opportunity to write about it.

CONTENTS

INTRODUCTION

I F YOU'RE LIKE a lot of people in their
twenties and thirties, you're worried about
money. And who can blame you? The nation's finances haven't
been this bad since the Great Depression, and the only saving grace
is that you probably didn't have all that much money to invest in
the stock market to begin with.

So how do you get on the right track when the whole financial
world is dealing with the wreckage of the Great Recession? It's a
challenge, for sure. But even in these tough times and even without
a big income, you *can* take control of your financial life. Now more
that ever, you need a playbook—a guide that teaches you the skills
and strategies of managing money. *This is that playbook.*

When I wrote the first version of *Get a Financial Life* more than
ten years ago, I was told that people in their twenties and thirties
don't think about their finances and the book would never sell. To
everyone's surprise—including mine—it became a *New York Times*
bestseller and is now in its fourteenth printing. Every week I receive
emails (in the '90s, I actually got letters) from readers, many of
whom are now in their forties, who say that this book changed their
lives. The reason, I think, is that the book makes clear that there are
just a few key steps you need to get out of debt, start saving, and
plan for the future. Once you nail these easy concepts, you'll be on
your way—in good times or bad.

This all-new version is totally rewritten to reflect what's going on in the world today. And unlike most personal finance books, this one focuses exclusively on what you need to know in your twenties and thirties—whether you earn $20,000 or $200,000, are single or married, financially flush or living paycheck to paycheck.

You'll learn how to eke out the most you can from your salary. You'll find out how to dig yourself out of debt. You'll discover where to stash your cash. You'll find the cheapest credit cards, car loans, and student loans. *Get a Financial Life* will help you understand and take advantage of automated savings plans, 401(k)s, and IRAs. You'll get no-nonsense, unbiased advice on how to select the best mutual funds. You'll pick up tax strategies that can save you hundreds of dollars a year. You'll learn how to avoid outrageous bank fees and how to determine which types of insurance you need—and which are a waste of money. You'll get well-vetted websites for every aspect of your financial life.

You'll get answers to specific questions that may have slowed you down in the past: What's my credit score and how can I improve it? Do I need a mortgage broker? How much should I contribute to my company's retirement plan? How do I figure out when it's time to stop renting and try to buy? Should I lease or buy a car? Where can I find help if I can't pay my bills? Also, if you're one of the millions of people in their twenties and thirties who are in the military (or recently finished serving), you'll get the details on education, home buying, and other special deals.

One more thing: If the thought of reading an entire book on personal finance leaves you cold, don't worry. Chapter 1 provides quick summaries of the most important steps. And throughout the book, "Financial Cramming" review sections highlight key concepts. So take the plunge, and read on. There's no better time for a personal finance overhaul. It's a lot easier than you might think— that is, if you take advantage of the one major benefit you still have on your side: *time.*

CRIB NOTES

A Cheat Sheet for Time-Pressed
Readers Who Need Help Now

I F YOU'RE OVERWHELMED by the idea of delving into chapter after chapter on personal finance, this section's for you. The advice below cuts to the chase and puts you on the road to a solid financial life. Adopting even one or two of these strategies will leave you ahead of the game, whether the economy is soaring or suffering.

Of course, as someone's mother once said, cheaters only cheat themselves. And while this chapter is a good launching pad, ignoring the remaining nine chapters is a little like relying on the *Cliffs-Notes* version of *Macbeth*: You'll get the basic plot line but never understand what all the fuss is about. Still, the following will give you the basics. I've tried to list them in rough order of importance, but your priorities will depend on your own situation.

1. Insure yourself against financial ruin.

There's been lots of talk recently about the health insurance crisis, but not much action. As a result, nearly 20 million people (18 to 34 years old) are uninsured. If you're one of them, you need to figure out a way to get some coverage. And even if you're insured through your job, you need to be smart about the choices you make. The right health insurance will protect you in case you have a serious accident or illness and guarantee that you don't bankrupt yourself or your family if you are beset with major medical problems. For that reason, health insurance should be your number one financial priority.

If you work for a company that offers employees health insurance, you're lucky; participating in your employer's group plan will almost always cost you much less than buying a policy on your own. You may be given more than one type of plan to choose from through your employer; make sure you consider not only the price but also the extent of the coverage you will receive. If, for example, you're thinking about joining a type of plan called a **health maintenance organization (HMO)**, inquire about exactly what is covered, ask about the procedure for seeing specialists, and find out what happens if you want to visit a doctor who doesn't participate in the plan. Before you sign up for any plan, talk to coworkers about their experiences with the various options.

If the company you work for does not offer health insurance, you'll have to pay for it yourself. If you recently graduated from college, see if you can extend coverage from your parents' plan for a few years. (Some states will let you stay on your parents' insurance until you turn 26; New Jersey is the only state that will give you until age 30.) If not, see if there are any organizations you can join—a trade association, for example—that will allow you to purchase health insurance at a group rate. If you're job hunting, at the very least get so-called "temporary" coverage that will protect you from true medical disasters. If all else fails, you'll probably need to purchase a policy on your own. Go online to compare prices for individual policies—either temporary coverage or longer term—from sites like eHealthInsurance (www.ehealthinsurance.com) and Net-Quote (www.netquote.com), as well as your local Blue Cross/Blue Shield company (www.bluecares.com).

For additional tips on purchasing all types of insurance, see Chapter 8.

2. Pay off your debt the smart way.

More often than not, the smartest financial move you can make is to take any savings you have (above and beyond money you need for essentials like rent, food, and health insurance) and pay off your high-rate loans. The reason is simple: You can "earn" more by paying off a loan than you can by saving and investing. Paying off a credit card that has a 16% interest rate is equivalent to earning 16% on an investment, *guaranteed*—an extremely attractive rate of return. (Actually it's even better than that; it's the equivalent of earning 16% *after taxes*.) If you want a full explanation of this concept, turn to p. 34. Otherwise, take my word for it.

If you can't pay off your high-rate debt immediately, take steps to reduce the interest rate you pay. Start by simply calling your credit card company and asking them to lower the rate. Also, see if you can qualify for one of the lower-rate cards listed on websites like www.credit.com, www.cardtrak.com, and www.lowcards.com.

If you have several different types of debt—say, a credit card balance on a card with a 14% interest rate, a car loan with an 8% rate, and a student loan at 5%—pay off the loan with the highest interest rate first. One strategy you may want to consider is asking your student loan servicer to stretch out your student loan payments over 15, 20, or even 30 years instead of 10 years. This will reduce your monthly student loan payment and leave you with extra cash, which you can use to pay off your credit card balance faster. Once you've gotten rid of your credit card debt, increase the payments on your auto loan. After you wipe out that loan too, increase your student loan payments to at least their initial levels.

The only time it doesn't make sense to kill your debt is when the interest rate you're being charged is *lower* than the rate you can receive on an investment. If, for example, you have a special student loan with a 3% rate and no other debt, you'd be better off maintaining your usual payment schedule on the loan and putting your cash into an investment that pays you an after-tax rate greater than 3%, if you can find it.

For detailed information on credit cards, auto loans, student loans, and home equity loans, see Chapter 3.

3. Start contributing to a tax-favored retirement savings plan.

You may be scared to part with your money right now, or you may just think retirement is so far away, why bother? But here's the reality. Saving money in a retirement plan is one of the smartest things you can do when you're young. If you're lucky enough to work for a company that offers a retirement savings plan like a **401(k)**, you should take advantage of it. There are several reasons to participate in a 401(k). For starters, many employers will match a portion of the amount you put into such a plan. That means the company will contribute a set amount—say, 50 cents—for every dollar you contribute, up to a specified percentage of your salary. That's free money, equivalent to an immediate 50% return! (In fact, if your company offers such a fabulous matching deal, you should probably contribute to the plan even before paying off your credit card debt.) In addition, the federal government allows you to delay paying taxes on the money you contribute to a retirement savings plan until you withdraw that money. That translates into an immediate tax break of hundreds of dollars each year. If, for example, you contribute $1,000 to a 401(k), you will reduce your taxable income by $1,000. If you're in the 25% tax bracket, that's a savings of $250.

Be forewarned that you're going to hear horror stories from people who lost huge amounts of money in their 401(k)s. But the benefits of matching and tax-deferred growth are so huge that this is still the best deal out there. And, if you're really nervous, there are ways to invest in your 401(k) without losing any of the money you contribute. (Learn all about this in Chapter 6).

Although you won't be able to withdraw your money until you reach age 59½ without paying a penalty, many plans allow employees to borrow against their retirement savings at favorable rates. If you switch jobs, you may be able to move your 401(k) money into your new employer's plan (or transfer it into something called an individual retirement account; see below).

Your employer might have already signed you up for its 401(k). If not, contact your employee benefits office and ask how you can have a set percentage of each paycheck automatically transferred into your company plan. Many companies allow you to do this online. Try to at least contribute the maximum amount for which you're eligible to receive matching funds.

If you aren't lucky enough to work for an employer who offers a 401(k) or a similar company retirement plan, you should start investing in an **individual retirement account (IRA)**. The most you can contribute to an IRA as of 2009 is $5,000 annually; if at all possible, contribute the maximum amount every year.

IRAs don't provide matching contributions, so putting money in an IRA is somewhat less pressing than enrolling in a company-sponsored plan that offers a match. Also, unlike a 401(k), an IRA does not permit borrowing. That said, certain IRAs known as Roth IRAs do offer a special benefit: You are allowed to withdraw the money you contribute to them at any time. (You're not allowed to withdraw the interest you earned on the money you contributed until after you turn 59½.)

Bottom line: Max out your company's 401(k) up until the matching limit if you have one. If not, go with an IRA.

For all your questions on tax-favored retirement savings plans, see Chapter 6.

4. Build an emergency cushion using an automatic savings plan.

If you find it impossible to save any money, you're not alone. But once you've gotten rid of your high-rate debt, taken care of Crib Notes 1 and 2, and started on Crib Note 3, it's time to begin stashing away three months' worth of living expenses in a safe spot.

Your safest choice is a bank savings account. You can have the money automatically withdrawn from each paycheck and funneled into your savings. That's a relatively painless way to force yourself to accumulate money.

A second choice is a special type of investment called a **money market fund**. Money market funds have historically been considered almost as safe as bank savings accounts and tend to pay higher interest rates. To find a money fund, check out websites like www.bankrate.com and www.imoneynet.com, which provide a list of the highest interest rates currently being offered. You can set up an automatic transfer from your checking account once or twice a month so it's as easy as saving in a bank savings account. (For virtually everything you need to know about money market funds, see Chapter 5.)

No matter what type of automatic savings plan you choose, focus on your goal of at least three months' worth of expenses. To figure out that amount, use the worksheet (Figure 2–2) in Chapter 2.

5. Consider investing in stock and bond funds.

Once you have your three-month savings cushion in place, you can continue putting money into low-risk bank accounts and money market funds, or you can choose to get more aggressive with your investments. The advantage of stocks and bonds is that they've historically tended to earn more for investors over long periods of time, allowing them higher returns to stay ahead of inflation. (For a discussion of inflation and why you'll need to worry about it, see Chapter 5.)

The downside of stocks and bonds is that they're riskier than money market funds. Translation: You can lose money by investing in them. Only you can decide how much risk you're willing to take for the chance to earn higher returns over time, but one common approach has been to put about half of the holdings you don't plan to touch for many years into stocks, one-third into bonds, and the rest in money market funds. This is a mix you may want to consider for your retirement savings plans, although some experts recommend putting somewhat more into stocks for IRAs and 401(k)s.

If you do decide to put some of your money in stocks and bonds, do so by investing in stock mutual funds and bond mutual funds. A **mutual fund** is a type of investment that pools together the money of thousands of people. It's headed by a fund manager, who invests the entire sum in a variety of stocks, bonds, and/or money market instruments. (To find out exactly what these are, you'll need to read Chapter 5.) Avoid investing in funds with **a load,** which is the commission that some mutual fund companies charge each time you put money in or take money out of a fund. They don't perform any better on average than no-load funds, so there's no point in paying extra for them. I recommend that you consider only **no-load** mutual funds with low **expenses.** Expenses are the annual fees charged by the fund and can take a huge bite out of your investment returns if you're not careful.

Although stock funds are considered somewhat riskier than bond funds, they have also performed somewhat better over long periods of time. If you decide to invest in a stock fund, I recommend you consider a type known as a **stock index fund**. "Index" means it tracks the performance of a recognized basket of stocks, such as the Standard & Poor's 500 Index.

Two companies that offer index funds with no loads are Vanguard (www.vanguard.com; 800-662-7447) and T. Rowe Price (www.troweprice.com; 800-541-6066). Vanguard has some of the lowest fees and the largest selection of index funds, but you'll generally need at least $3,000 to open an account there if you want to invest in its index funds. (It also has a special fund that only requires $1,000 to start; see p. 132 for more details.) T. Rowe Price has higher fees (still lower than the industry average) but allows investors to get started with a minimum of $50 a month automatically siphoned out of a checking account.

Bonds are generally less risky than stocks but riskier than money market funds and you can still lose money with them. Holding bonds as well as stocks will help to diversify your investments, reducing your overall risk. Vanguard and T. Rowe Price offer no-load bond funds as well. While there are several different types of bond funds, a reasonable approach would be to choose a **bond index fund** that invests in government securities or highly rated corporations.

To learn more about bond funds, stock funds, index funds, and investing in general—you guessed it—you'll have to read Chapter 5.

6. Find out your credit score and improve it.

A **credit score** is a number that tells lenders whether or not you're a good risk. It's basically a mathematical representation of your financial behavior, and it's contained in files at three national credit agencies: Equifax, TransUnion, and Experian. These files, which include information received by the agencies from your various creditors, are called your **credit reports**. You're legally entitled to one free report from each of the agencies every year. You should get them at www.annualcreditreport.com and check to make sure all the information included about you and your financial behavior is accurate.

You can think of your credit score as the SAT score of your financial abilities; the only difference is that unlike your SATs, your credit score is being recalculated all the time—and will have a huge impact on your life forever. If you want to qualify for a low-rate credit card, car loan, or home loan, and if you want to rent an apartment, get insurance, or change cell phone plans, your credit score will matter. To find out your credit scores from all three agencies (they often vary), go to www.myfico.com. It costs about $50 for all three. (See Chapter 3 for details.)

Once you've collected all this information, take steps to make sure your score is as good as it can be. The higher your score, the more likely you are to get a lower interest rate on a loan. The biggest component of your credit score is your track record for making on-time payments, followed by the amount of credit you're using and the length of your credit history. One of the easiest, most foolproof ways to keep your score in good shape is to pay all of your bills automatically, which you can do online.

7. Think about buying a house or apartment.

Despite all the havoc in the housing market, at some point in the next few years you may start to feel that it's time to purchase a home of your own. Deciding that it makes sense to buy involves more than simply comparing your monthly rent with the monthly mortgage payments you'd make as an owner. A whole range of financial factors, including the tax break you'll get from buying, the fees you'll pay when you buy, and how long you plan to live in the new home, should enter into your decision. For a discussion of some of these factors and ways to analyze your own situation, see Chapter 7.

If you do decide that it's time to buy, you may wonder if it's really as hard as they say to get a home loan, also known as a **mortgage,** these days. The answer depends on your situation. One of the toughest obstacles is coming up with the down payment required by the lender. You will likely need to have an amount equal to at least 10% of the purchase price of the home to qualify for a mortgage. In addition to that cash, you will need a good credit score and to be able to prove that your salary is high enough to make the monthly mortgage payments. Mortgage lenders also want to make sure that your other debts are manageable.

Once you are ready to buy, your next step is to look at sites like www.hsh.com, www.bankrate.com, and www.freeratesearch.com to find the best mortgage deal you can get. It's also a smart idea to check with your local bank or credit union—sometimes the best home loan deals are right in your own backyard.

But what if you're eager to buy and can't come up with the full down payment or don't have great credit? All is not lost. One option, for example, is to look into the Federal Housing Administration (FHA) loan program. FHA loans require only a 3.5% down payment and they're usually easier to qualify for, but you may end up paying somewhat more in interest and fees over the long run. Contact a lender or your local Housing and Urban Development office (www.hud.gov) for more information on FHA loans. You can also call your state housing office to see if it offers any low down payment mortgage options for which you're eligible. The advantage of these state programs is that they typically charge a lower interest rate than you can get on a bank mortgage. (For the website and phone number of your state housing office, see pp. 186–87.)

If you don't qualify for any of these programs, don't give up. Make it your goal to spend the next one to two years improving your credit score (by paying all your bills on time) and saving up for that down payment. You'd be surprised how quickly you can build your credit record.

For more housing-related tips for buyers and renters, see Chapter 7.

8. Get smart about income tax.

Want to stretch your paycheck further? One way is to decrease the portion that goes to Uncle Sam by taking as many tax deductions as you're eligible for. Deductions are specific expenses that the government allows you to subtract from your income before calculating the amount of tax you're required to pay. Taking advantage of these tax deductions is simple.

The easiest approach is to take the **standard deduction,** which is simply a fixed dollar amount ($5,700 for singles or $11,400 for couples in 2009) that you subtract from your income. But you might pay even less if you **itemize** your deductions instead. Itemizing means listing separately the specific items that are deductible under the tax laws and then subtracting their total cost from your income.

If you choose to itemize deductions, you'll have to fill out a tax form called a 1040 (also known as the long form). You'll then have to list your deductions on an attachment to Form 1040 called Schedule A. Among the types of expenses you may be allowed to deduct are state and local taxes you've paid (*or* sales taxes you've paid), charitable donations, and certain moving, job-hunting, business travel, and educational expenses. To figure out whether you should take the standard deduction or itemize, look at the list of deductions beginning on p. 273.

The only way to find out if you can save money on your taxes by itemizing instead of taking the standard deduction is to fill out a copy of Schedule A and see if the amount you're allowed to deduct is greater than the standard deduction. Even if you find that you won't save money by itemizing this year, this exercise will help get you better acquainted with some common types of deductions, and may help you plan things in a way that could reduce your tax bite next year.

One warning: If you don't earn a lot, you will be tempted to fill out the 1040EZ form, which is, well, easy to fill out. The problem is that you may miss out on some money-saving deductions. Although it may take a little more time, you should take a look at the more detailed forms like the 1040 and Schedule A so you don't pay more in taxes than you have to.

If you earn very little or have children or educational expenses, you may also qualify for valuable tax credits, which subtract money directly from the amount you owe the IRS.

Whether you owe money to the IRS or not, you will need to

file your taxes. Make sure you do it. If you earn less than $54,000, you can file online for free at the IRS website. Otherwise, try www .taxcut.com and www.turbotax.com, which will let you download the forms for roughly $40 to $50.

For specific ways to cut your tax bill, see Chapter 9.

2

GET A GRIP ON YOUR FINANCIAL LIFE

Figuring Out Where You Are
and Where You Want to Go

YOU MAY THINK that with all the
chaos in the economy, it's impossible to get
your own money in order. Well, the good news is that there's a lot
you can do—very easily—to take charge of your financial life.

You don't have to be that guy or gal who spends hours sifting
through receipts or color-coding tax folders. Life's way too short,
but (you knew there'd be a *but*) the longer you wait, the harder it is
to get organized. Yes, it's tempting to put off planning for the future
until you start making more money, or the economy soars. But remember, although your paycheck will increase as you get older (we
hope), your financial commitments will too. So get started today.
This chapter will help you get organized.

PUTTING A PRICE TAG
ON YOUR GOALS

You probably have one or two specific financial dreams that you'd love to realize within the next few years. You may want to buy a car. You may long to get rid of your credit card debt. You may fantasize about owning a house. Or you may simply want to move out of your parents' place as soon as possible.

The first step toward turning your financial desires into an achievable goal is calculating the dollar value of your dream. If you're not sure what that figure is, use the following guidelines:

- *A home.* The median-priced home for first-time home buyers in 2008 was about $165,000. To qualify for a home loan, you usually need to make a down payment of between 10% and 20% of the total price; you'll also need to pay 1% to 5% of the house price to the bank for "closing costs." So for a $165,000 home, you would need to have saved somewhere between $18,150 and $41,250. Of course, these figures could be higher or lower depending on the deal you get. (For details, see Chapter 7.)

- *A zero balance on your credit card.* The average college grad leaves school with about $3,000 in credit card debt. Say you make the minimum payment each month. At that rate, it would take about twenty years and cost more than $4,000 *in interest alone* to pay off the debt. And that's assuming you don't rack up even more debt. The lesson? The sooner you pay off your credit card, the sooner you can put your money to better use.

- *A new car.* Expect to make a down payment of between 10% and 20% of the total price. To buy a $25,000 car, you'll need between $2,500 and $5,000 in cash. Even a used car costs, on average, $14,000, in which case you would need to spend about $1,400 to $2,800 for the down payment.

- *A financial emergency cushion.* If you sock away at least three months' worth of living expenses, you'll have a reliable financial safety cushion. This amount will probably guard against a total disruption of your life if, for example, you lose your job. Although saving for a home, a car, or any other tangible item is a lot more exciting, accumulating enough for a financial emergency cushion is a real necessity that will give you the peace of mind to get started on the rest.

LEARNING HOW TO
REACH YOUR GOALS

Once you've figured out what your goals are, you're ready to work toward achieving them. Use the table in Figure 2–1 to help. It gives you a rough idea of how much you'll need to put aside each month to end up with a specific dollar amount in a set number of years. The table assumes that inflation will be 3% and the money you put away will earn an interest rate of 4% before taxes. (No one can know what will happen to inflation and interest rates in the future, but these are reasonable estimates.) It also assumes that your combined federal, state, and local tax rate is 30%* for the next 10 years. The table factors in tax rates because you'll have to pay taxes each year on the earnings you receive on certain investments. (For details on figuring out your tax rate, see Chapter 9.)

If you tend to be a good saver, you may not be fazed by the amount you'll need to save each month. If you're like most people, though, you'll probably have to set aside more than you think you can spare. Don't get discouraged. The next part of this chapter will help you figure out how to get this money from your current income. Even though you may ultimately decide you have to adjust

---

*Here's how I got the 30%: If in 2009 you're single and earn between $33,950 and $82,250 per year, or are married and together earn between $67,900 and $137,050, your federal tax rate is 25%. Depending on where you live, your state and local taxes might be about 5%; 25% plus 5% is 30%. One thing to keep in mind: If you itemize your tax deductions, you get to deduct the state taxes you pay. This will have the effect of reducing your rate somewhat. (See Chapter 9 for details.)

Figure 2-1

HOW MUCH DO YOU NEED TO SAVE EACH MONTH TO MEET YOUR GOALS?

Look across the top row and find the dollar amount that corresponds to your goal. Now look down the far-left column and locate the number of years in which you hope to achieve your goal. The point at which your goal and the number of years intersect is the amount you need to save each month.*

	YOUR SAVINGS GOAL										
	$1,000	$2,000	$3,000	$5,000	$7,000	$10,000	$20,000	$30,000	$50,000	$70,000	$100,000
Years to Reach Your Goal											
1	$85	$169	$254	$423	$607	$845	$1,691	$2,536	$4,227	$6,067	$8,454
2	43	86	129	215	301	429	859	1,288	2,146	3,005	4,293
3	29	58	87	145	203	291	581	872	1,453	2,035	2,906
4	22	44	66	111	155	221	443	664	1,107	1,549	2,214
5	18	36	54	90	126	180	360	539	899	1,259	1,798
6	15	30	46	76	106	152	304	456	761	1,065	1,521
7	13	26	40	66	93	132	265	397	662	927	1,324
8	12	24	35	59	82	118	235	353	588	823	1,176
9	11	21	32	53	74	106	212	318	531	743	1,061
10	10	19	29	48	68	97	194	291	485	679	969

* The goals listed across the top row of the table are in constant dollars. This means that if your goal is to buy a car in five years that's equivalent to a $20,000 car today you need to set aside $360 every month to end up with a sum that has the right purchasing power ($20,000 today is equal to roughly $17,000 five years from now). In other words, you don't have to worry about inflation eroding the value of the $20,000; the table factors it in for you.

your planned goal—or the amount of time it takes for you to reach it—at least you'll be on your way to making it happen.

FIGURING OUT WHERE YOUR MONEY GOES

Saving isn't easy for most people, and putting aside a fixed amount each month can seem like an impossible task. But the fact is you probably *can* save—even if you feel like you're barely making ends meet now. The key is getting a handle on your current spending habits and then reevaluating your priorities. This section will help you do the necessary financial soul searching it often takes to help achieve your goals.

The first step is to keep a detailed spending diary for one month so that you can get a clear sense of exactly where your cash goes. Keeping the diary is simple: Just get a little notebook and write down everything you spend money on, from your morning coffee to the quarter in the parking meter. (Attach the notebook to your wallet with a rubber band if it helps you remember to fill it out—or use the Notes program on your BlackBerry, cell phone, or iPhone.)

Once you've jotted down a month of expenses, you're ready to fill out the worksheet in Figure 2–2. You can do this online at my website (www.kobliner.com), and it will do the math for you. The point of the worksheet is to help you see where your money goes and then adjust your priorities.

Keep in mind when you fill out the worksheet that it's not necessary to be exact. Use your pay stubs and your bank statements to come up with reasonable estimates in the income section. For the outflow section, look at your spending diary, online bank statements, checkbook (if you use one), ATM receipts, and credit card statements. Don't forget that this worksheet is helping you examine your *monthly* expenses. For large expenses (like tuition, insurance, travel, and furniture), come up with monthly estimates. For expenses that vary from month to month (such as car repairs, clothing, and entertainment), take an average of four or five months' worth of spending. If possible, choose a month from each season so you can calculate a more accurate average.

Once you complete the worksheet, subtract your total outflow from your total income. If you come up with a negative number, that means you're spending more than you're taking in (obviously a problem). To do this, you'll need to think about your priorities and make some tough choices. Would you be able to save a bundle by cooking at home more often? Do you spend as much on clothes as you do on rent? Are you spending a ton of money on gifts? Are you subscribing to more magazines than you can actually read? Could you find a cheaper phone plan? Do you belong to a health club that you rarely go to? Is your car costing more than it's worth? Is recreational shopping making you broke? Are you overspending when you go out with friends after work? Could you save a few dollars by buying in bulk? These are some of the questions to consider.

With these questions in mind, go back over the entire outflow section. Consider where you can cut back—and by how much. To start, star those items that you feel are absolute necessities. (For most of us, that includes mortgage or rent, groceries, utilities, student loan payments, and health insurance premiums—although even here, many of us can cut back if we need to. There's more on that in Chapter 8.) Subtract your outflow on necessities from your total income. The answer (which is positive, hopefully) is the amount of discretionary income you have left.

Divide your discretionary income into two parts: the amount you'll save to meet your goals (like a car, a house, or your own retirement) and the amount you'll spend on things that aren't necessities (like movies, designer water, clothes you don't really need, and so on). At this point, it should become clear whether you need to adjust the size of your goal or the number of years in which you can realistically hope to attain it.

Of course it's hard to spend less, but this exercise will only work if you're ready to commit to putting limits on your unnecessary spending. Can you get by on $50 a week for eating out and entertainment? Is it worth it to you to forgo the latest cell phone or boots for a long-term goal? Once you start, it becomes easier than you think.

Figure 2-2

WORKSHEET:
A MONTH IN YOUR FINANCIAL LIFE

INCOME (what you take in each month):

Salary and bonuses (before tax)   _____
Pay from extra jobs (before tax)   _____
Interest on savings   _____
Interest on income   _____
Scholarship money   _____
Other   _____
TOTAL INCOME PER MONTH (BEFORE TAX)   _____

OUTFLOW (what you pay out each month):

Federal, state, and local income tax and FICA
   (get this figure from your pay stubs)   _____

Tax on interest income*   _____

Tax on investment income**   _____

Mortgage or rent   _____

IRA and 401(k) contributions   _____

Groceries   _____

Gas and electricity   _____

Cell phone and landline   _____

Eating out (including morning coffee, snacks,
   and lunches out)   _____

Nightlife   _____

Clothes and shoes   _____

Student loan payments   _____

Car loan payments   _____

Gas, car repairs, maintenance   _____

Public transportation (bus, train, taxi costs)   _____

Health insurance   _____

Homeowners/renters insurance   _____

Auto insurance   _____

Disability insurance   _____

Life insurance   _____

Home decorating   _____

Home repairs/maintenance   _____

Furniture   _____

Laundry   _____

Dry cleaning   _____

Tuition   _____

Child care   _____

Medical and dental expenses not covered by
    insurance   _____

Bank fees   _____

Hobbies   _____

Netflix, DVDs, movies, and theater   _____

Cable TV, Internet   _____

iTunes, CDs   _____

Gifts   _____

Vacation   _____

Magazines, newspapers, books   _____

Grooming (haircuts, toiletries, cosmetics)   _____

Health club fees   _____

Charitable contributions   _____

Pets, pet care   _____

Miscellaneous   _____

TOTAL OUTFLOW PER MONTH   _____

TOTAL MONTHLY INCOME   _____

minus   TOTAL MONTHLY OUTFLOW   _____

equals your   MONTHLY CASH FLOW   _____

---

* To estimate the tax on the interest, multiply the amount of interest you received for the month by your tax bracket. If you don't know your tax bracket, multiply the interest by 0.25 to get a rough idea.

** If you've held this investment for more than a year, multiply the investment income by 0.15 to get a rough idea. If you've held it for less than a year, multiply the investment income by your tax bracket—if you don't know your tax bracket, multiply the income by 0.25.

WHEN A SPENDER MARRIES A SAVER

Anne and Marc moved in together in June and started to plan a March wedding. Anne's parents said they'd be willing to contribute $20,000 for the event, so the couple figured out that they'd need to pitch in $10,000 of their own to have the wedding of their dreams.

The problem was coming up with the cash. Anne, who is frugal and likes being debt free, felt that with some careful planning, they could accumulate the money. After all, they each earned about $45,000. Marc, however, thought that raising that kind of cash was out of the question. He already owed more than $3,000 to various credit card companies and didn't see how he could possibly save the money. Why couldn't they just wait and see how much cash they received as wedding presents and then charge the rest?

After two weeks of discussion (actually, arguments), they decided to list their income and expenses and see if they could work out the problem. By writing things down, Marc quickly realized that if he cut out expensive lunches (he spent four times as much as Anne did) and put off buying clothes for work until the spring (he spent twice as much as she did on suits), he could come up with a good chunk of change. He also was forced to acknowledge that having Anne as his roommate would actually make saving much easier; it cut his rent, utilities, and phone charges in half. The compromise: Anne and Marc would each set aside $280 every two weeks in a joint bank account earmarked for wedding expenses only.

FINANCIAL RULES
OF THUMB

To help you evaluate whether your current spending and saving habits are right on track, wildly off base, or somewhere in between, I've listed a few financial rules. These will give you something to strive for. Realistically, they aren't always possible to attain, but it's good to set high goals. Use the worksheet you filled out to help with your calculations.

- **The Debt Target: Your debt payments (not including your mortgage) should be less than 20% of your monthly take-home pay.** To see if you meet this standard, list all the monthly payments you make on your student loans, credit cards, car loan, and any other lines of credit, and add these amounts together. If your total monthly payments exceed 20% of your monthly take-home pay, don't panic. Chapter 3 has tips on reducing debt, and as you adjust your spending, you'll free up more money to pay off debt faster.

  But it makes sense to analyze this often-quoted rule a bit. It's possible that monthly payments are artificially low—say you pay the absolute minimums on your credit cards—so the 20% rule could mask a dangerous amount of debt. For example, if you earned $40,000 a year (taking home around $2,985 a month) and you owe $20,000 in credit card debt, your monthly payment could easily be about $450, which is just 15% of your take-home pay. So while on paper you meet this rule of thumb, the reality is that you're drowning in debt.

  So in addition to the above rule, try this one as well: If the unpaid *balance* on your so-called consumer debt (that's your credit cards, car loans, and other lines of credit that aren't student loans or home loans) exceeds 20% of your *annual* take-home pay, you are probably carrying too big a debt load. (Of course, the percentage to shoot for in both cases is zero.)

- **The Housing Target: Spend no more than 30% of your monthly take-home pay on rent or mortgage payments.** This policy may be impossible in major cities like New York City, San Francisco, or Miami, unless you share a place with roommates. But if you're in a small town or a city like St. Louis or Albuquerque, it's reasonable. No matter where you are, it's something to shoot for.

- **The Savings Target: Save at least 10% of your take-home pay each month.** It's critical to think of your savings as a fixed monthly expense that's part of your budget, just like your car payments and your rent. While there's no magical reason to save exactly 10%, it's a good target to shoot for. Include in that 10% the money you set aside to meet your short-term goals as well as the funds you put in a company retirement plan. If you can save more, you should boost your goal to 15%. Chapters 4, 5, and 6 offer specific tips on improving your savings habits.

THE REAL COST OF SHOPPING

Because of the way our tax system works, the cost of buying something is higher than you think. Here's why: Say you find a great jacket for $75, and you buy it. If you were in the 25% tax bracket, you actually had to earn $100 in order to pay for the jacket. That's because $100 taxed at 25% is $75. Keep this in mind on your next shopping spree.

GETTING YOUR FINANCIAL
LIFE IN ORDER

It's easier to gain control of your finances if you're organized. Here are some tips:

- **Set up a financial filing system.** This is simpler than you may think, since most of your bank, credit card, and brokerage accounts are already available online. I recommend filing as many of your financial records as possible electronically; it saves time, paper, and space. Also, if you move around a lot or travel often for work, it will still be easy to keep tabs on your bills and balances.

  Filing records on your computer also minimizes the risk of identity theft. Surprisingly, even in this digital age, most thieves still access your personal information through traditional methods such as stealing paper mail. If it's not in hard copy form, there's less risk that your personal information will get into the wrong hands. To be extra safe, change your passwords a few times a year and use only your personal computer to check account information. And of course back up all your files in case of a tech disaster.

  You'll want to save copies of any financial statements you view online in a folder on your computer. Many financial institutions will only store your data for a relatively short period of time; after that, they'll charge you to get copies of older statements, which you may need if you get audited. I recommend keeping one folder for each account.

  There are, of course, certain items that are available only on paper, like receipts and the agreements you get when you open a credit card. If you want to keep these electronically, you can scan them. But since no one wants to sit by the scanner all day, you can simply file these documents in regular folders in a cardboard file cabinet. (This is also where you should keep any statements you may still get in the mail.)

Now you're ready to set up your system. Here are the folders you'll need (and some notes on what to keep inside each one):

Auto loans. Save loan agreements that list the terms of your loan.

Auto (other). Keep your purchase agreement, your certificate of title, and any warranty you may have. Also hold on to warranties and receipts from repair work. These are especially handy if you ever want to sell the car.

Bank statements. Your bank statements will show all your debit card transactions, so save statements showing purchases that may be deductible on your taxes and put them in the appropriate folder.

Brokerage accounts. Keep statements that show purchases and sales of investments. You'll also need to hold on to stock or bond certificates.

Credit cards. When you get these statements, make copies of any showing purchases that may be tax-deductible and put them in the appropriate folder.

Home improvements. Keeping track of these expenses could pay off if you ever decide to sell your home.

Home (purchase). Hang on to your closing statement and all the other documents related to the purchase.

Insurance. Within this folder, you'll need separate folders for auto, home, rental, life, health, and disability insurance. Keep your policies, descriptive literature, copies of any claims that you make, and statements of reimbursements.

Individual retirement accounts (IRAs). Hold on to your statements. If you have different types of IRAs, you'll need separate folders for each. See Chapters 6 and 9 for details.

Mortgage interest payments. If you own a home, hold on to statements related to all payments because they may be tax-deductible.

Mutual funds. File your year-end transaction statements.

Personal documents. Store important documents such as your passport, Social Security card, and marriage certificate here.

Property tax/real estate tax. These payments are tax-deductible, so hold on to statements related to them.

Retirement plan statements. Keep all "summary plan descriptions" you receive from your employer, and save quarterly statements from your retirement savings plan. Also hang on to documents relating to other employee benefits, such as profit-sharing plans.

Salary. Keep your biweekly or monthly pay stubs, your year-end pay form, and any written information you receive regarding your bonus.

Student loans. Save your original loan agreement and your monthly statements. A portion of the interest you pay every month may be tax-deductible.

Tax-deductible items (miscellaneous). If you don't have many deductible expenses, use this as a catch-all folder. Otherwise, you may want to set up separate folders for each specific type of deduction you can take. (See Chapter 9 for details on these deductions.)

Tax returns. Each January you receive W-2s from your employer and 1099s from a variety of sources including employers, banks, and mutual fund companies. Save them in this file. (You'll have to scan them if you want to store them electronically.) Also hold on to copies of your tax returns, your tax-related forms, and any supporting documentation. Create a new folder for each year.

Warranties, rebates, receipts, online order forms. Hold on to these for all major purchases. The receipts will help you if you ever need to verify to an insurance company that a particular item was stolen or ruined in a fire. When you order items online, print out or download copies of the order forms to serve as receipts until the item arrives.

* **Know what to save and what to get rid of.** Some people are pack rats who habitually save every scrap of paper. (I am the worst offender.) The fact is you don't need to keep all receipts and bills. In general, you'll want to hold on to receipts related to tax-deductible expenses or those you need in order to take advantage of a warranty. You'll also want to keep receipts of major purchases for insurance purposes in case of theft or fire. Below is a detailed list of what you need to keep and what you can throw away. Make sure you shred all papers and documents before you toss them, either with a machine or by hand.

Throw away now:

Old phone bills (unless you intend to deduct a portion of your phone bill from your taxes)

Supermarket receipts

Old utility bills

ATM receipts (once you're sure the correct amount has been credited to or taken out of your account)

Save for one year:

Store receipts (except those you need for tax or insurance purposes or for proof of purchase necessary for a warranty)

Pay stubs (your employer sends a W-2 at the end of the year)

Save for seven years:

Bank statements, credit card statements, receipts, and any documents you've saved for tax deduction purposes (which you may need to produce if you're audited by the Internal Revenue Service)

Save forever:

Birth certificate

College transcripts

Credit card agreement (for as long as you have the card)

Diplomas

Divorce decree and property agreement

Home improvement receipts (if you own your home; see Chapter 9 for details)

Home inventory (you'll learn about this in Chapter 8)

Insurance policies

Loan agreements

Marriage certificate

Passport (current one)

Pension plan and retirement plan documents

Receipts for major purchases (to use as proof in case of a fire or burglary)

Social Security card

Stock purchase agreements

Tax returns and additional tax forms

Warranties (for as long as they last)

Work performance reviews, memos on job performance

Year-end pay stubs and bonus statements

Year-end transaction statements from mutual fund companies

TIPS FOR SAVING MONEY NOW

Scaled back on lattes and lunches but still searching for extra cash? You can locate the best deals on everything from T-shirts to appliances when you compare prices at websites like www.smartbargains.com and www.pricegrabber. com. You'll find coupons for some of your favorite stores at www.retailmenot.com and www.dealsofamerica.com, and discount certificates for eating out at www.restaurant.com. There's a massive selection of off-price merchandise at www .overstock.com. And for a steady stream of money-saving tips, try blogs like www.getrichslowly.org, www.myopenwallet.net, and www.zenhabits.net.

KEEPING TRACK OF MONEY
COMING IN AND GOING OUT

When your parents were your age, keeping tabs on their money was pretty easy. They had a checkbook and added up the money going in and subtracted each expense coming out. Today, it's trickier because we have so many different accounts and means of accessing money. Here are some ways to help you organize your payments and track your spending. It doesn't matter which system you use—the point is to choose one that speaks to you so you'll stick with it.

- **Use your bank's online bill-paying system.** Most banks provide a free way to pay certain merchants electronically. Here's how it works: You have to list the merchants you pay regularly (power company, landlord, the gym), along with the amount you want to pay each of them and the dates on which you want the bank to send a payment. The bank then debits money from your account and deposits it into the merchant's account, or it will send a bank cashier's check (this could take up to five days to arrive). You can authorize the bank to make either a one-time payment or recurring payments for ongoing monthly bills.

  You can verify that a bill has been paid once the withdrawal shows up on your online statement. It will usually post a day or two after you request the payment be made. If you use this system, make sure to remember when you've arranged for payments so you don't accidentally spend money that isn't really there.

- **Arrange to have payments automatically deducted from your account.** Another way to make bill paying easier is to have the *merchant* electronically take payments (for example, your gym membership, your cell phone bill, or your electricity bill) out of your checking account on a designated date. Once you've signed up for this, the money will simply vanish from your checking account on the correct day of the month.

While this system is generally a good way to make timely payments, there are a few potential pitfalls. For one, the merchants could take out more than the actual amount owed, so don't sign up if you don't trust them. If you do, you should still monitor your account to make sure they don't make any mistakes. Furthermore, if your bill is unexpectedly large one month (for example, if you've run up your cell phone charges), a merchant could withdraw more money than you actually have in your account, so be sure you have a cushion in there to avoid getting fined for insufficient funds. If you don't like the idea of giving the merchant so much control, check to see whether he or she can send you an email to verify the amount before withdrawing it.

- **Have *savings* automatically deducted from your account.** The old adage is "pay yourself first," meaning you should contribute to your monthly savings just as diligently as you pay your monthly bills. And one of the smartest ways to do that is to make your savings automatic. Because you don't see the money that's being set aside, before long you won't even miss it. There are a couple of ways to do this: Ask your company's payroll office if you can have a fixed sum taken from each paycheck—say, $50 a month—and funneled directly into your savings account. If your employer doesn't provide automatic savings, set up a transfer to a savings or mutual fund account through your bank website. (See Chapter 5 for more on mutual funds.) If you set aside $50 every two weeks, at the end of the year you'll have $1,300—plus interest!

- **To help control spending, use online budgeting tools.** Truth is, if your financial life is fairly simple, you probably don't want to bother with anything more than your bank's online account services to keep tabs on your money. But if you have a more complicated situation, budgeting websites can help. Free sites like www.mint.com or www.wesabe.com or www.quickenonline.com make it easy for you to calculate what portion of your income goes to various categories, such as "housing," "clothes," and "dining out." If you had a grand time filling out my worksheet earlier in the chapter, these sites could help you hone in even more on where your money is going. At the end of a few months you can see how much you spent in each category, and you might learn something useful. (I know one friend who prided herself on not buying new clothes but was astonished one month to see that she spent almost 25% of her take-home pay on going out to eat). And if you and your partner fight about money, a computer budgeting program can be especially helpful because it offers an objective way to see where the money is actually going.

- **Use your checkbook.** If you still use checks, your checkbook can actually be a handy organizing tool. Every time you write a check, note the merchant, the amount, and the date in the ledger or save the carbon copy. Write down or save ATM receipts in the same place. This can be a good reminder of how much is going to be taken from your account when the check is cashed.

There are also some useful websites and publications that provide insights into saving and help with budgeting. Try *Money* (www.money.com), *Kiplinger's* (www.kiplinger.com), and *SmartMoney* (www.smartmoney.com).

FINANCIAL CRAMMING

- To calculate how much you need to save each month to reach specific financial goals, look at Figure 2–1 on p. 15. Although it's based on several assumptions about inflation, your tax bracket, and the rate you'll be able to earn on investments, it will still give you a rough idea of how much money you'll need to set aside.

- Keep a spending diary for one month. By forcing yourself to write down everything you spend money on, you'll get a better sense of why your cash seems to disappear.

- Consider these guidelines when evaluating your financial fitness: Spend no more than 30% of your monthly take-home pay on housing and dedicate at least 10% of your take-home pay to savings. Also, don't allow your monthly debt payments (not including your mortgage) to exceed 20% of your monthly take-home pay—or your *total* debt (not including your mortgage or student loans) to exceed 20% of your *annual* take-home pay.

- Gain control of your finances by setting up a filing system and developing regular bill-paying habits. And if you're having trouble controlling your spending, consider a site like www.mint.com or www.quickenonline.com, which can help you keep track of it.

- Automate your savings by having a certain amount siphoned from your paycheck each month.

DEALING WITH DEBT

Finding the Cheapest Loans and Getting Yourself Out of Hock

SUPPOSE YOU'RE 30 years old and you owe $3,500 on your credit card. The interest rate on your card is 17%. If you regularly make the minimum payment required by the credit card issuer, when will you have paid off your card? (Drum roll, please.) The answer is . . . when you're 65 years old. By then, you would have paid $7,662 in interest, plus the $3,500 you borrowed—a grand total of $11,162!

The point of this chilling example is clear: Carrying a lot of credit card debt—or *any* type of debt, for that matter—can be hazardous to your long-term financial health. Unfortunately, debt is a problem many of us are intimate with. The amount of money that Americans owe on their credit cards has nearly doubled in the last ten years.

Whether you're trying to pay off your debt or simply looking for a low-cost loan amid the credit crunch, this chapter provides tips on managing your credit card load, figuring out new student loan repayment strategies, locating affordable car loans, and avoiding the pitfalls of home equity loans. It will also provide you with an inside look at how your credit habits affect your credit report and your credit score, the SAT of your money management life.

FOUR POINTERS FOR
ANYONE WITH DEBT

Before we plunge into the nitty-gritty details of credit cards, student loans, and auto loans, there are four basic principles you should know:

- **If you have savings, use it to pay off your high-rate debt.** In most cases, the best investment you can possibly make is to pay off your credit card debts and car loans. This is because the interest rates on such debt are higher than the rates you can expect to receive from almost any investment. Paying off a loan with a 14% interest rate, for instance, is in effect paying yourself 14% interest, guaranteed and *tax-free*. That's a deal even Wall Street big shots would be thrilled to get.

   A lot of people worry that by paying off their debt, they're wasting their savings. But when it comes to high-rate debt, nothing could be further from the truth. To better understand this, consider the following situation. You have a $1,000 loan for which you pay an annual interest rate of 14%. You also have $1,000 in the bank—earning interest at a rate of 3%. If you keep the $1,000 in the bank for a year, you'll earn $30 in interest on it while paying $140 in interest on the loan, ending up with a $110 loss. With me so far?

   But if you take that money out of the savings account and pay off the loan immediately, you'll earn no interest but you will also pay no interest. Clearly, it's better to break even than to pay $110 in interest.

- **Transfer debt from high-interest-rate loans to lower-rate loans.** The process of transferring debt from high-rate loans to lower-rate loans is known as **refinancing**. Obviously it's better to pay 8% to borrow money than it is to pay 18%. So if you currently have credit card debt that you can't pay off right away, apply for a low-rate card that allows you to transfer your current debt to it. (All this will be explained in the section on credit cards later in this chapter.)

- **Pay on time.** Modern technology gives everyone from lenders to landlords and even potential employers the ability to look at your credit history (for more on this, see p. 70) and get a sense of how responsible you are when it comes to making monthly payments. People who appear to have trouble managing their debt get charged higher interest rates on everything from credit cards to car loans to home loans. (They are also more likely to get turned down as a potential renter or even as an employee.)

  You can't change your past, but you can make a huge difference in your future by paying your bills punctually now. One late $50 credit card or phone bill payment can literally cost you tens of thousands of dollars later by driving up the interest rates you'll get on a mortgage. The number one factor that goes into your credit score is your record of paying bills on time. Read that sentence again and commit it to memory. It's key. (For more, see the box on p. 77.)

- **Talk to your lender.** E-mail may be easy, but picking up the phone is a great way to remind people that you're a human being, not just an account number. If you have a debt-related issue (or even if you're just trying to get a better deal), call your lender and explain your situation. A lender might be willing to change the terms of the loan so that you can and will keep making your payments. If you're trying to negotiate for a lower rate, speaking directly with a supervisor is almost always the best route.

CREDIT CARDS

Many of us have become addicted to credit cards, and banks have been more than willing to feed this habit by dangling cards in front of everyone old enough to sign his or her name. Today, the card companies are tightening their standards and limiting credit lines as well as hiking interest rates and fees.

Whether you're a sensible user or a bit dysfunctional when it comes to credit cards, there are steps you can take to get the right card and reduce your costs. It's especially important that you know what to do these days; making credit mistakes can cost you a lot of money.

How to Find the Best Card for You

Despite what the ads say, whether your card has a Visa seal or MasterCard logo is not that important. These are just membership organizations. It's the bank or company that *issues* the card—such as Citibank or Bank of America—that matters. Issuers control the rates, fees, and other factors that are critical to you.

Look for a credit card that best suits your own personal spending habits. If you usually carry a balance from month to month, get the lowest interest rate—technically the **annual percentage rate** or **APR**—you can. But if you always pay off your balance in full, the rate doesn't matter. In that case, your priority is to find a card that doesn't charge an annual fee and offers a **grace period,** the stretch of time lenders give you to pay in full before they start charging interest.

If you pay off your entire balance each month, you may also want to consider special "reward" cards that offer frequent-flyer mileage or credits toward a car for every dollar you charge. If you have a troubled credit history, consider a secured card that requires you to have enough money on deposit to cover your charges, and if you have a tough time controlling your credit card spending, you may be better off just sticking with a debit card instead. (More on all these options follows.)

In any case, most of us don't need more than two credit cards total. Extra cards just make it easier to overspend.

How to Search for a Low-Rate Credit Card

If you find you don't have enough cash to pay off your credit card balance immediately, you'll want to get the lowest-rate card possible and transfer your debt to it. The way it generally works is that the new low-rate issuer pays off your other creditor(s) or gives you checks to settle your old accounts. The details vary from card to card, though, so you need to read the fine print (online, generally buried in the "terms and fees" page or in the paperwork the company sends you) before signing up. Some low-rate issuers, for example, offer you a twenty-day grace period before interest accumulates on the money you borrow; others tack on transfer fees (for transferring the debt, naturally) and start charging you interest the moment the checks are cashed by your old cardholders.

There are two kinds of low-rate cards: those with low rates that last and those with temporarily low introductory rates, also known as **teasers**. Teaser rates can be as low as 0% and last for six months to a year. After that period, the rate increases dramatically. While the low teaser rate lasts, however, it can save you a lot of money. Transferring a $2,000 balance from a 16% card to one with a 0% teaser rate, for example, would save you $156 in interest payments over six months—assuming there are no balance transfer fees, of course.

So if you know for sure that you can pay off the whole card before that teaser rate runs out, you're okay. The card issuer counts on the fact that you can't—which is the case for most people. If that's your situation and you're super-organized, you may be able to keep your rates low by going "credit card surfing"—transferring your balance to a new teaser-rate card whenever your teaser rate runs out. But you have to surf carefully and that's very hard to do. Credit card companies have gotten wise to credit card surfers, and most now charge transfer fees, so pay attention. Also, don't let the low rates seduce you into paying off your debt slowly; try to pay at least as much every month as you would with a higher-rate card.

In a perfect world, you'd be able to find a card with a low rate that lasts. The interest rates on such cards tend to be higher than teaser rates, but are far more stable in the long run. Unfortunately, after the wave of credit card delinquencies in recent years, banks have made it significantly more difficult to qualify for these cards. Here are details on some of the requirements.

- **Solid bill-paying habits.** If you've been 30 days late paying a credit card bill within the last four years or if you have ever been more than 60 days late, you'll have a hard time getting a low-rate card.

THE TRICKY TEASER

Rebecca is a dedicated credit card surfer who prides herself on her ability to pay the lowest possible interest rates on the $3,000 balance she tends to carry from month to month. Because she has a good credit history, she gets solicitations in the mail almost daily, offering her extra-low introductory teaser rates. Every few months, she switches cards and gets a new teaser rate, so she never ends up paying more than 5% on her debt.

Recently Rebecca transferred her balance to a card with a six-month teaser rate of 0%. She used the card to buy hundreds of dollars' worth of books and clothes. When she got her credit card statement at the end of the month, she was shocked to see that while the balance she had transferred from her old card was running up interest at 0%, the new money she had spent on books and clothes was being hit for 18.9%! What Rebecca hadn't noticed was that the teaser rate on her card only applied to balance transfers—*not to any new purchases she made.*

Determined not to pay interest rates in the double digits, she sent in a check that covered all the new purchases she

- **Stability.** Some issuers want to see that you've been at your job for at least a year. It also helps if you've lived in the same apartment or house for a year.

- **Moderate usage.** To measure credit card use, issuers look at the ratio of your outstanding debt to your potential debt (that's the sum of the credit limits on all your cards). This is called your **usage ratio.** For example, if you have two cards

had made that month. But when her next statement came, she found that none of that 18.9% debt had been paid off; instead, her check had gone toward paying off the older—and cheaper—balance she had transferred from her old card. She would have to pay off that entire $3,000 balance transfer (at 0%) before she could even make a dent in her more expensive new balance (at 18.9%). Ironically, her teaser rate was actually *preventing* her from paying off her high debt.

In the end, Rebecca was forced to engineer a complicated transaction to get at her 18.9% debt. She transferred all the debt on her card to *another* card, then immediately switched it all back. (That way, it counted as a balance transfer again.) Luckily, neither card charged a balance transfer fee. From then on, she made all new purchases on a second card and paid them off in full every month, avoiding interest payments altogether—and used her 0% card exclusively for her old balance.

The obvious moral of the story: Not all teaser deals are the same. New regulations prohibit the nastiest version of this trick, but you should still make sure to read all the fine print before you rush to switch cards. The hidden moral: Rebecca, like all card surfers, should stop wasting her time and pay off her debt once and for all.

with a combined $1,000 credit limit and outstanding debt of $900, your usage ratio is 90% ($900 divided by $1,000). This ratio should not exceed 30%. Borrowers who qualify for the best cards have a ratio of about 7%.

- **Long-term dependability.** Lenders favor borrowers who have established a lengthy track record of on-time payment— years and years of good behavior.

For the most comprehensive list of long-lasting low-rate and teaser deals, go to www.credit.com. Sites like www.cardtrak.com and www.lowcards.com also have a mix of advice and card offers. If you belong to a credit union, national association, or labor union, you might be able to get a card with a relatively low rate through one of those organizations. Also investigate local banks, which sometimes offer lower rates on cards than large national institutions do.

Pointers for Those Who Carry a Balance

About six out of every ten credit card users carry a balance from month to month. While your goal is to pay off your credit card debt entirely, until you can, take note of the following suggestions:

- **Pay your bill the day you get it.** Most credit cards have a grace period, which begins the day your purchases are made or posted (officially recorded) and lasts until the due date specified on the bill. As long as you pay your bill in full by the due date, you won't be charged interest. Unfortunately, with most cards, the grace period exists only for those credit card users who pay their full balance each month. If you don't regularly pay off your old bill in full, you'll be charged interest immediately on any new purchases you make. In other words, if you carry a balance from month to month— even a very small balance—you lose the grace period and everything you buy will start racking up interest from day one. To reduce your interest charges, pay your bill as soon as you get it.

- **Never miss a payment.** If for some reason you can't pay your bill the day you get it, at least make sure you pay it on time. Thanks to modern technology, late fees are usually applied to your account the minute after your payment is due—even if it's a weekend or holiday. And these fees are outrageous: Many banks now charge $40 for a single late payment. Worse, more and more banks punish payers who are late by 30 days or more by jacking up their interest rates to "penalty rates" of up to 32%. And don't forget: Late payments go on your credit report and affect your credit score, making it harder for you to get loans and low rates in the future. (There's more about credit reports and scores at the end of this chapter.)

  One tip: If you're transferring a balance from a high-rate to a low-rate card, keep making at least the minimum payment on your old accounts until you have confirmation that the transfer has gone through so that you avoid any late fees. If your old issuer ends up owing you money, just call to request a refund check.

- **Know how interest is calculated.** Most lenders calculate interest using a system called the **average daily balance method including new purchases.** Here's how it works. The issuer divides up the year into 30-day periods known as billing cycles. On the last day of each billing cycle, the issuer sends you a bill. Say you owe $500. If you pay the entire amount by the due date, you won't pay any interest. But if you leave even just $1 unpaid, it will have a negative impact on your next bill. Interest charges won't be calculated on just your $1 balance; instead, they will be based on the *average daily balance* of the billing cycle. In this case, your balance would be $500 for 25 days of the billing cycle and $1 for the last five days, resulting in an average daily balance of $417.

- **Pay more than the monthly minimum, and resist skip-a-payment offers.** Ideally, you should pay your balance in full each month. If you can't, pay as much as possible. Even paying just $10 more a month can save you hundreds if not thousands of dollars in interest. Many banks calculate your monthly minimum as 1% of your outstanding balance plus all interest and fees every month. Others ask for a flat 3% to 5% of your balance. However they do the math, the longer it takes you to erase your balance, the more money you'll end up paying in interest. (See Figure 3–1 to calculate how long it will take to pay off your debt.) Also, resist the temptation to go for the skip-a-payment deals offered by some issuers. What they often don't make clear is that you'll still be charged interest on your outstanding balance for that month. (There's no interest-skipping involved.)

A NASTY CARD SURPRISE

Kathy and Michael went on a honeymoon to Hawaii and charged all their expenses on a credit card. A week after they got home, the $5,000 credit card bill arrived. They had enough money to pay the whole bill, but Michael decided to pay it over the course of two months so he wouldn't fall below the minimum balance he needed to get free checking at his bank. He wrote a check for $4,900 and mailed it out by the due date. When the next credit card bill came, Michael was shocked to discover that although he owed only $100 from the previous balance, he also owed $63 in interest. Because he didn't pay off his balance entirely, he was charged interest for the average daily balance—in this case, about $4,180—of the billing cycle. The lesson: Don't carry a balance if you can help it.

If You Can't Get a Regular Credit Card, Try a Secured Card

If you've never had any credit, you've defaulted on a loan within the last few years, or just don't meet the lender's requirements, you may find it difficult to get a credit card. One option to consider is a **secured credit card**. With a secured card, the issuer requires you to provide collateral by depositing money into a special savings account. The issuer usually allows you to charge an amount up to the amount on deposit. You can't withdraw the money from the savings account while you have the card.

A secured card shows up on your credit record, so using it helps you build up a track record of managing credit responsibly. Once you've demonstrated that you can handle a secured card, issuers will be more willing to take a chance on giving you a regular credit card.

Be aware, though, that secured cards often charge higher interest rates than traditional credit cards, and most have annual fees of about $50. And though some issuers pay interest on the required savings account, most do not. That's why you should shop around. Sites like www.credit.com, www.cardtrak.com, and www.bankrate.com provide lists of secured card options and let you compare them side by side.

Should You Use Debit or Credit?

If you have trouble controlling your spending, consider cutting up your credit cards and using a **debit card** instead. Like a credit card, a debit card offers the convenience of not having to carry cash. Unlike a credit card, which allows you to borrow money, a debit card simply enables you to use money you already have. When you pay by debit card, the money is withdrawn from your bank checking account, usually overnight or within a few days. (Keep track of how much you have in your account to avoid penalties.)

Most debit cards have a Visa or MasterCard logo and you can use them wherever you would use an ordinary credit card, even

Figure 3-1
HOW MANY MONTHLY PAYMENTS
YOU'LL NEED TO KILL YOUR DEBT

This table can help you get a rough sense of how long it will take you to get rid of your credit card debt entirely, regardless of how much you have.

Here's how it works: Look down the far-left column and ask yourself what percent of your debt you can comfortably commit to paying off each month. If, for example, you have $1,000 in debt, you may decide that you can pay off 3% of $1,000, or $30, every month until the balance is completely wiped out. Now look across the top row and find the annual interest rate charged by your credit card. Say it's 18%. The point at which 3% intersects with 18% is the number of months it will take you to pay off your debt. In this case, the answer is 47 months. But, as you'll see from the chart, if you're able to refinance that debt with a credit card that charges only a 10% annual rate, the number of monthly payments you'll make will drop to 39.

If you want to do the math using your own numbers, you'll find a calculator at www.feedthepig.org, a fun site sponsored by the American Institute of Certified Public Accountants. (You know how funny they are!)

| | | ANNUAL INTEREST RATE | | | | | |
		3%	7%	10%	14%	16%	18%
	2%	54	60	65	75	83	93
	3%	32	34	39	42	44	47
	4%	26	28	28	30	31	32
Payment as a % of Initial Debt	5%	21	22	22	23	23	24
	10%	10	11	11	11	11	11
	15%	7	7	7	7	7	7
	20%	5	5	5	5	5	5
	25%	4	4	4	4	4	4

overseas. As you probably know, that same debit card can also be used with your personal identification number (PIN) to withdraw cash from an automated teller machine (ATM).

Here's where it gets a little tricky. You know how sometimes a store clerk will ask, "debit or credit?" when you hand them a card? Well, they're doing that for several reasons. If you're using a credit card, you simply say "credit" and the amount will be charged to your card. End of story.

But if you are using a debit card and the clerk asks "debit or credit?" what he or she is really asking is whether you want the money to travel through the PIN network (they call that "debit") or through the signature network (they call that "credit"). Either way, the money still comes from the same place—your checking account—and in roughly the same amount of time.

So here's the point. When you use a debit card and *say* "credit," it doesn't mean you're *getting* credit. Instead, it means you'll sign on what is basically an electronic check at the cash register, and if there isn't enough money in your bank account, you'll get slapped with penalty fees just as if you'd bounced a paper check. But if you say "debit," you'll enter your PIN and the money still comes straight out of your checking account. So why does it matter? Bizarrely, federal rules give you more protection (against fraud, for example) if you sign your name rather than enter your PIN, so make sure you understand them. (See the box on p. 46 to see why it's a good idea to use a signature whenever possible.)

Some Final Tips on Credit Cards

Whether you carry a balance or not, here are a few more pointers that will save you some money.

- **Ask your current card company for a better deal.** You may be able to talk your bank into lowering your rate or eliminating your annual fee, but you'll have to speak to an actual human being to get results. Call the toll-free number and ask for the "retention office." Explain in a friendly but assured manner that you're thinking of canceling your card if

DEBIT AND CREDIT CARD FRAUD

If your credit card gets lost or stolen, someone out there could be running up bills under your name. But you don't have to worry about paying the tab for their spending sprees. In cases of fraud, federal law limits your liability to $50—and most credit card companies won't ask you to pay anything at all. If you notice strange purchases on your credit card statement, let your card company know right away so that they can investigate and take the charges off of your balance.

Debit cards are trickier. If fraud takes place on a signature-based transaction, issuers will usually limit your liability to $50 (or even zero), and if you have an improper charge, they'll duke it out for you. Most major banks will also reimburse you within a few days for debit card losses due to fraud on signature-based transactions and then investigate, although some banks will wait until after an investigation.

With the PIN network, it's a different story. You want to tell your bank about a fraudulent PIN-based transaction as soon as possible. If you report it within 48 hours, your liability will be limited to $50. If you report it after two days, however, you could be held liable for up to $500, and if you take longer than 60 days, your liability could be unlimited.

Also, if someone cracks your PIN by hacking the machine you use to key in your number, they could raid your entire checking account (and even run up overdraft fees) by the time you notice the money is missing.

To make sure you don't get cleaned out, don't give anyone your PIN number, consider using the signature system whenever you can, and check your bank statement every month to see that it squares with your own records.

your request isn't met. Say that your other cards have lower interest rates and no fees (but be prepared for the phone rep to ask you to name names). There's a chance the rep will check your record and offer you some break on the rate or fee, if you've been paying your bills on time.

• **Open and read the mail your credit card company sends you.** Even if you're getting your monthly credit card statement online, you may still get old-fashioned paper mail from your issuer. Sometimes it's just little notices and advertisements, but sometimes it may be an important announcement from your credit card issuer. The company could be letting you know, for example, that it's charged you overdraft or late fees, lowered your credit limit, or raised your interest rate—it has to give you a written warning, and this may be the only notification you get. So when you get any mail from your credit card company, make sure you read it so you know your card's current rules.

• **Don't use your credit card for cash advances.** Most credit cards can be used to obtain cash from an ATM. When you use a credit card for a so-called "cash advance" from an ATM, you're borrowing money from the credit card company in a more expensive way. That's because many issuers charge higher interest rates on cash advances (up to 28%) than they do on purchases. And most cash advances don't have a grace period; interest begins accruing the moment you get the cash. On top of the interest, you may have to pay a one-time fee of as much as $35 or 4% of the amount you withdraw. You should also stay away from the "convenience checks" some issuers include with your statements (unless you're using them to transfer balances from higher-rate cards). These usually work the same way as cash advances, and you'll be charged accordingly.

• **Evaluate reward cards carefully.** With a reward card, whenever you charge, you earn points toward some product or service. Most reward deals make sense only if you pay off your entire balance each month. That's because the interest rates they charge are often higher than those of other cards. These higher rates can offset any rewards you get. Also, most reward deals—especially airline cards that allow you to earn frequent-flyer miles for every dollar you charge— pay off only if you charge a lot. You have to charge thousands of dollars (typically $25,000) in order to get one free round-trip ticket from an airline card. And that assumes you can use the ticket to get a seat on a flight you want! If you don't carry a balance and you don't spend very much, look for a reward card that does not charge an annual fee— for example, the Sunoco MasterCard, which offers rebates on gas, or the Citi CashReturns MasterCard, which will send you regular checks for 1% of the cost of everything you buy with it.

- **Watch your limits.** You've probably heard stories about the couple in the fancy restaurant who has to scramble for cash after the guy's card gets turned down because he's surpassed his credit limit. Not long ago, if you made a charge that would put you over your credit limit, the cashier or waiter would tell you your card was declined. While that still happens, credit card issuers have systems that let them approve some over-the-limit transactions—without asking you—and then tack on a fee (as much as $39) each time you cross the line. (This can happen with ATM cards too; see Chapter 4 for details.) They might also use this as an excuse to raise your interest rate or even lower your credit limit going forward.

- **Big Brother is watching (and raising your rates).** Credit companies have gotten so strict about monitoring cardholders' activity that they can detect late payments on any loan you have—even accounts with completely different lenders. As a result, messing up on one card can cause your other issuers to jack up interest rates on your future purchases to 30% or even higher. New regulations prohibit these issuers from raising rates on your *existing* balances.

- **Stay away from store credit cards.** Department store sales-people will often ask you that enticing question: "Would you like to open a store credit account? You'll get a 10% discount on your entire purchase." Don't do it! Interest rates on store cards are generally 20% or more—much higher than the national average. This means that if you put a $500 shopping spree on a store card to get the 10% off, and then pay only the minimum on your bill each month, you could easily end up spending an extra $400 in interest.

MEMBERSHIP HAS ITS PRICE

Traditional American Express cards may look like credit cards or debit cards, but they're actually a different species of plastic: **charge cards.** Charge cards work on a "pay-in-full" system, which means that you have to pay your bill completely at the end of every month, instead of carrying a balance. If you don't pay every cent you owe, you'll get hit with late fees, and eventually your card will be suspended. (American Express also offers a line of regular credit cards, so make sure you know what you're getting.)

Some people find that charge cards help them stay disciplined and avoid getting too deeply into debt. Problem is, they have high annual fees: Amex's basic card (the "Preferred Rewards Green") charges $95 for the privilege of membership and frequent flyer points. The fee on Amex's "Preferred Rewards Gold Card" is $150, and for that you get some extras that may or may not mean anything to you. Now that credit card issuers are offering gold and platinum cards with similar perks and no annual fees, think twice before you pay for a charge card. You could be better off just pretending you have one and paying off your bills in full every month.

That's one costly $50 discount. If you're sure you can pay off the purchase immediately and your starting purchase is truly large, it might be worth it, but otherwise use your own low-rate card.

STUDENT LOANS

Most students can expect to graduate from college with tens of thousands of dollars in student debt. If you're having trouble paying back your loans or you're simply looking for a way to reduce your interest payments, this section can help.

Most student loan debt consists of **Stafford loans,** which are guaranteed by the federal government. ("Guaranteed" means that the government will ultimately pick up the tab—though not without pain on your part—if you default on your payments.) Other kinds of federally guaranteed student loans include **PLUS loans** (which are made to students' parents) and **Perkins loans** (which are available only to lower-income families). Check your paperwork to see what kinds of loans you have; Stafford loans probably make up the majority of them.

There are two ways to get Stafford loans: The first is through a private lender, usually a bank, through the Federal Family Education Loan (FFEL) Program. The second is directly from the Department of Education, through the Federal Direct Loan Program (www.ed.gov/DirectLoan; 800-848-0979). You don't have a choice about whether your loan is a Direct Loan or a FFEL—it all depends upon the program in which your school participates. But either way, the rules for Stafford loans in terms of repayment and interest rates are set by the government.

One key difference between these programs: what they do with the loans once you start paying them back. The Federal Direct Loan Program keeps its loans throughout the repayment period. That means if you got your loan through the Federal Direct Loan Program, you'll be writing your check to the Department of Education until it's paid off. With private lenders, it varies. Some big banks will keep the loans and have you pay them back. But many private lenders sell off their loans to other companies, known as the **secondary market,** which take over the bill collection. The biggest player in the secondary market, Sallie Mae (www.salliemae.com; 888-272-5543), handles about one-fourth of all federally backed student loans.

Throughout this chapter, I'll be using the term **servicer** to refer to the company that actually deals with you when you're paying off your student loans—whether it's the federal government, your original lender, or the secondary-market company that has bought your loan.

How to Reduce the Cost of Your Student Loans

Here are four strategies to consider:

- **Sign up for electronic payment.** If you agree to make automatic payments each month, there's a good chance your loan servicer may reduce your interest rate by a quarter of a percentage point.

- **Pay all your bills on time.** It may be possible to find a program that rewards you for timely payments. For example, Sallie Mae will write you a check or directly credit your account for a fraction of your monthly payment after you make your first twelve consecutive monthly payments on time and sign up for automatic payment.

- **Prepay your student loans.** If you're not weighed down by credit cards or other high-rate debt, consider paying back your student loans faster than you're required to under your current payment schedule. This will save you a substantial amount of interest in the long run. Say you have $20,000 in loans with an interest rate of 6.8%. Assuming the interest rate remains the same and you pay back your loans over ten years, your monthly payment will be $230. If you can add just $50 a month to that amount and pay $280 a month, you'll pay off your loans in seven years and eight months and save almost $2,000 in interest. But remember, prepayment makes sense only if the interest rates on your loans are *higher* than the rates you can earn on an investment. (For an explanation of why this is so, see the box "If You Have Credit Card and Student Loan Debt" on p. 59.)

- **Deduct your interest payments.** The government gives students a tax break: You may be able to deduct *interest* payments on your student loans, up to a maximum of $2,500 a year. For example, if you're in the 25% tax bracket and you paid $1,500 in interest this year on your student loans, you'll get to cut $375 off your tax bill this year. You must fill out form 1098-E to get this. Money that goes toward repaying the *principal*, which is the total amount you borrowed, is not deductible. For more details, see Chapter 9.

Simplifying Repayment

If you feel overwhelmed by your student loans, here are three simple ideas that may help:

- **Find out where your loans are.** If you've lost track, you're not alone. If you're not sure where your paperwork is, either because you have changed addresses or your lender has given your loan to a loan servicer, or you're just at a loss, the National Student Loan Data System (www.nslds .ed.gov) can help you locate all federal loans.

- **Look into loan serialization.** If all your loans are with the same servicer, you may be able to simplify your monthly payments through **loan serialization,** which is a fancy way of saying that your lender will send you just one bill for all of the loans that they handle for you. Serialization (also known as **unified billing**) won't actually change anything about your loans, but it could make it easier for you to stay organized and make your payments on time. Check with your loan servicer to see if this option is offered.

- **Consider loan consolidation.** This is the process of combining various loans into one massive new loan with a new interest rate. The new interest rate is the weighted average of the rates on the loans you're consolidating rounded up to the nearest eighth of a point. It generally makes sense for borrowers who received federal loans before July 1, 2006, when those loans did not have fixed rates. If you're in the process of repaying loans like these, consolidating them will most likely let you lock in a rate that is lower than your current rate. But if your loans were issued after July 1, 2006 (when rates became fixed), then consolidating will not provide you with a lower rate. Check with your loan servicer to see if it offers consolidation, or try the Federal Direct Loan Consolidation Program (www.loanconsolidation.ed.gov). For more details on consolidation, go to www.finaid.com.

Choosing the Best Repayment Option

The standard way to pay back student loans is to make equal monthly payments for ten years. If you know where your loans are but you're having trouble making your monthly payments, you have several repayment options to choose from. The rules for these repayment options will depend on your servicer.

It's tempting to try to reduce your monthly payments, but be warned in advance that while these options may make your monthly payments more manageable, they could severely increase the total amount of interest you pay in the long run. Here are some common choices, whether you have a FFEL loan or a direct loan:

- **Extended repayment.** If you owe a lot, this option allows you to stretch out your repayment over a period of twelve to thirty years. For example, borrowers with more than $30,000 in federal loans may be eligible for a 25-year repay-

ment term. Generally, the length of time you'll be allowed
to extend your repayment period, if at all, is determined by
the amount you owe.

- **Graduated repayment.** This option allows you to make
  lower payments in the early years of your loan, depending
  on the amount you owe; your payments will then increase
  every two years.

- **Income-based repayment.** With this deal, you pay no more
  than a set percentage of your income; the lower your salary, the less you pay each month. If at the end of 25 years
  you still have not paid off your debt, the government will
  forgive you the remainder of what you owe. (It forgives but
  it doesn't forget. You'll have to pay income tax that year on
  the amount that's been waived.) For more information, go
  to www.ibrinfo.org.

How much will these various plans increase the amount of interest you pay? A lot. For example, if you extended the term of a
$20,000 loan (with a 6.8% interest rate) from ten years to twenty
years, you would have to shell out a whopping $9,021 in added in-
terest (although you would cut your monthly payments by a third).
For some useful calculators, go to www.ed.gov or www.finaid.org.

Special Breaks If You Can't Make Your Payments

The government has set up rules that spell out exactly why and for
how long you can put off repaying your student loans. Such a delay
is called a **deferment.** Deferment rules change every few years, so
figuring out whether you qualify for one can get pretty confusing.

Deferments are granted to people in a few different situations. If
you're unemployed, a part-time or full-time student, a professional
intern or resident, a full-time unpaid volunteer, or a recipient of an
approved graduate fellowship, you may qualify for a deferment.
Also, if you teach full-time in a public or nonprofit elementary or

EVERYTHING YOU NEED TO KNOW ABOUT THE STUDENT LOAN SCANDAL

The student loan business has come under fire in recent years after revelations of corruption throughout the system. It started when an investigation by the New York State attorney general found that financial aid officials at several big-name colleges and universities were paid kickbacks by private loan companies in exchange for sending borrowers their way. Once this collegiate Pandora's box opened, it became clear that the mess involved financial aid officers at other colleges and universities across the country, as well as several major banks. In some cases, school officials initiated the deals. In others, the lenders did everything from sending pricey bottles of wine to providing all-expense-paid junkets in order to drum up business. Unreal. But the very real outcome: a slew of resignations and firings, millions of dollars in settlements, increased oversight by the Department of Education, stricter legislation, and a renewed commitment by banks and schools to operate on the up and up.

However, the scandal has been so far-reaching that the fallout may not be over. The bottom line is that if you're trying to get financing to go back to school, do your homework (and get a second opinion) before you sign on the dotted line.

secondary school in what is considered a teacher-shortage area, you may be able to defer for up to three years. You can also get a deferment for up to three years if you're unemployed. During deferment periods, the government sometimes pays the interest for you. That's the case with some Stafford loans and Perkins loans. With most other student loans, you'll eventually have to pay the interest that

accrues during the deferment period. To learn more about deferments, contact your loan servicer.

If you don't qualify for a deferment, all hope is not lost. For
those who simply can't make the payments, servicers can offer time
off from paying through a process known as **forbearance**. Like a
deferment, this is granted at the discretion of the lender. You'll be
responsible for the interest that accrues on any type of loan during a
period of forbearance. If you find yourself in a situation where you
need to apply for forbearance, speak to someone at the institution
that's servicing your loan to get more details.

What you want to avoid at all costs is **defaulting,** as there are
serious repercussions. For one, you may have to pay hefty penalty
fees and collection charges of up to 25%. In addition, you could
find that the government withholds your tax refund and reduces
your future Social Security payments.

Special Breaks for Those Who Help Out

There are also a number of **forgiveness** programs, which essentially
cancel your student debt after a certain period of time. The laws
vary by state and by loan type, so to find out more, visit www
.studentloanborrowerassistance.org and www.finaid.org. You may
be eligible if:

- **You teach.** Teachers who work in a school designated as
  "low income" by the government can apply to have their
  loans (both Direct and FFEL Program) partially cancelled
  after five years. Benefits vary by state, and there's more information available at the American Federation of Teachers
  website (www.aft.org). There are also specific benefits for
  people who join the AmeriCorps teaching and community
  service program (www.americorps.org).

- **You work in public service.** People working full-time in public service careers (such as law enforcement) can get their
  remaining debt canceled after ten years of employment. You

have to be in the Direct Loan Program or have consolidated
your loans into it in order to take advantage of this.

- **You join the Peace Corps.** Volunteers may apply for deferment of Stafford loans (either through the Federal Direct
  Loan Program or the FFEL Program) and Perkins loans as
  well as partial *cancellation* of Perkins loans (15% for each
  year of service, up to 70% in total).

- **You work in health care.** Doctors and nurses who are willing to work for two years in regions that are remote or eco-
  nomically depressed can also have their Direct and FFEL Program loans partially forgiven through the National Health
  Service Corps (nhsc.bhpr.hrsa.gov) and the Nursing Education Loan Repayment Program (bhpr.hrsa.gov/nursing/loan
  repay.htm).

- **You enlist.** If you sign up to join the Army, Navy, or Air Force,
  you may qualify to have up to $65,000 (or up to $20,000
  for reservists) of your student loan debt paid though the Student Loan Repayment Program (www.military.com). Perkins,
  Stafford, PLUS, and consolidation loans are considered. For
  more on military benefits, see Chapter 10.

Understand the Perils of Private Loans

With tuitions skyrocketing, many students and their families have
turned to **private loans,** also known as alternative loans, from banks or
other financial institutions. These are different from the federal loans
you may get under the FFEL Program from a "private" bank. All this
gets very confusing, but the bottom line is that private loans are often
much more expensive for borrowers. You need to be on guard.

One problem with private loans: The interest rates are generally
not capped. In fact, due to the credit crunch, private lenders have
jacked up the interest rates by as much as two or three times the
rates on federal loans.

If you're already stuck with several private loans and you find that your credit history has improved over time, you might want to consider folding them all into a new private consolidation loan at a better rate. Or try to get a cosigner with good credit to apply with you for a new lower-rate loan.

If you're in college now and have used all the federal loans you qualify for, talk to your parents before you sign up for any private loans. If they haven't had any major credit problems (i.e., a recent foreclosure or bankruptcy), they may be able to help by getting a Parent PLUS loan. Rates on these loans are generally a little higher than on Stafford loans, but they're still a much better deal than most private loans. This can save a lot of money. The PLUS program allows parents to borrow up to the full amount of their child's tuition, fees, on-campus room and board, and even a living allowance. They have the option of deferring payments until six months after you graduate.

Bottom line: Max out your federal loans and get a private loan only when you really cannot find the money anywhere else. Private loans are a last resort.

Good News if You're Going to Grad School

For years, once grad students maxed out their federal loans (Staffords top out at $20,500 per year for graduate students), they had to resort to high-rate private loans to pay for school. However, in 2006, a new loan called the Grad PLUS made it easier to borrow more affordably. The program's fixed-rate loans, which tend to charge several percentage points less than private loans, can be used to fund the entire cost of your education (tuition, books, and living expenses) minus whatever other financial aid you receive. If you have a decent credit record—meaning you haven't had a recent foreclosure or bankruptcy—these could be a great option.

These loans are administered by the college or university you attend, but to apply you have to fill out a Free Application for Federal Student Aid (FAFSA), which is available online (www.fafsa .ed.gov).

IF YOU HAVE CREDIT CARD AND STUDENT LOAN DEBT

The interest rates on your student loans are probably lower than the interest rates on your credit cards. If this is the case, you should pay off your credit card debt faster than you pay off your student loans. By extending the number of years over which you pay back your student loans, you can reduce monthly student loan payments and free up some cash to speed up credit card payment. (Of course you'll need to resist the temptation to spend this cash instead of using it to pay down your more expensive debt.) Once you've wiped out your credit card debt, increase your student loan payments to at least their original levels.

CAR LOANS

It's a tricky time to get a car loan—while manufacturers are eager to make sales, banks are choosier about giving out auto loans. Another problem is that once you get a car loan, you may be stuck with it; it's hard to find a lender who will refinance your loan at a lower rate.

And that can make a difference on your bottom line. For instance, getting a 7% rate instead of a 9% rate on a $24,800 six-year loan would save you almost $2,000. It might also mean the difference between being able to make your payments on time and having your car repossessed.

Even people with great credit reports have to do their homework in order to get the best deal. This section will offer advice on finding the right car loans and leases for you.

How to Get a Good Deal

You're going to need to do some legwork. Here are some pointers:

- **Shop around.** There's more than one place to get a car loan: directly from a dealership, bank, credit union—or even online. Before you set foot in a dealership, do some research. Consult your local newspaper to look for the best deals offered in your area, then go to websites like Bankrate (www.bankrate.com) and LendingTree (www.lendingtree.com) to gather more options. Credit unions tend to charge lower auto loan rates, so if you belong to one, check. See if a bank is willing to bargain; you can sometimes get a half-percentage-point break if you're willing to have your payments deducted automatically from your bank account.

- **Ask a lender with a good rate if you can get preapproved for an auto loan.** Preapproval is a process by which the lender looks at your income, debts, and other financial information to determine how large a loan you can handle. The benefit is that if you end up going to a dealership, you'll know that you're approved for financing. Also, you'll be better equipped to negotiate once you have a ballpark figure of how big a loan and what rate you can qualify for. You can do this online or at your local bank or credit union.

- **Negotiate with car dealers and settle on the exact price of the car before you discuss financing.** Sometimes dealers will give you what seems like a break by offering you a low-rate loan—but then jack up the price of the car to compensate. In general, the sticker price is about 5% to 10% higher than the price the dealer paid for the car. For all but the hottest models, you shouldn't pay the sticker price. To get an idea of what you can expect to pay, look at the comprehensive write-ups of specific cars on consumer-oriented websites like Edmund's (www.edmunds.com) and Kelley Blue Book (www.kbb.com). Armed with the information from those sites, you're ready to haggle with the dealer. Aim to pay just 5% or so above the price he paid (the sites will tell you how much that is).

- **Don't tell the dealer how much you can afford to spend on monthly payments.** This is often the first question a car dealer will ask. Although you should have a rough idea of the answer (see Figure 3–2), don't share that information with the dealer. The reason: Once the dealer knows, he can adjust the terms (for example, the price of the car or the interest rate you're charged) to his liking while matching your monthly payment figure. Instead, say you want to check out the different cars you're interested in and settle on the price before you discuss financing.

- **Steer clear of low down payment loans.** Even if you find one of these deals, don't take it. The lower the down payment, the more interest you'll pay over the life of the loan. That's because a low down payment increases the size of the loan you need. Of course, if you can afford it and don't have other high-rate debt, the best move is to pay the entire cost of the car upfront. If not, try to put down at least 20%. If you can't afford that, get a cheaper car—or better yet, a used car.

- **In general, go with the shortest-term loan you can afford.** The average term on new auto loans is about five years (up from four-year terms just a few years ago). That may be appealing in terms of lower monthly payments, but remember that you'll be paying more interest overall by the time you pay off the car. Many owners have ended up owing more than the car was worth by the time they sold it or traded it in. Just as troubling, some auto makers are offering loans of seven years or even longer to tempt people into buying even more expensive cars, since a longer-term loan reduces the monthly payments. Try to get a loan with a term of four years or less.

FIGURE 3-2

HOW MUCH YOU'LL PAY EACH MONTH
WITH AN AUTO LOAN

This table can help you get a sense of what your monthly car payments will be, given a specific term and interest rate on a $24,000 auto loan. Although your monthly payments are lower with a longer-term loan, the total amount you'll pay is higher. To figure out the total cost of the car loan, multiply the monthly figure by the number of months it will take you to pay it off. So, for example, if you're paying 9% on a five-year loan (currently the national average), you can expect to pay about $498 every month, adding up to $29,892 over the course of five years.

| | INTEREST RATE | | | | | | | | |
	3%	4%	5%	6%	7%	8%	9%	10%	11%
24	$1,032	$1,042	$1,053	$1,064	$1,075	$1,085	$1,096	$1,107	$1,119
36	698	709	719	730	741	752	763	774	786
48	531	542	553	564	575	586	597	609	620
60	431	442	453	464	475	487	498	509	522
72	365	375	387	398	409	421	433	445	457

Term (Months)

- **Weigh low-rate vs. rebate.** If you're lucky enough to qualify for a really good car loan, you may have a choice between taking the loan and getting a cash rebate; do the math to see which deal makes the most sense. There are good calculators available on the Kiplinger's website (www.kiplinger .com/links/carincentive). Don't get seduced by advertisements touting 0% financing; you need a very high credit score to qualify.

- **Consider buying a used car.** Buying a used car in good running condition can cost about half as much as a new car on average. That means that your auto loan will be half as expensive. And although there are some risks in terms of quality control, you can minimize these, especially if you look for a make with a great reputation. If you buy from a dealer, ask for the car's inspection history and pay an independent mechanic to inspect it for you. To find a good one, consult your state auto association. If you buy from a private owner, run the car's VIN (vehicle identification number) at www .carfax.com to do a more thorough background check.

Some Advice if You Lease

If you can afford it, it is generally better to buy than lease a car. That said, if you can't come up with the down payment, leasing is an option you may want to consider. But you should know what you're getting into.

When you lease, you're essentially renting a car for a fixed number of years. Although it's most common to lease a car through a dealership, a dealer is actually just the middleman who works on behalf of a leasing company. As a leasing customer, you pay for the amount the vehicle *depreciates,* or loses value, during the lease period—typically three years—plus interest on this amount. Your monthly payments are based on the price of the car, your interest rate, the number of years in the leasing period, and the car's expected resale value at the end of the lease.

At the end of your contract, you have the option of buying the car you've been leasing. If you don't want it, you can usually return it and lease a new one—without the time, expense, and hassle of trying to sell a used car. But you won't have anything to show for the money you've put into your auto payments.

Look Before You Lease

Leasing typically makes sense for people who want to drive a new or almost-new car at all times. (Of course, if you're watching your money, that's not exactly a priority.) If you plan to keep your car for many years, you'll probably save money by buying. That's especially true if you drive a lot or aren't great about upkeep, because you'll have to pay for damages and extra mileage when your leasing contract is up.

Before you make a decision about buying or leasing a car, take some time to crunch the numbers. Several good calculators are available on websites such as Kiplinger's (www.kiplinger.com) and Bankrate (www.bankrate.com). Another helpful website for leasing options is www.leasecompare.com. The Federal Reserve publishes a useful guide called *Keys to Vehicle Leasing*, which you can get by going to www.federalreserve.gov/pubs/leasing or by phoning (202-452-3244).

Leasing agreements have their own jargon and can be pretty complicated. As a result, it's easy to get taken for a ride. Here's the key data you should collect if you're considering leasing a vehicle.

- **The "price" of the car on which the lease is based.** In leasing lingo, the term **adjusted capitalized cost** is basically the purchase price of the car you're leasing, as set by the dealer (the manufacturer's suggested retail price), *plus* tax and *minus* your down payment and the value of any trade-in. This serves as the basis for determining your monthly lease payment. It may also include extras like insurance, extended warranties, and other optional services. Make sure these extra charges are itemized so you can decide which ones you really want before you agree to include them in your contract. Also, bargain down the suggested purchase price in the same way you would if you were buying the car, following the steps outlined above.

A few companies offer what are known as **manufacturer-subsidized leases**, which get financial support from carmakers. You can find updated information on the best manufacturer-subsidized deals at Edmund's (www.edmunds.com).

- **The probable value of the car at the end of the lease.** This is known as the residual value. This isn't a number you can negotiate, but you can find out if the dealer is quoting you a fair residual value. One source is www.cars.com. To make a leasing deal more attractive, some car manufacturers are willing to make the residual value artificially high. If all other factors are equal, a high residual value is better for you, because your monthly payments are based on how much the car is expected to depreciate during the time you lease it. A high residual value means that the car will not depreciate much during your lease; as a result, your payments will be lower.

  But high residual value can be a drawback if you're planning to buy the car when the lease is over. If you do decide you want to buy the car, you may be able to bargain with the leasing company and get them to sell it to you for less than the residual value you previously agreed to in your leasing agreement. The best time to negotiate is just before the lease is up.

- **Your monthly payments.** Unlike when you buy a car, when you lease an auto, you want to focus on those monthly payments—and you want them to be as low as possible. The lower the payments, the less you'll pay out over the life of the lease. It's clear cut.

- **The lease term.** You want to keep the length of the lease at about 36 months. If you opt for a longer term, you'll inevitably get stuck paying for expensive maintenance, like tire replacements or new brakes, which cars need as they age. Also, be sure you know what the penalties are for getting out of the lease early, and make sure this information is included in your agreement.

- **The total mileage you're allowed.** You'll also want to settle a few issues such as the total mileage you're allowed without being charged extra; compare this mileage limit to how much you actually drive.

HOME EQUITY
LOANS

If you own a home, you may be able to borrow money from your bank in the form of a home equity loan (HEL). Here's how it works. You're usually allowed to borrow a percentage of your home's value (traditionally 80%), *minus* the balance on your mortgage. So, for example, if you own a home valued at $200,000 and you have a $120,000 mortgage, you may be able to borrow $40,000 (that's 80% of $200,000—or $160,000—minus $120,000).

So why would someone want to do this?

One of the main advantages of a home equity loan is that it offers you a tax break that you don't get with credit cards or auto loans. (I'll explain how this works in a minute.) For this reason, in addition to using HELs to pay for home improvements, you could in fact take out home equity loans and use the money, which comes in one lump sum, to pay off higher-rate debt like credit cards or auto loans.

While all this *sounds* really good, there's also a huge pitfall you should know about. If you end up having trouble making your payments, you risk losing your home and still ending up owing money to the bank. That's exactly what's happened to millions of people across the country in recent years.

In the early 2000s, home prices were rapidly rising and banks and mortgage companies were aggressively peddling HELs (often with complex terms that borrowers didn't understand). A growing number of homeowners took out these home equity loans and in some cases started using the money to pay for lifestyles they really couldn't afford. Before long, many people found themselves deep in debt. Even worse, when home prices started to decline, millions found themselves owing more than their homes were actually worth. For that reason, lenders are now much more cautious about giving out home equity loans.

Home Equity Lines of Credit

Most banks offer both home equity loans and **home equity lines of credit (HELOC)**. With a home equity *loan*, you get all the money at once in a lump sum and you repay it over five to fifteen years. The interest rate on a home equity loan is typically a fixed rate, meaning it's the same throughout the life of the loan. Home equity **lines of credit,** which are twice as popular as traditional home equity loans, are quite different. Home equity lines are similar to credit cards in that borrowers get a set credit line on which to draw over time; they can choose when, how often, and how much to draw from that loan. Each month they can make the minimum payment or pay more if they want to. Home equity lines generally have variable interest rates, which means they change on a monthly or annual basis when interest rates rise and fall throughout the economy. But they are also available with a fixed rate if you shop around.

As I mentioned, you may want to transfer your car loan to a HELOC, but because you can decide how much you want to pay back each month with a home equity line, it can be tempting to make small monthly payments. Don't. Dragging out repayment gets expensive, so you have to be disciplined, which is why it's a smart idea to pay off your home equity line over the same number of years it would have taken to pay off your car loan. Remember, if for any reason you can't make your payments—say you lose your job or have a medical emergency—your home is on the line.

One hidden danger of home equity lines: Banks reserve the right at any time to drop your credit limit to what you currently owe and stop you from using any more credit. In recent years this nasty move has become more common, so beware.

Before You Take Out a HEL or a HELOC, Read This

As you've seen, it can be very risky to transfer your high-rate debt to either a home equity loan or line of credit. Do not consider it unless you do the following:

- **Know how the tax break works.** The interest you pay on a home equity loan or line of up to $100,000 is deductible, meaning you can subtract it from your taxable income when you fill out your tax return. The interest on amounts over $100,000 is not deductible unless you're using the money for home improvements; in that case, you can deduct the interest on a loan of up to $1 million.

  Here's what that tax break means in dollars. Say you owe $1,000 on your home equity loan and your interest rate is 8%. If you pay it off in one year, you will also pay $80 in interest. If you're in the 25% tax bracket, you will save $20 (25% of $80) at tax time if you itemize your deductions. So after you factor in your tax savings, the interest you actually paid was just $60. ($80 minus $20 in tax savings is $60.) Another way to look at it is that the after-tax interest rate on an 8% equity loan is 6%. (See Chapter 9 for more on tax breaks for homeowners.)

- **Factor in up-front fees.** Some lenders charge hundreds or even thousands of dollars in initial fees when they grant home equity loans and lines of credit. But many lenders waive these fees entirely. Look carefully. And make sure that after you factor in the fees, it still makes sense for you to refinance.

- **Shop for the best deal for you.** If you've made up your mind to get a home equity loan, check out the websites of several different banks to get an idea of what's being offered where. You can also compare interest rates on HELs at www.credit .com, www.cardtrak.com, and www.bankrate.com.

BORROWING FROM FRIENDS AND RELATIVES

Jim wanted to pay off the $3,000 balance he owed on his credit card, which charged a rate of 18%. His parents were willing to lend him the money to do it. Here are some steps they followed to make the transaction harmonious:

- **They made sure the deal was good for both parties.** Jim agreed to pay his parents back with interest, and they settled on a rate of 8%. Not only was this a good deal for Jim, but it was also beneficial to his parents, whose money had formerly been sitting in a bank savings account earning just 4%.

- **They put everything in writing.** Jim's parents wrote up an agreement that included the interest rate charged and the dates payments were due. It might sound formal, but this helped avoid confusion. You can download sample contracts and get advice from www.nolo.com.

- **They made sure there weren't any negative tax consequences.** Bizarre as it may seem, the IRS sets a minimum interest rate—**the applicable federal rate (AFR)**—that family members and friends are required to charge on certain types of loans. Even if your parents, for example, want to lend you money without charging you interest, they may owe tax on the interest they would have received had they charged you the AFR. If you borrow less than $13,000 to buy an item like a car or to pay off debts (as Jim did), you don't have to worry about these rules. But if you borrow the money to purchase assets like stocks and bonds or if you borrow more than $13,000 for any purchase, your parents, friends, or relatives may be expected to charge you interest.

- **Know the worst-case scenario with a variable interest rate.**
  The adjustable interest rates on some home equity lines can
  seem enticingly low at first, but many have first-year rates
  that can increase several percentage points in year two. Ask
  the loan officer how much the rate can rise and know how
  bad it could get.

CREDIT REPORTS AND
CREDIT SCORES

A credit report is a document that offers a snapshot of your financial history. It is created by companies known as credit agencies or credit bureaus. They gather information from an array of
credit card companies, businesses, debt collectors, and merchants
with whom you've done business. Then, when you apply for a
loan or credit card, they supply the lender with a detailed record
of your bill-paying habits. Creditors can buy reports from one or
more agencies and evaluate your history. The bureaus also offer
credit *scores*—numerical summaries of your credit report based on
a complicated mathematical formula. These scores are supposed to
predict how likely you are to keep up with your bills.

Because so much rides on a credit agency's evaluation of your
history, it's essential to check your credit report and know your
credit scores (each agency uses a somewhat different calculation)
before applying for a major loan.

Q: How do I get a copy of my credit report?

A: There are three major credit agencies that maintain these records: Equifax, Experian, and TransUnion. You're entitled to one
free credit report within a 12-month period from *each* bureau. You're
also entitled to an additional free report from each agency if you're
unemployed. You can access your free reports by filling out the request form at the agencies' joint website (www.annualcreditreport
.com), or by calling 877-322-8228. If you want more than one report
from an agency in a given year, you can purchase it from the credit
bureaus separately: Equifax (www.equifax.com; 800-685-1111),

Experian (www.experian.com; 888-397-3742), and TransUnion (www.transunion.com; 800-888-4213). They charge about $10 per report. (Don't pay attention to the various credit monitoring services and other credit-related products listed on the sites; they're expensive and usually not necessary.)

Q: What kind of information is in my credit report?

A: Your report lists the basics, such as your age, birth date, Social Security number, current and previous addresses, current and previous jobs, and spouse's name if you're married. The credit information describes all the credit relationships you have, such as bank credit cards, store credit cards, and student loans. Included is the date you opened each account, how much you owe, the maximum amount you can borrow, and your payment history. It will also indicate whether you've ever had any major financial problems, like defaulting on a loan or declaring bankruptcy.

Q: How is my credit score calculated?

A: The most commonly used scoring model is called FICO, named for the developer, Fair Isaac Corp. There are five main factors that determine your overall FICO score. Most important is your payment history, which accounts for 35%. How much you owe counts for another 30%, and your credit history represents 15%. The last two factors, the type of credit mix and the number of new credit applications you have, each account for 10%. Scores range from 300 to 850—the higher, the better.

Q: Where do I get my credit score?

A: Although you're entitled to a free credit report from all of the agencies each year, you're not entitled to a free credit score. If you're curious and want to get a rough idea of your score, you can get a free ballpark figure at websites like www.bankrate.com and www.creditkarma.com. Remember, though, that these are only estimates. The score most lenders will look at is your FICO score, which you can get for about $16 at www.myfico.com. If you're serious about getting a loan, know your FICO score before applying.

Q. Why would I need to get a FICO score from all three bureaus?

A. For one thing, FICO develops slightly different models for each of the three bureaus. Also, the agencies have different information in their files on you, depending on what they may have received or not received from various lenders. So the material in the report used to concoct your score varies from one bureau to another. That's why it's especially important to get your score from all three bureaus: to make sure you know how you're viewed by each. Again, the good news is that you can get all three at www.myfico.com.

Q: How will a high score help me?

A: The higher the score, the better you are viewed by lenders; they will want your business and offer you lower rates. The lower your score, the higher your interest rates on credit cards, mortgages, and loans. Consider just one example. Let's say you have a $200,000, 30-year fixed-rate mortgage. The table below shows how your credit score would affect your monthly payments and ultimately how much you pay over the life of the loan.

Q: If I'm turned down for a loan, do I get to find out why?

A: Yes. The Equal Credit Opportunity Act says that if your application for credit is denied, the lender must either give you an

THE COST OF A WEAK CREDIT SCORE

SCORE	INTEREST RATE (NATIONAL AVERAGE)	MONTHLY PAYMENT	TOTAL COST (MORTGAGE PLUS INTEREST)
760–850	5.68%	$1,158	$416,880
700–759	5.90%	$1,186	$426,960
660–699	6.18%	$1,222	$439,920
620–659	6.99%	$1,329	$478,440
580–619	9.02%	$1,613	$580,680
500–579	10.31%	$1,801	$648,360

Source: MyFICO.com

explanation for the rejection or inform you how you can get an explanation. If you ask for a specific reason, the lender is required to provide you with one. According to the Federal Trade Commission, explanations should be fairly specific—for example, you earn too little money or you haven't worked long enough. Vague reasons—such as not meeting the creditor's "minimum standards"—aren't acceptable.

Under the Fair Credit Reporting Act (FCRA), if the denial was due to something in your credit report, the lender must tell you the name and address of the credit agency that provided information about you. If you're denied credit, credit agencies are required by law to send you a free credit report if you request it within 60 days. The same is true if you've been turned down for a job or an apartment because of your credit history. (Unfortunately, you aren't entitled to get a free copy of your scores.)

Q: How long will my credit report show my misdeeds?
A: Most negative information will be deleted from your report after seven years. If you ever file for bankruptcy, it could take ten years before your credit report will be clean. This doesn't mean you won't be able to get credit before then. Your behavior in the last two years or so counts the most.

Q: There are a lot of companies, including online operations, that claim to repair credit ratings. Should I consider one?
A: Definitely not. Don't waste your money on sleazy firms that promise to fix credit reports. At best, these fly-by-night companies work the legal fine print to trip up the credit bureaus and force them to remove negative information. But most of the time, they do nothing for you. Instead, go to the FTC's website (www.ftc.gov) and get a copy of the agency's free publication "Credit Repair: Self Help May Be Best." Or call 877-FTC-HELP.

Q: What should I do if I find a mistake in my credit report?
A: Credit bureaus have a reputation for making mistakes. Sometimes it's simply misspelling your name or giving a wrong address, but sometimes it's a potentially damaging error, such as incorrectly indicating that you've defaulted on a loan.

If you find a mistake on your report, contact the credit agency right away to dispute it. You can do this online, by mail, or on the phone at all three agencies. Be specific about your concerns. The agency has to investigate your complaint—usually within thirty days—unless it considers the dispute unjustified. If it can't verify the information on the report, the agency is legally required to delete it. If this happens, you can ask that copies of the corrected report be sent to any lender who has seen the report within the past six months or any potential employer who has seen it within the past two years. (You'll find a list of these people on the credit report itself.) If you don't agree with the outcome of the investigation, write a short statement (100 words or fewer) and send it to the credit agency to include in your credit report. They won't let you do this online; you'll have to send it through the mail.

Q: Will "credit card surfing" hurt my credit score?

A: Hopping from credit card to credit card whenever your low teaser interest rate runs out can save you money, but it could also slightly lower your credit rating. Every time you apply for new credit, an inquiry is noted on your report. Credit scoring systems tend to punish people with a lot of inquiries on their credit report, because those inquiries may be a sign that they're applying for more credit than they can handle.

Q: How can I fix my credit report if I've been the victim of fraud?

A: **Identity theft** is the fastest growing crime in the country. It's easier than ever for thieves and con artists to get hold of your personal information, including your Social Security number, driver's license number, and even your PIN codes. Using this information, they can pass themselves off as you and set up accounts or work in your name, run up huge bills, and leave you to clean up the mess.

Under federal law, you can't be held financially responsible for false charges made in your name, but your credit report might well be wrecked. If this happens, it's important to start cleaning up your record right away.

The first step is to call the fraud departments of the three major credit bureaus (or contact them online) and request that a so-called "fraud alert" be placed on your file: Equifax (www.equifax.com, 800-525-6285), Experian (www.experian.com, 888-397-3742), and TransUnion (www.transunion.com, 800-680-7289).

The alert will stay on your file for at least ninety days and will notify lenders that there's been an identity breach; double-check with your lenders to make sure they're aware of it. You should ask all three credit bureaus for free copies of your credit reports and review them carefully. If you find that fraudulent or inaccurate information has made its way onto any of your reports, you will

CLOSING YOUR ACCOUNTS

People often ask me whether they can improve their credit scores by closing their credit card accounts once they pay them off. The old advice was that if you keep the card open, potential lenders might think you have too much available credit already. That's no longer the case. Closing one of your accounts could actually hurt your score in the short term. Here's why. Lenders like to see that you're only using a small percentage of your potential credit (called your usage ratio). Because canceling a card lowers the total amount of credit you have available, it will up your usage ratio, and that could hurt your score.

Here's how it works. Say you have four credit cards, each with a $1,000 limit, and you owe a total of $2,000 spread across all four. Your total credit limit is $4,000 and your usage ratio is 50%. (You are using $2,000 of the total $4,000 in credit.) If you close one card, you still owe $2,000 but your total limit shrinks to $3,000, so your usage ratio will jump to 67%. Lenders will look at you as a higher risk, and your credit score will probably slip a few points.

What's more, the further back your current accounts go, the better. Closing the account means it stops getting any older, and you have to restart the clock with a new card. Definitely cut up the cards or hide them in a drawer, but think twice before you cancel them.

have to take further action before contacting the agencies to get it removed.

Your next step is to contact your local police station to file an official police report. Then send a copy of the police report (or at least the report number) along with a copy of the ID Theft Complaint and the form letter to the fraud departments of each of the credit agencies as well as any businesses where the thief used your information—use certified mail and request a return receipt to make sure all this paperwork doesn't get lost in the mail. The credit bureaus have fifteen days from the time they receive your material to ask for any additional information they may need.

Clearly, this process is something of a nightmare, so to minimize the danger of your identity being stolen, develop a few basic precautionary habits: Carefully review your credit card and bank account statements; never give out personal information over the phone or online to anyone you don't know; tear up or shred personal documents before throwing them in the garbage; check your credit reports on a regular basis. For more information on identity theft, contact the Privacy Rights Clearinghouse (www.privacyrights clearinghouse.com; 619-298-3396).

Q. I've heard a lot about a credit freeze. How is that different from a fraud alert?

A. A credit freeze is a relatively new way to add another layer of protection to your credit report. While a fraud alert notifies lenders that your identity has been stolen, a freeze simply restricts all access to your report. To put a freeze on your credit, go to the appropriate link on each of the credit bureaus' websites and submit a written request. After the freeze is activated (which can take anywhere from fifteen minutes to three days and costs about $10), companies that you already do business with will still have access to your credit report, but no new third parties, including potential lenders, can get a copy. You can temporarily lift the freeze if you need to apply for new credit, but it could take a few days.

Q: I'm married. Does that mean my spouse and I have the same credit report?

A: No. If you have a joint credit card or loan, this account will be noted on both your individual credit reports. Keep in mind that whenever you share a card or cosign a loan, you're liable for each other's debts. It's important for you to keep at least one loan or credit card in your own name and for your spouse to do the same, so that each of you establishes a separate credit history. If you don't, you'll have trouble getting credit if you get divorced or if your spouse dies.

Q: Who can look at my credit report?

A: The law says that credit bureaus can disclose information about you to any person or organization with a "permissible purpose" for seeing the information. That can include a lender, an insurance company, a landlord who wants to find out about your past

THE $51,000 LATE PAYMENT

Although she'd never been late on a credit card payment before, after Anna returned from vacation, she ended up paying her bill a month past its due date. Anna paid the interest and the $35 penalty charges and assumed it was all behind her. But it wasn't. When she started shopping around for a home loan a few months later, she was shocked. Although people with great credit were qualifying for 5.9% interest rates, her one late payment lowered her credit score to the point where she could only qualify for a rate of 7%. That didn't sound like a big difference, but she did the math and discovered that 1.1% meant she'd pay $51,000 extra in interest over the life of her thirty-year loan. (See the chart on p. 72 for how the math worked out.)

After consulting a few more lenders, Anna learned she could build up her score again by reestablishing her old pattern of paying all her bills on time. She decided to wait, and over the next three years her score slowly but steadily climbed back to where it was in the first place.

financial habits, or even a potential employer who wants to know more about you. (Potential employers, unlike lenders or landlords, must get your written permission before requesting your credit history.) A copy of your report will show who has made inquiries about you in the past two years.

IF YOU'RE IN SERIOUS DEBT

If you're like a lot of people these days, you may be having severe trouble paying your bills. The first thing you should do is go straight to your lenders and explain your financial situation. You may be surprised to find them willing to work with you to come up with a more flexible repayment schedule. After all, they have a vested interest in making it possible for you to pay them back.

If your creditor has hired a debt collector to get you to pay up, know your rights. Debt collectors can contact you by phone, mail, fax, or in person. They must contact you during reasonable hours (not before 8 a.m. or after 9 p.m.) unless you agree to a different arrangement. They can't harass you or repeatedly phone you with the intent to annoy you. You can stop a debt collector from continually contacting you by sending a letter to the collection agency he or she represents. Under the Fair Debt Collection Practices Act, the collection agency must stop contacting you at your written request, except to notify you of plans to bring legal action against you. Debt collectors are forbidden to contact you at your workplace once you tell them your boss doesn't allow it. It's also illegal for them to discuss your debt with your boss or fellow employees.

If you need help negotiating with lenders to lower your monthly payments and possibly reduce the interest rates on your loans, you may want to contact a nonprofit credit counselor. You can work with a counselor face-to-face, over the phone, or online. Two places to start looking for a good match are the Association of Independent Consumer Credit Counseling Agencies (www.aiccca.org) and the National Foundation for Consumer Credit (www.nfcc.org). Both organizations hold their members to strict certification and counselor training standards. The Justice Department also keeps a list of agencies that meet the official standards for helping people considering bankruptcy. For one near you, take a look at www.usdoj.gov/ust/eo/bapcpa/ccde/cc_approved.htm or call 202-514-4100.

You may also want to look into other nonprofit counseling services available in your area. Some colleges and credit unions, for example, offer help, and you might be able to get a referral from a local bank or consumer protection office.

One thing you don't want to do is sign up with a so-called debt settlement firm that claims to help you pay off your bills for a fraction of what you owe. These companies generally advise people to make monthly payments into a special account instead of paying creditors. They promise to use the accumulated cash to settle debts for pennies on the dollar, but in the end they don't actually settle anything. Their tactics could result in you losing your cash—or worse, in a major blow to your credit score.

WHY YOU SHOULD TAKE A PASS ON PAYDAY LOANS

One loan you should avoid at all costs is a **payday loan,** which is a wildly expensive way to borrow money to tide you over until your paycheck clears. A lender will give you money as an advance on what you'll soon receive, but this will cost you about $15 for every $100 that you borrow for a period of two weeks. Over the course of a year, that's a percentage rate of 391%!

If you're so desperate for money that you're considering a payday loan, see if there's some other way to go, like asking family or friends for a loan. (For more information on borrowing from friends and relatives, look back at the box on p. 69.) Some employers will allow you to borrow from your own paycheck, usually for a small fee but sometimes at no cost at all, so make sure to investigate.

WHEN TO CONSIDER BANKRUPTCY

At first blush, declaring bankruptcy, especially a certain type known as Chapter 7, can seem appealing if you're deep in debt. You have to fill out some paperwork and submit it with a fee (recently $299) to a federal bankruptcy court, and you'd also probably need to pay a bankruptcy lawyer to help make your case. But if your petition for bankruptcy is accepted, your debts will be "discharged," meaning you'll be absolved of responsibility for the money you owe to creditors such as your landlord, doctors, and credit card companies. Some of your assets can be seized to pay off these creditors, but depending on which state you live in, you may be able to work out a deal where you get to keep your car, home, and household possessions. And it may not be long before you can start borrowing again. One study found that even people who recently declared bankruptcy can get credit. (But most debtors, wisely, didn't accept.)

Although declaring bankruptcy may sound like a good deal, it's not an option that many of us should choose. For starters, there's a long list of debts that can't be discharged, even if you file Chapter 7. Student loans, for instance, usually can't be wiped out. What's more, bankruptcy is noted on your credit report for ten years. True, you may be able to get some form of credit sooner, but you probably won't be eligible for low-rate credit cards or other attractive loan deals for a long time. Finally, keep in mind that prospective employers will learn from your credit report that you declared bankruptcy—you may have trouble changing jobs, especially if you're trying to get a position that requires you to be financially responsible.

Even if all this is not enough to dissuade you, you should know that recent changes to the bankruptcy law also make it harder for people with higher incomes to use Chapter 7. To figure out whether you can file for Chapter 7, you have to measure your current monthly income against the median income for a household of your size in your state. If your income is lower than or equal to the median, you're eligible for Chapter 7. But if your income is higher than the median, you have to go through another hoop and take what's called "the means test." It's designed to figure out whether you have enough disposable income, after subtracting certain allowed expenses and required debt payments, to qualify for what's known as Chapter 13.

With Chapter 13, you'll pay less to file, but your debts won't be wiped clean. The court will instead set up a repayment plan that will make it easier for you to pay off all or part of what you owe creditors. It's not, however, all that simple. Chapter 13 filers with incomes above the median in their state, for example, have to hand over all of their disposable income. They're allowed to keep a certain amount, which is decided by the IRS, for expenses. There are some other drawbacks, such as the fact that personal property is valued at its replacement price, meaning how much it would cost to buy it if it was new. That makes the Chapter 13 filer look richer on paper than in reality, so the official in charge of recovering the debt has greater leeway to confiscate and sell the goods. Also, filers will have to pay the full amount of a car loan if they want to keep their car, even if the vehicle is now worth less.

Before you can file for bankruptcy under either Chapter 7 or Chapter 13, you have to complete credit counseling with a U.S. Trustee's Office–approved agency to determine whether it's really necessary. Counseling is required even if it's clear that an informal repayment plan wouldn't work. You don't have to agree to any repayment plan the agency proposes, but you do have to submit it to the court along with proof you completed the counseling before you can file for bankruptcy.

Before your case is over, you'll have to go to another couseling session to learn how to manage your personal finances. Again, you'll need proof you completed the counseling before you can get a bankruptcy discharge wiping out your debts.

Consider bankruptcy only as a last resort. If you're in deep trouble and have no choice, do some research at sites like www .thebankruptcysite.org or visit the American Bankruptcy Institute online at www.abiworld.org.

FINANCIAL CRAMMING

- Take any savings you have and pay off your high-rate credit card debt. Paying off a balance on a credit card that charges 14% is the equivalent of earning more than 14% interest on your money after taxes. This is the best investment you can make.

- If you have a decent credit history and you can't pay off your high-rate credit card debt immediately, try to get a low-rate card and transfer your debt to it. You can find listings of low-rate cards on sites like www.credit.com, www.cardtrak.com, and www.lowcards.com.

- If you're having trouble paying off your student loans, speak with your loan servicer to find a repayment plan that works better for you. See p. 52 for details.

- Before you visit a car dealership, shop around to get an idea of current auto loan rates and car pricing information. Then, once you find the car you want, negotiate an exact price for a car with the dealer before you discuss the financing he has to offer.

- If you own a home, think twice before taking out a home equity line in order to pay off your high-rate debt. Plan to pay off your home equity line as fast as you would have paid off the loans you're refinancing.

- Get free copies of your credit reports from www.annualcredit report.com (877-322-8228) and buy your credit scores from www.myfico.com.

- If you've been a victim of identity theft, call the credit bureaus' fraud departments to have a fraud alert placed on your file. (See p. 74 for more details.)

BASIC
BANKING

How to Keep Your Costs Low
and Your Money Safe

THERE WAS A time when people's financial lives revolved around their local bank.
They got their mortgage there. They obtained their first credit card
there. They kept their checking and savings accounts there. They
may have even gotten their toaster there.

But that's not true for you, because today many of the services
that were once the domain of your local bank are better handled
online. You probably went online to shop for an auto loan or to
apply for a credit card. Or you may even keep your savings in an
Internet-based bank because it pays you higher interest.

So why do you need a bank at all? The main reason is that
banks offer two services that are still difficult to get elsewhere: an
all-purpose checking account and easy access to your cash through
ATMs (automated teller machines). You don't want to settle for just
any bank. Your goal is to find the one that gives you those things
for the lowest fees and the least hassle.

This chapter will show you how to shop for a bank and how to
manage the money you keep there. It will also give you tips on how
to cut costs and maximize savings when you bank online. And it
will explain how you can keep your money safe, despite the recent
turmoil in the banking industry.

A BANK BY ANY OTHER NAME

For our purposes, it doesn't matter whether an institution calls itself a bank, a savings bank, or a savings and loan (S&L). These
classifications only reflect the government agency that oversees the
institution—they're all the same to you. A **credit union** is slightly
different: a sort of not-for-profit bank formed by people who have
something in common, such as their workplace or profession. Credit
unions tend to offer lower-priced services than ordinary banks. (For
details on the advantages of credit unions and how to join, see the
box on p. 89).

Nearly all banks, savings banks, and S&Ls in the United States
are covered by something called federal deposit insurance, which
guarantees that, if the institution fails, the money in your account
is protected. The government agency behind this is the Federal Deposit Insurance Corporation (FDIC), and it normally protects accounts up to $100,000 (the government has raised that limit to
$250,000, but it may be temporary), so you have nothing to worry
about. Check for FDIC stickers in banks that you're considering or
consult the FDIC website (www.fdic.gov/deposit) to find out if your
accounts are insured and for how much. At credit unions, look for
the NCUA sign, which indicates that accounts are protected by the
National Credit Union Share Insurance Fund. If you don't see a sign
or sticker at your institution, ask. Keep in mind that many banks,
savings banks, S&Ls, and credit unions also sell uninsured investments these days (which will be explained later in this chapter), so
it is important to make sure that the type of account you're opening
is covered by federal deposit insurance.

For simplicity, I'm going to stick with the term "bank" when
discussing all these financial institutions.

WHAT TO LOOK FOR IN A BANK

Whether you need a bank or you're just thinking about switching
to a new one, here's what you want:

- **Free checking.** Most banks offer this—you just have to
  wade through the choices and sign up for the right account.
  Look for one that allows you to write as many checks as
  you need in whatever amount you want without requiring
  you to maintain a minimum balance. Some banks may require you to have a regular paycheck automatically deposited into your account in order to qualify for free checking.

- **Nearby ATM or branch locations.** Free ATM access is key.
  Banks don't charge you for using their own machines, but
  you will be charged for using ATMs that are affiliated with
  other banks. The fee your bank charges you for using a
  "foreign" ATM, as it is called, is on average $2, but could
  be as high as $3. So if you tend to use the ATM a lot, make
  sure you open a checking account at a bank with ATM locations near your work or home.

- **Online account access.** Online banking is a great way to
  monitor your accounts. You'll spot any bank errors much
  faster if you check your accounts online every week, instead
  of waiting for the monthly paper statement to arrive in
  the mail. Almost all banks offer free online account access
  with a checking account. This includes your statements and
  transaction history. Some banks will actually charge you for
  requesting paper statements, so if that matters to you, ask
  about it in advance.

- **Mobile banking.** If you're on the road a lot and can't get
  to a computer, see if your bank offers mobile banking. It
  will allow you to check your balances, pay bills, and transfer money between accounts, all from your cell phone—
  a handy tool for those on the go.

MANAGING YOUR CHECKING ACCOUNT

Make sure you're managing your checking account wisely. If you don't, you could find yourself paying hundreds of dollars in fees. These fees are big business for banks. Here are some tips that will help you avoid such outrageous charges:

- **Monitor your checking account balance.** You should check your balance at least once a week in order to spot anything that isn't right. For example, I know someone whose account mysteriously showed her balance to be *minus* $600, even though she knew she had $400 in the account. If she hadn't kept tabs on her balance, she wouldn't have caught what turned out to be a bank error and would have lost the equivalent of $1,000. (Save all your debit card and ATM receipts until your transaction shows up online in case you have a dispute with the bank.)

- **Be wary of overdraft protection plans.** For years, banks got a bad rap for charging as much as $30 for each bounced check, in addition to the $20 to $30 you would owe the merchant to whom you wrote the check. These days, most major banks will automatically enroll you in what they call a **courtesy overdraft protection program** in order to shield you from these charges, but don't let the name fool you. Often, this type of "courtesy" protection is more expensive than the charges from which it allegedly protects you. Some courtesy.

  Here's how this system works. If you write a check or use your debit card (or at some banks try to withdraw money from an ATM) for an amount greater than what you actually have in your checking account, the bank has the option to cover the shortfall and let the transaction go through. If it does this, you'll be charged a flat fee (generally $30 to $40) each time. And here's where it can get really bad: Some banks will increase the fee each additional time you're caught short or for each day your balance remains below zero ($5 to $15 per item, or $5 to $10 per day). In theory, these fees could end up in the hundreds of dollars.

But there's a way around this that still protects you from the possibility of bouncing a check. When you open a checking account, tell the bank that you don't want courtesy protection, but instead want to link your checking account to your savings account. This is your cheapest option. If you're worried that you don't have enough savings, your next best move is to sign up for something called an **overdraft line of credit**, which is essentially an automatic loan that kicks in to cover you. Although it's not a great deal either—the interest rate on the overdrawn amount can run to 18% or higher—it's generally cheaper than either courtesy overdraft protection or a bounced check charge.

If you opt for this plan, keep in mind that you'll probably have to make a separate payment to cover the account if you have an overdraft; not all banks will automatically use your next deposit to pay it off. Also, be aware that some banks allow you to access your overdraft line of credit via your ATM—which can actually be really dangerous. I have a friend who ran out of money and simply withdrew the $1,000 in overdraft protection via the ATM to cover the cost of a trip to France. It took her three years and more than $300 in interest to pay off the loan.

Bottom line: The only real protection is you. Make sure you don't spend more than you have.

- **Link your accounts.** If you link your checking account to a savings account (or even a low-rate credit card you have with the bank), it can automatically transfer funds to your checking account as needed. Some banks do charge transfer fees (so know what they are), but they're usually much lower than overdraft fees.

- **Avoid interest-bearing checking accounts.** Checking accounts that pay interest sound appealing, but they're often bad deals. Many require you to keep thousands of dollars in your account while paying you next to nothing. At one major bank, for example, in order to earn a pitiful 0.05%, you have to maintain a minimum balance of $10,000. At that interest rate, you'll make all of $5 at the end of a year. And that's assuming your balance doesn't dip below the required minimum—in which case you'll be dinged with a $20 fee. At the same time, by leaving your money in such a low-paying account, you're not keeping up with inflation, so you're actually losing purchasing power. (For more on beating inflation, see Chapter 5.) You're better off using an ordinary checking account and finding a higher-paying savings account for extra funds.

- **Pay your bills online.** Most banks provide free electronic bill payment. (For more details, see Chapter 2.) You simply go to your online checking account and find the link to paying bills, where you provide the names of merchants, the amounts you owe, and the dates on which you want each payment to arrive. These may be recurring bills or one-time payments. The bank will either take money from your account and send a certified bank check or simply make an electronic transfer.

- **Use direct deposit for your paycheck.** If you have a regular paycheck, ask your employer to electronically transfer it straight into your checking account. Some banks will not only waive minimum balance requirements if you have direct deposit, but also reduce monthly service charges or even offer you a small cash bonus.

- **Pick up the phone.** Many banks will waive fees if you contest them. If you find a fee on your statement, call the bank to explain why the fee occurred and why you think it should be erased. If it's your first offense—an overdraft mistake, for example—there's a good chance you can talk the service rep into removing it. A friend of a friend of mine moved to a city where her bank had no branches and found she was paying the bank a $2 fee every time she used another bank's

CONSIDER A CREDIT UNION

Credit unions tend to charge lower rates on loans and pay higher rates on savings accounts than ordinary banks (better even than some online banks). And credit unions typically charge less for everything from money orders to bounced checks. As with your deposits in a traditional bank, the money you have in a credit union (up to $250,000 until at least December 2009) is federally insured.

But before you sign up with a credit union, see if it offers all the services you want. Although more and more credit unions belong to ATM networks that are controlled by fellow credit unions, they still operate a relatively small number of machines compared to what banks offer. That means credit union members must often use a bank's ATM and pay high fees for the privilege. Also, not all credit unions offer online access to accounts.

Still, if you like the idea of doing your banking with a nonprofit community outlet, look into a credit union to see if it's right for you. If you work for your city, chances are there's a credit union available to you. Contact the Credit Union National Association (www.cuna.org; 800-358-5710) to find a website or phone number for your state's credit union league. The league will help you locate a credit union that you may be able to join. For example, your church, synagogue, or alma mater may have one, or your community may have a credit union whose members are people who live in the neighborhood. If you have a relative who belongs to a credit union, you might be eligible to enroll; some credit unions accept immediate family members only, while others allow members of the extended family to sign up.

ATM. She called her bank and explained that since there were no branches in her city, she had no choice but to use other banks' ATMs. The manager removed three months of fees, saving her $44.

USING THE ATM WISELY

Not that long ago, banks didn't charge you for using ATMs at all. They wanted to encourage customers to bank by machine so they could save money on tellers' salaries. It worked. And then, when everyone started getting hooked, banks started charging consumers to use them. Today, people spend billions of dollars a year on ATM fees; I know plenty of people who throw away hundreds of dollars a year on their cash machine addictions. Here's how I suggest you keep those ATM habits—and your spending—in check:

- **Find out what your bank charges you to use another bank's ATM.** Your bank probably won't charge you for using its ATMs, but will charge you as much as $3 for using machines that are affiliated with other banks. Your bank won't warn you about this fee—you'll just see it on your next statement. So stick with your own bank's ATM whenever you can.

- **Find out what other banks charge too.** It's the nasty one-two punch of ATM fees: In addition to the fees your own bank may charge you for using another bank's ATM, you will almost certainly also have to pay so-called **surcharges** of as much as $3 to that other bank. These surcharges can be especially high in places where people need to get money fast, like malls and casinos. I know of one ATM in Las Vegas that charges $20 per withdrawal! Remember which ATMs carry high surcharges and avoid them when you can, or be sure to withdraw as much as you'll need for the week when you're at your own ATM.

THE $33.50 PACK OF GUM

When Adam moved to New York City, he signed up for a checking account at a bank near his office and got a debit card linked to the account. The officer who helped him never mentioned that by signing up for the new account, he was automatically enrolled in a courtesy overdraft protection plan. Adam assumed that if he didn't have enough money in his account, he wouldn't be able to use the card to buy things. The Thursday after getting his first paycheck (his company didn't have direct deposit) Adam deposited it into his brand-new account and allowed two days for it to clear. That weekend, Adam figured the funds were already in his account and began to use the card for small purchases. On Saturday, he bought the following things:

Gum	@Pharmacy	$1.50
Cappuccino	@Coffee shop	$4.50
Dinner	@Pizzeria	$19.00
Groceries	@Grocery store	$25.00
Total		$50.00

On Monday, Adam checked his account online and discovered that he had been charged an extra $32 for *each* of the things he purchased. Since his paycheck hadn't cleared until that morning, the bank had slapped him with fees of as high as 2,100% on the $1.50 pack of gum. (And if he weren't able to pay it off right away, it would have been even higher.) The total bill: $128 in "insufficient funds courtesy fees."

- **Know the different ATM fees your bank charges.** Avoid using ATMs for more than deposits and withdrawals. Some banks actually charge for other transactions like finding out your balance or transferring funds between accounts. Make a habit of handling those transactions online. Or look for a bank with low transaction fees or one that waives all ATM charges when you maintain a certain minimum balance.

- **Limit yourself to four ATM withdrawals per month if possible.** Not only can it be expensive to withdraw, say, $20 a day from an ATM belonging to a bank other than your own, but it's also a bad way to keep track of where your money goes. Use the worksheet you filled out in Chapter 2 to estimate how much cash you need each week. Then pick one day a week to withdraw cash from the machine—say, every Monday. Make a pact with yourself to make that cash last for the entire week. Promise yourself that once it runs out, you won't get more. This strategy will also help you rein in your spending.

- **Consider "cash back" rather than ATM withdrawal.** You can often make ATM-style cash withdrawals at the supermarket or drug store, though you'll usually be limited to $50 or $60. If your grocery bill comes to $20, for example, say "yes" when the cashier asks if you want cash back. The money he or she gives you from the till is generally fee-free—a better deal than going to an ATM.

- **Keep your ATM receipts.** Hold on to those little slips until you can check them against your online statement to make sure the bank hasn't made an error in recording your transaction.

WHEN TO GO INTERNET-ONLY

You may choose to go with an account that's offered only online, or an **Internet bank account.** This could mean that your bank has few or no brick and mortar branches, or it may mean that you've signed up for an online-only account at a traditional bank. Either way, Internet bank accounts have become extremely popular recently, largely because they pay higher interest on savings accounts. Since the costs for that bank are so much lower than those of a brick and mortar bank (branches, tellers, ATMs) it can pass on these savings to you in the form of higher interest.

You'll most likely get an ATM card for cash withdrawals and debit card purchases. Some banks will offer paper checks as well or will enable you to make online payments. There are some drawbacks, however. (For example, you may not be able to communicate with anyone at the bank in person.) If you're thinking about signing up for an Internet bank account, here are some things to consider:

- **What kinds of deposits will you be making?** If most are from your paycheck, no problem: Sign up for direct deposit. But many Internet banks don't have a wide ATM network, which means that in order to make most any other kind of deposit, you'll have to *mail* it to the bank. This could be a major problem if you need to get a check into your account right away or if you're paid in cash. Some Internet banks are affiliated with brick and mortar banks and therefore have wider ATM access—important if you make a lot of cash deposits.

- **What will it cost to use ATMs?** Check the bank's ATM policy. Find out if you can use its ATM network. If you can't, or if the bank doesn't have one, this could add up to hefty surcharges. Some Internet banks may credit you automatically for ATM surcharges, while others may require you to mail in your ATM receipts in order to get reimbursed, which can be a pain. Some may not credit you at all.

- **Will you need to write paper checks?** While some Internet-only banks have begun to issue checkbooks and debit cards, most of them provide electronic bill-paying services. This can be convenient in many situations, but not when you need to give someone a check right away.

- **How much time does it take for a check to clear?** Internet banks sometimes take *longer* to process checks than traditional banks. You may have to wait as long as five business days after the bank receives your check to see the funds in your account. If your online bank doesn't have ATMs that allow you to make a deposit, this could mean a week on top of the length of time your check is in the mail.

- **Will you miss speaking with a bank teller?** Truth is, I don't know anyone other than my dad who regularly speaks to a teller. But if you're so inclined, customer service at an Internet bank is sometimes limited to phone calls and e-mails. Even if your Internet bank is affiliated with a brick and mortar bank, you won't be able to walk into a branch office and consult tellers.

WHAT TO DO WITH YOUR SAVINGS

No matter what kind of bank you use, bank savings options don't offer the potential for phenomenal gains, but that's not what you're after here. When it comes to savings, safety and access—not phenomenal returns—are the goal. Banks can be a good place to accumulate the "three-month emergency cushion" discussed in Chapter 2. You might also want to consider putting savings beyond that into something called a money fund, which I will discuss in Chapter 5. Your goal is to find a safe, high-paying account with **liquidity,** meaning you can withdraw your cash whenever you want without any penalty.

Check on www.bankrate.com or www.bankingmyway.com to find the best deals on savings accounts that pay the highest interest. Here are some details on the interest-paying accounts you will encounter:

- **Basic savings accounts.** This plain-vanilla type of account is the simplest way to keep money in the bank and earn interest on it. Most major banks require you to maintain a minimum balance (usually $300 to $500) or they'll charge you a monthly fee. The bummer about savings accounts in traditional banks is that they tend to pay very low—almost negligible—interest. Banks eventually raise the rates on savings accounts when interest rates in the economy rise, but they're very slow in doing this.

- **Internet savings accounts.** In recent years, rates on Internet-only accounts have been higher than those on traditional bank savings accounts. Internet banks are able to offer these rates because their expenses are much lower than regular banks, although there's no guarantee those rates will remain so high. Generally you can open an online savings account in less than five minutes with no minimum cash requirement (though it will take about a week for the money to appear in your new account). The money you keep in a federally insured Internet bank account is normally protected for up to $100,000 (the government upped it to $250,000 until at least December 31, 2009), just as it would be at a traditional bank, so if the bank goes out of business you won't lose your savings. Check by searching the Federal Deposit Insurance Corporation's website (www.fdic.gov) or contact the FDIC Call Center on 877-ASKFDIC (877-275-3342).

- **Money market accounts.** A money market account (MMA) is little more than a savings account with a relatively high minimum balance requirement and a complicated name. You will most likely need $1,000 to $3,500 to open a money market account, and you may have to keep at least $1,000 in your account at all times to avoid paying a monthly account maintenance fee. Like savings accounts, MMAs are liquid (except for the minimum balance requirement), but they may also pay more interest, depending on how much you have in the account.

Because they require you to tie up so much cash, I'd say skip these. One exception: MMAs at many Internet banks tend to offer decent rates, so they're worth investigating.

- **Certificates of deposit (CDs).** A certificate of deposit is a so-called "savings product" that usually pays a fixed interest rate if you keep your money in it for a specified period of time (known as the CD's **term**). You can find a CD with as short a term as three months or as long a term as ten years. CDs almost always pay slightly better rates than savings or money market accounts at traditional banks. With a CD you make a one-time investment and earn interest until the CD's term is complete. You do not continually add money to a CD; if you want to invest more money, you can open a new CD.

   At many banks you need at least $1,500 to open a CD, but some banks will allow you to open one with just $500. Basically, you're giving up the liquidity you have with a sav-

THE BEAUTY OF SAVING AUTOMATICALLY

Although you're probably not going to keep your life savings in a bank forever, a bank savings account is a great place to start. If you haven't been able to accumulate much savings on your own, have someone save *for* you. "Forced" savings methods that pull money from your checking account into a savings account offer an effortless way to build up a nest egg. (For more details, see Chapter 2.) One idea: Ask your employer to put the bulk of your salary into a checking account and the rest into a savings account. Or have your bank transfer a certain amount into your savings account once your paycheck has been deposited into your checking account. This will take you less than five minutes on your bank's website.

ings or money market account in exchange for a higher rate. If you take out the money you've deposited before the CD's term is complete, you'll be hit with a steep early withdrawal fee. In some cases, you could lose all your interest plus part of your initial investment. So CDs are best for money you know you won't need for a while.

When you put money in a CD, you're sort of placing a bet that interest rates at the moment are higher than they will be in the near future. Here's an explanation: Say you deposit money in a one-year CD that promises to pay you 4%. Now suppose six months later, interest rates in the economy increase dramatically, and banks are now paying 5% on one-year CDs. You're stuck with a 4% CD for another six months. Though you would like to get out of the 4% CD and into a 5% CD, the early withdrawal penalty you'd have to pay might be so large that it wouldn't be worth it. You won't face this risk with a money market fund or a savings account because the rate you receive will rise (slower with the savings account than the money fund) as interest rates in the economy rise. Of course, this works in reverse too. If interest rates fall and new CDs are paying 3%, you'd be a winner with your 4% CD.

JOINT VERSUS SEPARATE ACCOUNTS

Before you open a joint account with anyone, give it serious thought. With a joint savings or checking account, either person has complete access to all the money. What's more, if you have a falling-out with that person, dividing up the money could get ugly.

Many people in serious relationships do decide, though, to open joint accounts both for the sake of convenience and to ensure that their partner has their money if anything happens to them. But this can be very tricky. Having a **joint account** with what is known as the **right of convenience** does not entitle one person to inherit all the money that's in it if the other dies. Having a joint account with what is known as the **right of survivorship**, however, does. Yet it still doesn't provide total protection for the surviving partner; parents and other family members can challenge the arrangement in court, especially if there isn't a marriage license or will.

Even if you're married, you and your spouse should discuss the joint account question. If you favor separate accounts but your spouse wants a joint one, there's a way to compromise: Consider putting a certain percentage of each paycheck into separate accounts and keeping the rest in a joint savings account. This way you'll have the freedom to spend some of your money independently. You should also discuss what will happen in case of death. In some states your parents would split your assets with your spouse if you die without leaving a will.

If you and your spouse decide to have a joint account, you're going to need to develop a system for managing it so that you can avoid penalty fees—with two people writing checks, it can get complicated.

One person should assume responsibility for the account and keep track of the balance. You might want to keep a box or a folder in a commonly used area (maybe where you drop the mail) where you can stick both debit receipts and ATM slips. If you use a checkbook, get one with carbon copies. Whoever monitors the account can go through the paperwork every week or so to make sure everything's in order. It's also a good idea to set a price limit for individual purchases and agree that you won't buy anything over that amount without consulting the other person.

A WARNING ABOUT
BANK-SOLD INVESTMENTS

Banks used to offer only savings options—savings accounts, MMAs, and CDs—all of which are federally insured. Today many banks also offer a wider array of investment choices, including mutual funds. Although you'll learn everything you ever wanted to know about mutual funds in Chapter 5, I want to mention something right away: Mutual funds, even those sold in banks, are *not* protected by federal deposit insurance. That means you *can* lose money with a mutual fund. Bank salespeople, who like to call themselves "financial counselors," are supposed to explain this; they sometimes forget.

As a rule, you're almost certainly better off buying mutual funds directly from low-cost mutual fund companies than from banks, because most banks offer limited choices and charge commissions. So skip the investments at the bank no matter how persuasive the salesperson is. Chapter 5 will tell you all about working with low-cost mutual fund companies.

WHY IT PAYS TO KNOW YOUR BANK MANAGER

You don't have to present your bank manager with a shiny apple each time you visit, but it's a good idea to get acquainted. You can simply say that you've signed on as a customer and wanted to introduce yourself. If you think this sounds a little weird, invent a reason—ask about loan choices or something. The point is to make sure the manager recognizes your face. It may even make sense to add your bank manager to your holiday card list. If you ever have a problem, it can really help to have someone at the bank who knows you as more than just another multidigit account number. And if you ever encounter an outrageous fee, don't hesitate to speak up. When a friend of mine was charged $30 for two certified checks—an amount he felt was too high—he protested to the bank manager, who waived the fee. The fact is bank managers often forgive fees for customers who complain, especially customers who have clean banking records. And if you're penalized for something you had no control over—like unknowingly depositing a bad check—you should definitely talk to the bank manager; he or she may be willing to give you a refund.

FINANCIAL CRAMMING

- Find a bank that has conveniently located ATMs so you can avoid the fees incurred by using another bank's ATM.

- Avoid insufficient funds charges by checking your account activity and balance regularly online.

- Look into Internet-only interest and check out websites like www.bankrate.com and www.bankingmyway.com to compare rates.

- If you've been charged an outrageous fee for a bank service, complain. Being firm but polite will often help you persuade the bank's manager or customer service rep to waive the charge.

- Resist buying mutual funds from your bank. Instead, look into some of the low-cost mutual fund companies discussed in Chapter 5.

ALL YOU REALLY NEED TO KNOW ABOUT INVESTING

Getting a Foothold in this Rocky Landscape

EVERYONE KNOWS THE stock market can be risky. Stocks skyrocketed in the 1990s, tumbled from 2000 through 2002, recovered, and then had one of the worst years in history in 2008. Clearly, volatility is the name of the game. But whether the market is rising or falling, one thing is certain: Nobody really knows where it will go next.

So what do you do?

No matter what's happening in the stock market, once you have enough to cover your living expenses and are getting started on your emergency savings cushion, you should at least learn the basics of investing. There are some simple rules for putting your money in everything from safe investments that pay a little more than a bank account to riskier alternatives that give you the chance to earn more. Whatever your comfort level, you should be thinking about an investment known as a mutual fund. In fact, you can consider mutual funds your entire investment universe, at least for now. This chapter will explain what mutual funds are and how you might want to use them to meet the goals you formulated in Chapter 2. Later in this chapter, you'll learn how to actually go about investing in them.

MUTUAL FUND FUNDAMENTALS

Before I get into the details, you'll need to know what a mutual fund is. Mutual means shared, or in common. A fund is a sum of money set aside for a particular purpose. A **mutual fund** is a type of investment that pools together the money of thousands of people. At the helm is a fund manager—the person (or company)—in charge of investing the money. Depending on the type of fund, the fund manager generally invests the fund's money in a mixture of stocks, bonds, and money market instruments; these are all known as **securities**. (I'll explain all of these things in a moment.)

What's So Great About Mutual Funds?

Pooling your money with the money of other people works to your advantage because it allows you to reduce the risk you take as an investor. A mutual fund is typically invested in hundreds or even thousands of different stocks, bonds, or money market instruments. If you bought just one of these securities on your own, your success or failure would depend solely on the performance of that one security. When you invest in a mutual fund, though, you avoid putting all your eggs in one basket. So even if half the securities in the mutual fund lose value, you won't necessarily lose money; the other half may be profitable and may offset the losses with gains. The term for this investing principle is **diversification**.

Some people would argue that you're not really an investor unless you put money in individual stocks. And there's no doubt that it's much more exciting to follow one stock closely and watch it rise or fall. But I don't recommend individual stocks for people who are just starting out—or even for people who have been investing for a while—unless they can afford to lose that money. Buying individual stocks does not offer the diversification you get with mutual funds. (But if you still want to buy individual stocks despite my warnings, see p. 134 for the best way to go about it.)

Mutual Fund Shares and Where They Are Sold

When you invest in any type of mutual fund, technically you're purchasing units known as **shares**. As shareholders, you and thousands of others are in fact the owners of the fund. The fund's share price—meaning the price at which you can buy or sell a share in the fund—is called the **net asset value (NAV)**.

There are several ways to invest in a mutual fund. The simplest is to buy it directly from a **mutual fund company** (a company that sells—you guessed it—mutual funds). Both traditional and Internet **brokerage firms**, which tend to specialize in trading individual stocks and bonds, offer mutual funds as well. So do financial planners, banks, and insurance agents. Your best bet is to go with a low-cost mutual fund company. I'll explain why in this chapter, and I'll offer recommendations about specific mutual fund companies.

Two Pointers for New Investors

Before I get into the details of the various types of mutual funds, I'd like to take a minute to acknowledge the sad truths of investment life. Though these points may seem obvious, they're often lost on investors who should know better.

- **There's no easy way to pick a winner.** The fact that a given stock did well last year, for example, provides little or no information about how well it will do in future years. More generally, there's no proven investment strategy that will always beat the others. If people tell you otherwise, don't believe them—including the analyst from a major brokerage firm who appears on CNBC, the distinguished economist who is quoted regularly in the newspaper, or your favorite uncle on your mother's side who had the foresight to buy stock in Microsoft in the 1980s.

• **In general, you don't get something for nothing.** With rare
exceptions, the only way to get an unusually high rate of
return on your investments is to accept an unusually high
level of risk. So if anyone promises you a very high return
with "no risk," be skeptical.

MONEY MARKET FUNDS

Money market funds are a specific type of mutual fund that provides
a relatively safe alternative to bank savings accounts. Though it's not
a bad idea to keep money you need for your three-month emergency
cushion (see Chapter 2) in a plain old savings account, you may also
want to consider a money market fund for further savings. Usually
known simply as money funds, they're typically the safest, most stable
type of mutual fund, and the returns they pay tend to be higher than
the rates paid on most bank savings accounts.

Don't let the name confuse you. Money market *funds* (MMFs)
are very different from bank money market *accounts* (MMAs),
which you learned about in Chapter 4. For one thing, the cash you
put into a money fund is not federally insured like a bank money
market account is. (During the financial upheavals of 2008, though,
the government did temporarily insure some money funds.) Although it's rare for one of these funds to lose money—only two
have done so since MMFs were first created in 1970—it can happen. (More on that in a minute.)

As with bank accounts, it's easy to withdraw your cash from a
money market fund, but some MMFs have a minimum starting balance of $1,000 or more. And there are times when money market
funds pay less than a high-rate Internet bank savings account, so
always make sure to compare when choosing a place to park your
emergency cushion. (To learn more about high-rate Internet savings, see Chapter 4.)

What Are Money Market "Instruments"?

To better understand what money funds are, you'll need a crash course in money market instruments, the securities that money funds invest in. When large companies or governments need money for very short periods of time, they issue **money market instruments** in exchange for the cash they need. These money market instruments are basically IOUs from reliable institutions like the federal government, various state governments, and big-name corporations that promise to repay these debts very quickly. And for the most part they've kept their word. But as recently as 2008, a fund called the Reserve Primary Fund lost money (leaving investors with a bit less money than they had put in). The catalyst: the Reserve Primary Fund held IOUs from the Wall Street firm Lehman Brothers, which eventually declared bankruptcy.

How You Make Money from a Money Market Fund

As with any mutual fund, when you invest in a money fund, you're actually purchasing shares of that fund. Money fund managers try to keep the price (known as the **net asset value** or **NAV**) of each share equal to a dollar at all times by investing in short-term debt securities they believe to be very safe. So when you invest $250 in a money fund, what you're actually doing is buying 250 shares of the fund. The fund manager then puts your $250 together with the money from other investors and loans it to various governments and/or corporations, receiving IOUs (money market instruments) in return.

In addition to repaying their debts, these governments and corporations must pay the money fund interest on the money they're borrowing. Now here's the good part. The fund then passes these interest payments on to you in the form of **dividends**, typically credited to your account every business day. If you like, most money market funds will deposit these dividends into your bank account or mail them to you (usually once a month). Many investors, however, choose to have their dividends automatically reinvested in the money fund. In this case, their dividends are used to buy them more shares in the fund. This is a smart thing to do; in addition to saving you the hassle of bookkeeping, it's a painless way to increase the size of your account and keep yourself from spending your dividends.

The **yield** of a money fund is expressed as a percentage and is analogous to the interest rate paid on a savings account. It's calculated by dividing the fund's **dividends per share** by its share price (with most funds, the share price is a dollar, making this really easy math). The yield of each money fund fluctuates day to day. Since money funds all calculate their yields in the same way, you can (and should) compare the yields of several money funds before selecting one. You can comparison shop online at www.bankrate.com, www .imoneynet.com, and www.cranedata.us.

Money funds send monthly or quarterly statements indicating the number and value of the shares you own. The two figures are usually the same because the price per share is almost always a dollar.

Different Types of Money Market Funds

There are a variety of types of money funds to choose from. Your tax bracket and the state you live in will have some influence on which fund you choose. Also, some types of money funds are slightly riskier than others.

The choices are detailed below, divided into two basic categories: taxable money funds and tax-exempt money funds. Although you don't need to memorize all the specs, you'll probably want to refer to this information when you're ready to choose a money fund.

- **Taxable money market funds.** If you are just starting out and are in a low tax bracket, these make the most sense for you. With all taxable money market funds, you're required to pay federal taxes on the dividends you earn (although in some cases, you may be exempt from certain state or local taxes on those dividends). Here are the major subcategories (basically the gory details) of taxable money funds:

» *U.S. Treasury money funds* invest in short-term federal government IOUs called Treasury bills. These are the money funds that are closest (in terms of safety) to bank accounts since Treasury bills are issued by Uncle Sam and are said to be backed by the "full faith and credit" of the U.S. government. (This basically means that the government promises to pay you everything you're entitled to, even if it has to raise taxes or print more money to do so.) The dividends you receive will be taxed by the federal government; they may be free from state and local taxes, depending on which state you live in.

» *U.S. government money funds* invest in various types of money market instruments issued by the U.S. government itself and/or by federal agencies like the Small Business Administration. Because U.S. government agency securities are backed only by the "moral obligation" of the federal government, not by its "full faith and credit," they're considered just a little bit riskier than U.S. Treasury bills. To compensate investors for this slight additional risk, the yield on government money funds is a touch higher. Some of the dividends are free from state and local taxes in certain states.

» *Corporate money funds*, also known as **prime money funds,** invest in money market securities issued by companies in the United States and abroad. (The Reserve Primary Fund I mentioned earlier was a corporate money fund.) Because the risk that a corporation will fail to repay its debts is considered higher than the risk of default by the federal government or a federal agency, and because the dividends paid by a corporate money fund are not exempt from state tax, corporate money funds tend to offer somewhat higher yields than money funds that invest in government instruments. Neither the additional risk nor the additional yield is very large, however.

- **Tax-exempt money market funds.** If you earn a relatively high income and are in a higher tax bracket, you should consider these. When people refer to a money market fund as tax-exempt, they generally mean only that its dividends are exempt from *federal* tax. The dividends of tax-exempt funds are sometimes exempt from state (and in certain cases, local) tax, but this is not the case for all such funds. In either case, the yield on tax-exempt money funds is lower than the yield on taxable funds, but since the dividends aren't subject to federal income tax, you may end up earning more money in the end with a tax-exempt fund. Here are your choices:

  » *Federal tax-exempt money funds* (sometimes referred to simply as tax-exempt money funds) invest in money market instruments issued by various states, counties, cities, and towns, along with tax-exempt entities like utilities. The dividends paid by these funds are not subject to federal tax, but if you live where there's a state or local income tax, you'll have to pay these taxes on all or most of your dividend income. In most cases, federal tax-exempt funds invest in the securities of a number of issuers and in a number of different regions, in an effort to reduce risk through diversification.

  » *Double tax-exempt money funds* invest in money market instruments issued by a single state (or by counties, cities, towns, or utilities) and pay dividends that are exempt from both federal *and* state income taxes, as long as you're a resident of that state. Because such funds are not able to invest in the securities of as many issuers in as many regions, they may be somewhat riskier than multistate federal tax-exempt money funds.

  » *Triple tax-exempt* money funds may be right for you if you live in a city like New York or Philadelphia where residents pay income tax not only to the IRS but to the state and city as well. These funds are similar to double tax-exempt money funds but restrict their investments to a single city, not just a single state. Although they offer a triple tax break (federal, state, and local) for residents of that city, such funds are even less diversified (and thus a bit riskier) than double tax-exempt money funds.

Taxes and Money Funds

Remember, if you want to go with the absolutely safest type of money fund, choose a U.S. Treasury money fund. If you're willing to take a little bit more risk, the main thing to focus on is the yield— or to be more precise, what's left of the yield after you pay your income taxes. For this reason, as I suggested above, your choice of a money fund may be influenced by your federal income tax bracket, and if you live in an area where you're required to pay state and city income taxes, by those tax brackets as well. (To figure out your tax bracket, see Chapter 9.)

Here's why taxes matter. Say you're considering investing in a corporate money fund that pays 5%. Assuming that there's no state or city income tax where you live and that you're in the 25% federal tax bracket, 25% of that 5%, or 1.25%, will go to Uncle Sam, leaving you with an after-tax yield of only 3.75%. So you'd need to earn more than 3.75% from a tax-exempt money fund in order to beat the return you'd get on the taxable fund. In this case, a tax-exempt fund paying 4%, for example, would be a better deal for you than the 5% taxable fund. Since the yields on money market funds fluctuate, you should repeat this comparison every year. If you discover at some point that you'd be better off investing in, say, a taxable fund instead of a tax-exempt fund, it's easy to transfer your money from one to the other.

If you're subject to state and/or city income tax, do the above calculation using your combined federal, state, and local tax rate. You can then decide whether a double or triple tax-exempt money fund would give you enough additional after-tax yield to make it worth taking a bit more risk. This is probably much more than you'll ever need (or want) to know. Still, it's here for reference when you need it.

Where to Find a Money Market Fund

Because money funds hardly ever lose money, some people ignore all these details and simply go for a money fund that offers them the best after-tax yields. To find lists of the highest interest rates currently being offered on money market funds, check out bank rate.com, imoneynet.com, and cranedata.us. If you're a one-stop shopper, you might want to get your money fund where you will eventually do other types of mutual fund investing. (For recommendations on specific mutual fund companies that might satisfy all your fund needs, see the section "Deciding Where to Buy Your Mutual Funds" later in this chapter.)

A WORD ABOUT INFLATION

You may wonder why people don't keep all their money in nice, relatively secure money market funds. After all, even if your money won't grow quite as fast in a money fund as it might in some riskier investment, at least it will be growing, right?

Well, maybe not—at least in the way that matters most. After paying taxes due on your earnings from a money fund, you'll probably have a hard time even keeping up with **inflation**—the tendency of prices to increase steadily over the years. If you earn, say, a 5% yield on a taxable money fund one year but are in the 30% tax bracket, you'll be left with only 3.5% at the end of the year. While this doesn't *sound* terrible if inflation is at 3.5%, that means everything you buy costs 3.5% more on average at the end of the year than it did at the beginning. So your investment didn't really get you anywhere.

It's easy to forget about the effects of inflation when you're thinking about long-term investments. To help put things into perspective, take a look at the way inflation has weakened the "purchasing power" of the dollar over the past few decades. Say your parents bought a new car for $3,500 in 1969. If you bought a comparable car today, you'd pay about $25,000. Put another way: $3,500 today buys only about one-seventh of what it could buy back in the late '60s. Amazing.

Inflation has bounced around a lot over the years—it was more than 6%, for example, in 1990, less than 2% in 1998, nearly 5% in 2005, and then plunged to 1% in late 2008—and it's hard to predict where it will be in the future. One thing that seems pretty likely, though, is that inflation will continue to erode the value of the dollar over the next few decades. That's why it's important to earn interest on your money. If you put $20,000 under your mattress and inflation increases at, say, an average of 3% a year, after 30 years, your $20,000 will have reduced in value to the point where it buys only what you can now buy for $8,268. If you'd been earning 3.1% interest on that money, you'd have the equivalent of about $20,608.

The rate of return you receive on an investment (known as the **nominal rate of return**) minus the rate of inflation is called the **real rate of return.** So if an investment is paying 5% and the inflation rate is 3%, your real rate of return is 2%. Take a look at Figure 5–1. It shows the nominal and real rates of return (without considering taxes) associated with various investments between 1926 and 2008. Don't worry for now about the exact definitions of these different securities; I'll explain that later. For now, the thing to notice is that stocks and bonds (and although it's not shown in this table, the mutual funds that invest in them) have done a much better job of overcoming the effects of inflation over this period than Treasury bills (which are often found in money funds).

It's clear from the table that if you'd kept your money in a money market fund that invests in Treasury bills, you would barely have kept pace with inflation. Although Treasury bills had a *nominal* return of 3.7%, the real rate of return, after accounting for inflation, was a pitiful 0.7%. And things look even worse when you take taxes into consideration. Although after-tax returns vary depending upon an investor's tax bracket, most investors would actually have *lost* money by investing in Treasury bills over this period. By investing in stocks and bonds, they would have done considerably better.

As mentioned at the beginning of this chapter, the fact that a particular stock has done better historically than most other stocks tells us little or nothing about how well it's likely to do from now on. But it's all we've got. So it's the best guess of many investment experts that over the long term, stocks and bonds *as a whole* will continue to offer rates of return that are significantly higher than the rate of inflation. Although there's no guarantee that this will actually happen (or even that you won't *lose* money by investing in the stock and bond markets over the years), my guess is that these analysts are guessing right.

Low-risk money funds and bank savings accounts are good places to keep your three-month emergency savings cushion. But if you can tolerate more risk, you should consider investments that will give you a fighting chance to get a rate that's a bit higher than inflation. In that case, your next step should be to consider two more aggressive types of investments: stock mutual funds and bond mutual funds.

STOCK FUNDS

Just as money market mutual funds invest in money market instruments, **stock mutual funds** invest in—you guessed it—stocks. The downside of a stock fund is that you risk losing money. The appeal is that your return over the long term may be significantly higher than the return you'd get with a money market fund.

What Is Stock?

To understand stock mutual funds, you must first understand stock. Stock is sold in units known as shares. A **share of stock** represents a small piece of a company; if you buy stock in a company, you become the owner of a fraction of that company. The more shares you buy, the more of the company you own. The amount of money paid for one share is called the **stock price** or the **price per share**.

A stock's price rises and falls depending on supply and demand.

FIGURF 5-1

HOW VARIOUS INVESTMENTS
HAVE FARED OVER TIME

Type of Investment	Average Return (Nominal)*	Average Return (Real)*	Highest Return (Nominal)**	Lowest Return (Nominal)**
U.S. Treasury bills	3.7%	0.7%	14.7%	0.0%
Government bonds (long term)	5.6%	2.6%	40.4%	−9.2%
Government bonds (intermediate term)	5.4%	2.4%	29.1%	−5.1%
Corporate bonds (long term)	5.8%	2.8%	42.6%	−6.8%
Large company stocks	9.8%	6.8%	54.0%	−43.3%
Small company stocks	11.9%	8.9%	142.9%	−58.0%

*Compound annual total return, 1926–2008
**Best and worst years, 1979–2008
Data © 2008 Morningstar. All rights reserved. Used with permission.
Year-to-date performance and annualized returns reflect performance as of November 30, 2008.

When a lot of people want to buy a stock, that tends to "bid up" its price, the same way that rival bidders at an art auction might bid up the price of a painting. If, on the other hand, there are more scllers than buyers, the price tends to fall. Anything that might influence investors to buy or sell a company's stock may affect the share price. New information that might lead investors to believe that a company will make more money than previously expected, for example, will generally cause its share price to rise. Unanticipated bad news typically leads to a decrease in price.

In some cases a company's stock price will move up or down for reasons that have nothing to do with changes in the firm's expected profitability. A stock may fall, for example, because a large investor decides to sell lots of shares to raise money for some other purpose and has to settle for a lower price in order to cash out quickly. And in many cases, stock prices go up or down for what appears to be no particular reason at all.

Stocks don't pay interest like a savings account. You make money from stocks by selling your shares for more than you paid for them. The difference between the price you sell for and the price you paid is called a **capital gain**. Certain types of stocks pay **dividends**, which are regular cash payouts companies make to keep shareholders happy. Typically, older, well-established firms pay dividends on their stocks, while newer firms do not.

There are fund managers whose job it is to pick and choose stocks to put in their mutual funds. Some stock fund managers invest in stocks they believe will reap hefty capital gains; others focus on companies that have historically paid substantial dividends on a regular basis, even if they're unlikely to increase much in price.

What Is the Stock Market?

You've probably heard reports on television that the stock market was up or down. Loosely speaking, the stock market is said to have gone up if the prices of most stocks have risen that day. The barometers most people use to keep track of "the market," though, are not based on *all* the thousands of stocks that people trade but on a representative sample. The prices of all stocks in the sample are averaged in some way to calculate what's known as an **index**.

The most widely known index is probably the **Dow Jones Industrial Average**, which, despite its fame, is actually based on the stock prices of only 30 large companies, and for that reason, doesn't provide an especially accurate reading of the direction of the market as a whole. Another well-known indicator is the **Standard & Poor's Index of 500 Stocks.** The S&P 500, as it's called, is more representative because it tracks changes in the stock prices of 500 large companies. Someone who tells you that "the market" has gone up is usually referring to one of these two indexes.

Different Types of Stock Funds

Stock mutual funds can be divided into two basic categories. The vast majority are **actively managed funds,** which means a fund manager uses his or her own judgment to pick and choose among the thousands of stocks available. The other major type is an **index fund.** An index fund invests in nearly all the stocks that make up a particular index, such as the S&P 500. Some people refer to index funds as **unmanaged** or **passively managed** since the fund manager doesn't pick which stocks go into the fund. With an index fund, the manager's job is simply to come as close as possible to matching the performance of the index it tracks.

I recommend that you go with an index fund. A number of studies suggest that over long periods of time, stock funds managed actively by "expert" fund managers do no better on average than passively managed index funds. (In his extensive research on this topic, for example, Burton Malkiel, Princeton economics professor and author of the classic finance book *A Random Walk Down Wall Street,* has found that most active managers have underperformed the S&P 500 in the long run.)

But in an actively managed fund, you'll pay much more in fees for the fund manager. Most index funds will provide you with the same or better diversification and allow you to participate in the (historically higher) returns associated with the stock market without paying too much.

This is not to say that index funds are in any way a sure thing. Whether you invest in index funds or in actively managed funds, you're always taking a risk when you put money in the stock market. Still, the lower expenses associated with index funds have given them an edge over time.

Let's put some numbers on this. In 1996, in the first edition of *Get a Financial Life*, I strongly recommended index funds. Over the next eleven years, the average S&P 500 index fund had an annual return of 9.32%. Meanwhile, the average actively managed stock fund returned 8.34%. In fact, according to experts at mutual fund research firm Morningstar, index funds have beaten their actively managed counter-

---

A FINANCIAL JOURNALIST COMES CLEAN

Many readers think I'm holding out on them. "Sure, you recommend index funds in your book," they tell me, "but what investments do you *really* like?" People believe there's an insider trick to investing, and that if only they knew the truth they'd strike it rich. Various financial magazines feed into that dream by promising big returns with every issue—if you follow their sage advice. But just how good are their stock tips?

Back in 1994, before I found index fund religion, I was asked to write a cover story for *Money* magazine called "Eight Investments that Never Lose Money." Being a diligent reporter, I did a thorough search of investments, and interviewed dozens of Wall Street gurus to determine which stocks were expected to continue to do well.

How did the advice pan out? If you had spread out $10,000 among the eight investments I recommended, you would have $31,993 today. Not too shabby, and it's true that my recommendations didn't lose money. But if you had simply put that cash in an S&P 500 index fund, you would have beaten *Money*'s hand-picked portfolio an astounding 13 out of 15 years. And you wouldn't have had to spend all the time and effort to do the research.

The bottom line: Go with index funds.

---

parts over the last twenty years. So, for example, if two people had put $10,000 into the stock market twenty years ago—one in an actively managed fund and one in an index fund—the index fund investor would have an extra $9,000 today, once you factor in expenses.

But don't expect to hear this from a salesperson at a brokerage firm or mutual fund company. Higher expenses may be bad for you, but they're great for the companies that offer actively managed funds. (I'll say more about fund expenses later in this chapter.)

Questions and Answers on Stock Funds

Q: If the market is tanking, wouldn't I be best off choosing a top-performing actively managed stock fund?
A: Yes, if you knew which funds were going to perform well in the future. But you don't. If there's any advantage at all to betting on past winners, it's probably not large enough to justify paying the higher fees that active managers charge. In fact, David Swensen, the chief investment officer of Yale University, argues in his book *Unconventional Success: A Fundamental Approach to Personal Investment*, that the high fees of actively managed funds eat up your returns. That's why I prefer low-cost index funds. Of course, you don't always do better with them. But even in late 2008, when index funds were down sharply, actively managed funds on average did even *worse*.

Q: But what about those few fund managers who've done well year after year?
A: Maybe they're brilliant, and maybe they're not. But before jumping to conclusions, it's worth remembering that given the number of stock funds that have been formed over the years, it would be surprising if some of them didn't do better than average for a number of years by sheer chance.

Let's talk odds for a minute. Suppose all fund managers pick their stocks completely at random. The chance that a particular fund will perform better than average (that is, better than half of all the funds out there) during any given year is 50%, or one chance in two. There's one chance in four (two times two) that this fund will do better than average for two successive years, and one chance in eight that it will be in the top half of its class for three years in a row. Do this ten times, and you'll discover that there's one chance in 1,024 that a given fund will beat the average for ten years running through sheer luck. These may sound like pretty slim odds, but with thousands of fund managers out there picking stocks, we should expect a handful of them to do better than average ten years in a row—enough to convince most anyone that they're financial geniuses even if they're in fact choosing their stocks at random.

To be fair, this doesn't prove that there aren't any mutual funds whose managers are genuine stock-picking geniuses. But even if there are, how are you going to tell them apart from the ones who've just been lucky? My advice: Don't try.

Q: What kind of stock index fund should I invest in?
A: Later on in this chapter I'll list some of the different mutual fund companies that offer funds based on various stock market indexes. First, though, you'll need to know a little more about the indexes themselves. Here are a few of the better-known ones:

- **The S&P 500.** The most popular index is the S&P 500, which is based on 500 of the largest U.S. companies, including such major players as General Electric, Microsoft, and Coca-Cola. There are a lot of S&P 500 index funds out there, some of which have very modest fees and are willing to accept a relatively small initial investment. While this is a fine place to start, especially if you don't have much money to invest, the S&P 500 has its drawbacks as well. Though large-company stocks (also known as "large capitalization" stocks, or large caps) did incredibly well throughout the 1990s, they didn't do as well as small-company stocks (small caps) between 2000 and 2007. No one knows where the trend will go, so for better diversification, you might want to invest in an index that includes the stocks of small- and medium-sized companies as well (see the next index)— or invest in a few different index funds.

- **The Dow Jones Wilshire 5000 Index.** This index comes closest to reflecting the performance of the U.S. stock market as a whole. Despite its name, the Dow Wilshire 5000 is actually made up of approximately 4,800 stocks, including those of a wide range of small, medium, and large companies. If you invest in only one, this is a good one to consider.

- **The MSCI US Broad Market Index.** This index is somewhat less inclusive than the Dow Wilshire 5000. It leaves out 900 of the smallest companies but still reflects about 99.5% of all the money in the U.S. stock market.

- **The MSCI EAFE Index.** If you're looking for more diversity, you may want to consider investing a small portion of your money in the stock markets of other countries. The MSCI EAFE Index tracks the performance of about 1,000 companies based in Europe, "Australasia" (a mash-up name for Australia and New Zealand), and the Far East (hence the acronym EAFE). Going with a mutual fund that mirrors this index is a good way to diversify your U.S. investments. Of course, some foreign stock markets are notoriously volatile, and the fees charged by international fund managers tend to be slightly higher on average than those of U.S. funds.

BOND FUNDS

Bond mutual funds invest in bonds, which I'll talk about in a minute. First, though, you should know where bond funds fall on the risk/return spectrum. While the exact answer depends on the type of fund, bond funds are generally riskier than money market funds but less risky than stock funds. Not surprisingly, the returns of bond funds have historically been somewhere between those of stock funds and money market funds.

WHAT'S DEFLATION AND WHY SHOULD I CARE?

Whenever the economy takes a nosedive, people start chattering about **deflation.** It's an economic term that means prices are declining over time. In other words, you get more for your dollar on everything from electronics to oil. Sounds like a good deal, right?

Here's the catch: Deflation creates a nasty downward spiral. Clothes may be cheaper, but because you think the sale will be even bigger next week, you wait . . . and everyone else does too. In the meantime, the store closes and the employees lose their jobs. That's where the vicious cycle kicks in. As more people start losing their jobs, there are more people who can't *afford* to buy. The economy stalls, and eventually you may be the one getting the axe.

But don't panic yet. Although talk of a prolonged downturn has resurfaced in recent years, most economists believe the chances of full-blown deflation are slim to none.

What Is a Bond?

Like a money market instrument, a bond is an IOU issued by a company, a government, or some other institution. The main difference is that in the case of a bond, the issuer has more time to repay its debt.

When you buy a bond, you're basically lending a sum of money (the **principal**) to the issuer for a fixed period of time (the **term**). In return for the loan, the issuer pays you interest, computed at a fixed rate called the **coupon rate.** Interest is generally paid monthly or quarterly, but in the case of a **zero coupon bond** you won't receive any interest at all until the end of the bond's term. (The bonds you received as graduation or bar mitzvah gifts may have been zero coupon bonds.) When a bond reaches **maturity** at the end of its term, you're entitled (at least in theory) to get back your full initial investment.

So What's Risky About a Bond?

The risks associated with buying a bond can be divided into two categories. The first, which is often referred to as **default risk** or **credit risk**, is the possibility that the issuer may fall on hard times, and be unable to pay you interest or repay your principal the way it's supposed to.

The second, which is somewhat more complicated, is known as **interest rate risk.** Here's one way to think about this kind of risk: If interest rates rise unexpectedly fast during the period in which you own the bond, you won't be able to take advantage of them. You'll be left with the same fixed coupon rate, which will start to look worse and worse compared to prevailing market rates. And since inflation tends to rise along with interest rates, the dollars you receive when the issuer finally pays you back probably won't buy as much as you'd originally thought.

So why not simply sell your bond if interest rates rise unexpectedly and buy another one with a higher coupon rate? Unfortunately, you're not the only one who's thought of this. To do that, you'd need a buyer. And nobody is going to buy your low-coupon bond if a new, high-coupon bond can be had for the same price. Since the bond market, like the stock market, obeys the laws of supply and demand, the price you'll be able to get for your bond will drop as soon as interest rates rise. The higher interest rates climb, the less your bond will be worth. So you're stuck with it.

A bond that doesn't have much time left until its final payback date, though, won't drop in value all that much when interest rates rise. This is because its holder won't have to put up with a lower-than-market coupon rate for very long and because inflation won't have much time to erode the value of the principal. A bond with many years left until its final payback, on the other hand, will fall much further when interest rates go up by the same amount.

So far, I've talked only about how interest rate risk can hurt you when interest rates increase. The other side of the coin is that when interest rates *fall* more than the market expects, bonds tend to *rise* in value. Before you quit your job to become a bond trader, though, you should review the exact wording of the previous sentence. It's not enough to know that interest rates are likely to fall if everyone else knows that too, since those expectations will almost certainly already be reflected in the price you'll have to pay to buy bonds. To "beat the market" you'd have to outguess thousands of experts who spend their time thinking of little else.

My recommendation: Don't even try. The point of this discussion is not to teach you how to make extraordinary profits by predicting the future direction of interest rates but simply to help you understand the two major factors—default risk and interest rate risk—that contribute to the uncertainty surrounding a bond's future performance.

Different Types of Bond Funds

Bond funds differ according to the type of bonds they invest in. There are two key variables to look at. The first is who is issuing the bond. This affects the degree of default risk you're exposed to and determines whether the income you receive from the bond is taxable or tax-exempt. As in the case of money market funds, there are bond funds that invest in bonds issued by the U.S. Treasury, by various federal agencies, by cities, states, and counties, and by corporations.

From a tax perspective, these different types of bond funds work in pretty much the same way as the corresponding types of money market funds. This is true of default risk as well, except that the stakes are higher. Even a somewhat shaky corporation may be able to stay afloat for long enough to repay a three-month money market instrument, but whether it will last long enough to make good on a twenty-year bond may be another story.

That doesn't mean that shaky corporations don't issue bonds. In fact, there's a whole class of bonds (most commonly known as "junk bonds," though brokers understandably prefer the term "high-yield") that are issued by financially troubled firms. They pay higher coupon rates to attract investors. Because a junk bond fund typically invests in the bonds of a *number* of "junky" companies, the failure of any one company may not constitute a disaster for the fund's investors. If many of these companies were to fail and therefore default on their bonds, though, investors could earn a much lower return and might even lose a substantial part of the money they originally invested.

The second variable is the average number of years before the bonds in the fund come due, or "mature." **Short-term bond funds** typically invest in bonds that will mature in fewer than four years, **intermediate-term bond funds** in instruments with maturities of between four and ten years, and **long-term bond funds** in bonds that won't mature for at least ten years.

Because changes in both overall interest rates and the financial stability of specific companies have a big impact on long-term bonds, these bond funds are generally riskier than short-term funds. But the relative safety of short-term bond funds comes at a price: Historically, short-term funds haven't performed as well as intermediate- and long-term funds

The upshot: It's all about how much risk you're willing to take. Funds that invest in the bonds of less stable companies are riskier than those that invest in solid companies; funds that invest in long-term bonds are riskier than funds that invest in the short-term bonds of similar companies. Only you can decide how much risk you're willing to accept for the possibility of a higher return. The choice is yours.

If you have the energy and enthusiasm to evaluate and keep track of more than one bond fund, consider spreading your money among several types of funds that fall at different points on the risk/return spectrum. If not, don't worry; the guidelines in the next section will allow you to hedge your bets while dealing with a single bond-fund approach.

Questions and Answers on Bond Funds

Q: Where can I get information about the types of bonds in a bond fund?
A: Look at the fund's **prospectus,** a document you can get by going to the fund company's site. You may also want to look up the fund's most recent **shareholder report,** which gives a breakdown of the **credit ratings** of the bonds that the fund recently held. These ratings are assigned by one of several rating agencies, like Standard & Poor's and Moody's. (Figure 5–2 explains the meaning of various ratings.)

Q: Within a given category of bond fund, how should I pick a particular fund?
A: Concentrate on one thing: fees. Studies have shown that bond fund managers have little effect on the performance of bond funds, so there's no point in researching managers and paying extra for someone who claims to be better than average.

Q: Are there bond index funds?
A: Yes, there are several dozen. The most common bond index is the **U.S. Aggregate Market Index,** which tracks the performance of all three types of bonds: short-, medium-, and long-term. I'll offer advice on finding a bond mutual fund a little later on in this chapter.

THE RIGHT MIX OF INVESTMENTS

As I've said, your first investing move should be to save three months' worth of expenses in a combination of a money market fund and a bank savings account. But what happens after that?

FIGURE 5-2
BOND RATINGS

	S&P	Moody's	Description
Investment grade	AAA	Aaa	Highest quality
	AA	Aa	High quality
	A	A	Good quality
	BBB	Baa	Medium quality
High-yield (junk bonds)	BB	Ba	Risky elements
	B	B	Risky
	CCC	Caa	Riskier
	CC	Ca	Highly risky
	C	C	Extremely poor prospects
	D	—	In default

Sources: Standard & Poor's, Moody's, and Investment Company Institute

If times are bad and you're nervous, you can keep all further savings in money funds or bank accounts. If you're willing to take more risk for a shot at higher returns, you can consider stock funds and bond funds.

Unfortunately, there's little agreement even among experts on how much you should risk on the stock market. Historically, a fairly typical recommendation has been to allocate roughly 50% of your assets to stock funds and 30% to bond funds, while keeping 20% in "cash"—meaning money market funds or bank savings accounts. Some financial advisors have said over the years that young people should put even more of their assets—say 80% to 90%—in stock funds, since they have much more time to ride out the downturns of the stock market. But others (including Paul Samuelson, winner of the Nobel Prize in economics) have questioned whether it really makes sense to allocate your assets based on your age.

INFLATION-PROTECTED BONDS

If you want to own bonds as an investment, but can't meet the minimum requirements for any of the funds I've mentioned, there are still alternatives. You should consider **Series I** savings bonds, or **I Bonds,** a little-known type of savings bond issued and sold by the U.S. Treasury. They're different from the old-fashioned savings bonds that your parents knew about because they have built-in protection against the negative effects of inflation. As of this writing, I Bonds pay a guaranteed real rate of 0.70%—*after* inflation. That may not be very impressive, but they would still beat most bank savings accounts after inflation, and they're just as safe.

There's another advantage to I Bonds: Because they're government-issued, there's no state or local tax on the interest you earn. You do have to pay federal tax, but not until the bonds are cashed in. This means your money grows tax-free for as long as you hold the bonds. (See p. 142 for an explanation of the magic of tax-free compounding.) And depending upon your income, you may be able to avoid paying any tax on the

Once again, you'll have to decide for yourself how much risk you're willing to take in pursuit of bigger rewards. To help determine the right mix for you, consider these questions:

- **What's your risk tolerance?** Are you a risk taker by nature? Do you like to gamble? Are you willing to lose $10 for the chance of earning $30? If so, you might be willing to put a lot of your money in stocks. But if you're afraid of risk and sickened by the thought of losing money, a large percentage of your investment portfolio should probably be in a money market fund.

interest I Bonds earn if you use the money only for educational expenses.

Another plus is that you don't need a lot of money to get started. I Bonds can be purchased in electronic form with as little as $25 directly from the Treasury website, www.treasurydirect .gov. The Treasury will also let you set up an automatic investment program that allows your employer to deduct a certain amount from your paycheck and deposit it into your Treasury account. You can also get paper I Bonds at most banks, credit unions, and savings institutions in increments of $50 and up. Either way, they can be cashed in any time after twelve months, up to thirty years (but there's a three-month interest penalty if you cash them in before five years).

For investors who have a bit more money to start with, there's another type of inflation-protected bond offered by the government: **Treasury Inflation-Protection Securities,** or **TIPS.** These come in minimum denominations of $100. You can get TIPS directly from the Treasury or through banks, dealers, and brokers (where you'll pay a commission). For more details, visit www .treasurydirect.gov and go to the "Individual Investors" section.

- **Are you diversified?** As mentioned above, to reduce the overall risk in your portfolio, you'll want to have a mix of investments. Before you make any decisions, examine the types of investments in your company retirement plan. If you invested your company 401(k) plan mainly in stocks, for example, you'll probably want your other savings to include some bond and money market funds. (For details on 401(k)s, see Chapter 6.)

- **What are your goals?** If you have $10,000 that you'll need to use in the next year or two for a down payment on a home, don't invest it in a stock fund or a long-term bond fund, where you could lose a lot of it if the market crashes or interest rates soar. But if you're just trying to build up your savings over the next ten or twenty years without a fixed goal in sight, you might want to take some risk in the hope of bigger returns.

One final note: Don't be discouraged if you can't create the perfect investment mix immediately. If you don't yet have enough money to meet the minimums required for separate investments in both a stock fund and a bond fund, don't let that paralyze you. Start with a stock index fund, and then begin investing in a bond fund after you've accumulated some more savings.

MUTUAL FUND EXPENSES

Because there's little evidence that one mutual fund manager is any more likely to beat the market than another, it makes sense to focus on the one thing that will *definitely* affect your investment results: the fund's **expense ratio**. This ratio is computed by dividing the fund's **total annual operating expenses** (which I'll talk about in a minute) by the value of all securities held by the fund. The fund's operating expenses are passed on to its investors, so the higher the expense ratio, the less you'll earn on your investment. If, for example, you invest in a fund that earns a 10% annual return on the securities it holds but has a 2% expense ratio, your investment will grow at a rate of only 8% per year.

One component of a fund's total annual operating expenses is the **management fee** paid to the fund manager (or fund company) for investing and managing the fund's money. Management fees typically range from 0.5% to 1.0% of the fund's assets per year. Other expenses include legal fees and administrative charges. Some fund companies also charge investors what's known as a **12b-1 fee**, which is used to cover the fund's marketing costs. Why should you pay for this? You shouldn't. Find a fund without 12b-1 fees.

As of this writing, expense ratios average about 1.5% a year

ETFs: TO BUY OR NOT TO BUY?

Always eager to get more business, several Wall Street companies have been marketing so-called **ETFs** (exchange-traded funds), which are increasingly popular, but you probably don't need them.

Basically, an ETF is a lot like an index fund with one key difference. While you can (and should) buy index funds through a mutual fund company, ETFs are bought and sold like stocks, which means you'll have to go to a brokerage firm (and pay fees) to invest in them. These fees can offset the slightly lower annual expenses that ETFs charge.

That said, if you're really eager to make some sort of investment in the stock market, but you have very little money, an ETF may be your only option. You can buy just a share of an S&P 500 ETF (called a Standard & Poor's Depositary Receipt or SPDR), for example, for around $100—a lot less than buying into a low-cost mutual fund. But make sure to use a discount broker so that any gains aren't eaten away by excessive commissions. To learn about how to find a good discount broker, go to p. 135.

for stock funds, about 1.1% for bond funds, and around 0.6% for money market funds. As you'll see in the next section, though, the expense ratios of some funds are much lower, and there's no reason to believe that low-expense funds will perform any worse than high-expense ones. The moral of this story is simple: Invest in funds with the lowest expense ratios you can find, and ignore anything a broker, financial advisor, or bank employee might try to tell you about the great track record or bright prospects of the high-expense fund he or she is trying to push.

One other trap you should look out for: **loads**. Loads are typically one-time fees paid when you buy and/or sell shares in certain mutual funds (which are often referred to as **load funds**). They aren't included in the fund's expense ratio, so you'll have to look for them as well. Loads typically range from 3% to 6% but can be as high as 8.5%. Studies show that load funds perform no better on average than **no-load funds**. So why does anyone pay a load? Because they've been talked into a load fund by an aggressive salesperson. Loads are commonly used to provide generous compensation to the people who sell them, so they're highly motivated to convince you that the fund's performance will justify the load. Just say no. What you want is a no-load fund with a low expense ratio. The salesperson will get over it.

To get the scoop on a fund's fees, loads, and expense ratio, go to the company's website and read the prospectus. It will spell them all out in detail. For many, this sounds as painful as having four wisdom teeth pulled. But it's actually not so bad.

DECIDING WHERE TO BUY YOUR MUTUAL FUNDS

Today there are more than 500 mutual fund companies in the United States alone, many of which offer dozens or even hundreds of funds. Don't be alarmed, though. I'm going to make this easy. As I said earlier, there are three places to purchase a mutual fund: brokerage firms, banks, and mutual fund companies. I recommend focusing on mutual fund companies. Why not the others? Brokerage firms tend to sell funds with loads and substantial fees, and their minimum investment requirements are usually high. Even if you go with a "discount broker," there's often some kind of fee involved. Banks offer a limited selection of index funds and also tend to charge loads. So mutual fund companies are the way to go.

You should be able to meet all your fund needs at a single mutual fund company. The main advantage of getting all your funds from the same company (sometimes called a "fund family") is con-

START WITH JUST $50 A MONTH IN AN AUTOMATIC INVESTMENT PLAN

Some no-load mutual fund companies will waive or lower their minimum initial investment requirement if you sign up for their automatic investment plan. With these plans you can have a fixed amount—as low as $50 or $100—siphoned off once or twice a month from your checking account and funneled into your mutual fund. When you choose a mutual fund company, simply indicate on the application that you want your money to be automatically invested and specify where you want the money to come from.

You can set this up online with your initial investment. After that, you won't have to do much except sit back and watch the money accumulate—although you may also want to check your investment mix occasionally to make sure it's still in the proportion you want. If one type of investment—say, stocks—does really well for a number of years, you may find yourself more heavily invested in stock mutual funds than you intended.

venience: You'll get a single statement every month covering all your holdings, and you'll be able to move your money from one fund to another without much hassle. Depending on your situation, though, you may want to split your money between two or more fund families.

Choosing a mutual fund company is surprisingly easy. What you're looking for is a company that offers no-load funds with low expense ratios and minimum investment requirements that you can meet. In this section, I'll direct you to a few mutual fund companies that currently fit the bill. Although others might tell you differently, I don't believe it's necessary for you to subscribe to *Institutional*

Investor or spend your evenings scouring the Internet. Just pick a fund company that fits the criteria I mentioned at the beginning of this paragraph, then go to its website to open an account.

One company worth considering is The Vanguard Group (www .vanguard.com; 800-662-7447). (Just for the record, I don't get any kickbacks, discounts, or free slide rules from Vanguard or any of the other firms I mention in this book.) Vanguard is a no-load firm that has some of the lowest expenses in the business and the largest range of stock and bond index funds around. As of this writing, Vanguard's S&P 500 index fund has an expense ratio of 0.15%, one-tenth of the industry average for actively managed stock funds, and its "Total Stock Market Portfolio" (which tracks the MSCI US Broad Market Index) charges 0.15% as well. The only problem with Vanguard is that it has a minimum initial investment requirement of $3,000 per fund. There's one exception, though: the Vanguard STAR Fund, which has a minimum initial investment of $1,000. It's about 60% stocks and 40% bonds, and is a "fund of funds," which means it invests in 11 other Vanguard funds. The expense ratio is 0.32%, still much lower than most actively managed funds. So if you don't have $3,000 at the beginning, once you build it up to $3,000 in STAR, you can then transfer to Vanguard's index funds.

But what if you don't have even $1,000? Build it up in your bank account until you get there—or try T. Rowe Price (www.troweprice .com; 800-638-5660). It will let you start investing in its slightly more expensive index funds with just $50 as long as you commit to invest at least $50 a month through an automatic plan. (For details on automatic investment plans, see the box on p. 131.)

If you serve or have served in the military or have a parent who did, USAA (www.usaa.com; 800-531-8181) is a good option. It offers some low-cost actively managed bond and stock index funds, charging just 0.19%. It will also waive its usual $3,000 minimum if you sign up for its $20 per month automatic investment plan.

SOCIALLY RESPONSIBLE INVESTING

People often ask me to recommend "socially responsible" invest-ments. There are more than two hundred mutual funds that fall into this category, but each has a somewhat different idea of what it means to be socially responsible. Some of these funds don't invest in certain industries, such as tobacco, liquor, or firearms. Others zero in on firms that treat employees well by providing child care services and promoting women and minorities, as well as green companies that deal with energy conservation and environmental issues.

A socially minded company might perform about the same as the market as a whole. But some people argue that the outlook for these types of companies is stronger in the long run because they pay attention to good business practices. It's really about your personal priorities rather than your financial goals. If it feels mean-ingful to you to support socially responsible companies, choose a mutual fund with this focus. As always, steer clear of any fund that charges a load or that has an unusually high expense ratio.

Vanguard has its own socially conscious fund, the Vanguard FTSE Social Index Fund. The expense ratio is just 0.24%, mak-ing this one of the cheapest funds in the category, but you'll still need $3,000 to get into it. Pax World (www.paxworld.com) offers a balanced fund that requires only $250 to start, but it's a lot more expensive, charging 0.96% in fees. Most other social funds charge at least 1%. For more information, go to www.socialfunds.com, which analyzes and links to socially aware mutual funds.

BUYING INDIVIDUAL STOCKS

By now you know that my advice to anyone wanting to get involved in the stock market is to stick with mutual funds— specifically index funds. But I feel compelled to offer some advice to readers who want to ignore me and buy individual stocks. Here are some tips:

- **Cut your costs and buy direct.** Many companies, particularly large ones like General Electric and AT&T, allow you to purchase shares from the company (that is, without going through a broker) through something called a **dividend reinvestment plan,** or **DRIP.** DRIPs often have low minimum investment require- ments ($100 or less) and charge very low or no commis- sions. Although some companies do tack on annoying fees (read the DRIP prospectus carefully before you sign up), for the most part DRIPs can be even cheaper than using a discount broker. One technicality: Some compa- nies require you to buy at least one share of company stock through a broker before they'll let you buy shares directly. For a free list of hundreds of companies that offer DRIPs, see www.moneypaper.com.

- **If you feel compelled to use a broker, stick with a discount broker.** A typical transaction that would cost you on average $10 at a discount broker could cost $50 at a full-service firm. Also, full-service firms often charge annual maintenance fees of about $150 a year. But there's no evidence that these would-be experts' advice justifies the steep commissions they charge. And keep in mind that all these brokers, including discount brokers—who are salespeople, not stock analysts—generally make money by getting you to buy or sell stocks. So even if you're comfortable stock-picking on your own, you're clearly better off paying lower commissions and going with a discount broker. Every year, *SmartMoney* magazine (www.smartmoney.com) publishes an excellent ranking of the best discount brokers, based on a variety of factors, including price and service. Read it. Magazines like *Kiplinger's* (www.kiplinger.com) and *Money* (www.money.com) also run articles on this topic from time to time.

FINANCIAL CRAMMING

- The first phase of your investment plan should be to build an emergency savings cushion equal to at least three months' worth of living expenses. Keep that in money market funds or a bank savings account so it's available if you need it.

- Your next move will be to begin investing in stock and bond mutual funds. Invest in index funds, since actively managed funds tend to charge higher fees and have not performed any better historically.

- Invest only in no-load funds. There's no point in paying hefty sales commissions or fees to invest in a load fund since there's no evidence that they're better investments.

- Choose a mutual fund with low expenses. As of this writing, expense ratios average about 1.5% a year for stock funds, about 1.1% for bond funds, and around 0.6% for money market funds. Find a fund that charges less.

- Sign up for an automatic investment plan. These plans allow you to have small amounts of money—say, $50 each month—withdrawn from your bank account or paycheck and funneled into a mutual fund. If you invest automatically, some funds will waive the minimum investment requirements.

THE BRAVE NEW
WORLD OF 401(K)S

Don't Let the Market Meltdown
Be Your Excuse for Missing the
Best Savings Deal Around

I T'S EASY THESE days to write off the idea of contributing to retirement savings accounts like 401(k)s. You've heard scary stories of people losing half their life savings in the chaos of the market. Plus, you don't feel like you have any money to squirrel away for the year 2040. You're off the hook, right? Wrong. 401(k)s are the best savings opportunity you can possibly have—in this or any economy. And not taking advantage of them while you're still young is a huge (and costly) mistake.

Retirement accounts aren't just about retirement. They're really more like supersmart savings accounts. They offer terrific tax advantages that allow your money to grow exponentially fast. In many cases, they bring you *free money* from your employer; many companies will put 50 cents in your account for every dollar *you* put in. A matching contribution like this amounts to an immediate guaranteed 50% return on your money—that's a payoff you can't get anywhere else in good economic times or bad.

Here's why it's so important to start now: The government limits the amount you can put in a 401(k) each year, so if you fail to contribute now, you won't be able to make it up (and enjoy the matching funds) when you're older and perhaps wiser. Now, for an example to get you motivated: Suppose you set aside $1,000 a year (about $19 a week) from age 25 to age 64 in a retirement account earning 5% a year (historically, stocks have returned more like 8%, but I'm being conservative). By the time you turn 65, you'll have $126,840. But if you don't start saving until you're 35, you'll have only $69,760. Starting just ten years earlier would have almost *doubled* your total. Yes, doubled.

Okay, so now you might be asking about all those people who lost money in their 401(k)s. Yes, that's the reality of the times. Nobody can tell what will happen with the market. But what you do know is that the tax break and the free money match from your employer (if you get one) are great deals. And because of this, even in the worst economy, 401(k)s—or, if that's not available to you, IRAs (individual retirement accounts)—are an offer you can't refuse. Details on how to approach your retirement savings appear later in this chapter.

Now that I've gotten your attention, there's one big-picture point you should know. Saving for retirement is more pressing today than ever before. That's because the Social Security Administration currently predicts that by the year 2017 it will be paying more than it collects, and unless Congress finds the money for an overhaul by about 2041, there won't be enough money in the fund to pay out full benefits. While Social Security will probably be around in some form when you retire, it will almost certainly provide less support for you than it has for your grandparents.

This chapter will teach you everything you need to know about retirement accounts. It will demystify the ins and outs of your options and answer the questions that may have been getting in your way. So go forth and save—there's no excuse not to.

WILL SOCIAL SECURITY BE
THERE FOR YOU?

One reason Social Security has generated so much attention in the past is that investment companies stood to gain huge fortunes if they had control of the money. While it's true the system has some problems, letting Wall Street take over isn't the answer—a point that has become painfully obvious in recent years.

Social Security was built on the idea that there would always be more workers paying into the system than older people taking money out. Enter the Baby Boom, a group that is now beginning to retire, and suddenly it's clear that there's just not enough cash being paid into the Social Security pot anymore.

That said, there's a lot that can be done, such as raising the retirement age a tad or reducing benefits a bit. These small changes would go a long way toward fixing the system and making it better. And here's what the Wall Street analysts rarely tell you: Even if nothing is done, the program will still be taking in enough money for you to receive most of the benefits (the current forecast is about 75%) that previous generations enjoyed—for the rest of your life.

Besides, even if it's just a myth that Social Security is going broke, the program was never meant to be your main source of income in retirement. That's why you need to work now to max out your contributions to the retirement plans discussed in this chapter.

WHAT ARE RETIREMENT
SAVINGS PLANS, ANYWAY?

Back in the early 1970s, when Microsoft was just a glimmer in Bill Gates's eye, Congress decided to give savers a break by creating tax-subsidized retirement savings programs. Today, most of us have access to some sort of tax-favored plan whether we have a traditional job or work freelance. In a traditional set-up, you probably have a 401(k) plan. If you work independently (or if your company doesn't offer a 401(k) plan), you can go for an IRA (individual retirement account). Bill Gates probably isn't worrying much about his retirement savings, but you need to.

Here's an explanation:

- **401(k)s** are retirement savings plans available to employees of most major companies and many small ones. **403(b)** plans (also called tax-sheltered annuities) are a version offered to employees of public schools and certain religious or charitable organizations. (Since 403(b)s are similar to 401(k)s, I'll refer only to 401(k)s throughout this chapter.)

- **IRAs** are available to working people (and their nonworking spouses) and are especially attractive for those who work for companies that don't offer retirement savings plans. There are two main types of IRAs: **traditional IRAs** and **Roth IRAs**. I'll get into the details in a minute.

The main tax-saving principle behind all these retirement savings plans is simple: Uncle Sam agrees not to tax the money in your retirement account while it is accumulating interest and other earnings until you take it out—and in return, you agree not to take it out until you're 59½ or older. That may not sound like such a big deal. But allowing untaxed interest to pile up year after year could result in thousands of dollars more for you over your lifetime, especially because your interest, as it's added to the pot, earns interest

on itself. The effect of your interest earning interest is known as
compounding. I've heard some financial types call this "The Eighth
Wonder of the World." (Okay, maybe they need to get out a bit
more.) When money compounds without being taxed for, say, forty
years rather than thirty, it not only grows for a longer period of
time, but it also grows more quickly, as the example at the beginning of this chapter shows.

HOW YOUR RETIREMENT SAVINGS ACCOUNT WORKS

Whichever type of retirement plan you have, the money doesn't
just sit there; it's channeled into investments so it can grow. When
you sign up for a plan, you're given a choice of investment options.
You pick the ones you want and decide how to divide your money
among your selections.

Your choices will depend on the kind of plan you are in. With
a 401(k), the employer typically narrows down the investment options for you. Many plans offer you a menu of about twenty alternatives, which might include shares of your company's own stock,
some actively managed stock mutual funds, some index funds, a
few bond mutual funds, balanced mutual funds (which have a mix
of stocks and bonds), at least one money market fund, and an international fund or two.

Every time you contribute, the money is automatically divided
up according to your initial specifications. If you don't provide any
input, your money will be put into a "default" investment plan—
usually one that's a mix of stocks and bonds. (See the box on
p. 150.) You may not be permitted to choose how to invest your
employer's matching contribution. Many large companies will provide only their own company's stock as a match.

One side note: Since retirement accounts allow your money to
grow in a tax-favored way, you may want to consider the advantages (and disadvantages) of putting certain investments in them.
For instance, it doesn't make sense to put tax-free bond funds into

an IRA or 401(k); stick with taxable investments only. (For a discussion of different investment options and suggestions on the pros and cons of each, see Chapter 5.)

CONTRIBUTING TO
YOUR 401(K)

Contributions you make to a traditional 401(k) actually benefit from two tax breaks—one up front, the other in the long term. (There's an exception to this rule with the newly introduced Roth 401(k), but I'll talk about that a bit later in this chapter.) First, the government allows you to delay paying taxes on the money you contribute to a 401(k) each year until you withdraw it from your account down the road. This is known as a **pretax** contribution. So if you earn $40,000 in a year and you put $1,000 into a 401(k), you're taxed as if you had earned only $39,000 that year. Assuming you're in the 25% tax bracket, you'll save $250 that year—the 25% of that $1,000 you would otherwise have had to pay in taxes. (See Chapter 9 for more on how to calculate this kind of tax deduction.) The other, longer-term benefit of a 401(k) is that you get to delay paying taxes on the *interest* (or other earnings) your retirement account generates over the years.

It's true that when you withdraw the money at the time of your retirement, you will pay taxes on the whole sum—the amount you contributed plus your earnings. But because the money is able to grow untaxed for many years, paying taxes later rather than sooner could result in thousands of dollars more for you when you retire.

If you go to work for a company that has a 401(k) plan, it's possible that your employer will automatically enroll you and divert a bit of your salary (generally 3%) for you into the 401(k). More and more companies are beginning to do this in order to increase participation. Of course, you could decide that you want to opt out (or reduce your contribution), but you'll have to make a conscious effort to do so—and the financial gods would breathe a tragic sigh for years to come. If your company doesn't automatically enroll you, all you have to do is go to your company's benefits site or benefits officer and get the details on how to enroll. I hope that by the time you finish this chapter, you'll not only keep your contribution level where it is, but also add more to it.

A lot of you are probably thinking, "But I need every single penny of my paycheck!" I know you feel that way, but you simply have to take advantage of these plans, even if it means saving just a small amount every month. I get more mail from people saying how glad they are that they forced themselves to do this than I get on just about any other topic. In the end, these people didn't really miss the $20 a week they would have spent elsewhere, and they know that when it really counts, they'll be happy they have something to show for it.

As of 2009, the maximum amount of annual *before-tax* income an employee can contribute to a 401(k) is $16,500. (Actually, the maximum you're permitted to contribute may be less, depending on factors such as your salary and your employer's contributions, if any, to your plan.) If you've just started your first job, this may seem like an insane sum, but remember, it's the *maximum*. You can start with much less.

One of the biggest benefits of a 401(k) is that many employers match a portion of the amount you contribute with a contribution of their own. Many companies contribute fifty cents or a dollar for every dollar you put in, up to a fixed maximum (often 2% to 6% of your salary). That's the equivalent of an immediate 50% (or even 100%) return on your investment. (Of course, in these tough economic times, some companies are cutting back on their matches.) To take advantage of a match, if you have one, try to contribute at least the maximum amount for which you are eligible to receive matching funds. If your so-called "adjusted gross income" is $30,000 and your company matches $1 for every $1 you contribute up to 6% of your salary, you'd want to contribute at least $1,800 to make sure you get the full $1,800 the company will match—in total, you'd be putting away $3,600 a year.

Contributions to 401(k)s are siphoned from your paycheck by your employer. The truth is, after a while, most people don't even notice the money that's being skimmed off and discover that they're saving faster than they ever thought possible. Now is the time to act.

CONTRIBUTING TO AN IRA

The other major type of retirement savings plan—great for free-lancers with no 401(k)—is the individual retirement account, or IRA. Unlike 401(k)s, IRAs are not offered by employers. They're private accounts set up through brokers, banks, and mutual fund companies. (My first choice for an IRA is a low-cost mutual fund company, but more on that later.)

The maximum you can contribute to an IRA as of 2009 is $5,000 a year, plus an additional $5,000 to your spouse's IRA if he or she doesn't earn any income. If both you and your spouse work, you can each contribute up to $5,000 to your own accounts. These limits apply to your total IRA contribution—whether to a traditional IRA, a Roth IRA, or any combination of IRAs. Even people who do have a 401(k) can open an IRA. I'll explain the details below.

First we'll start with the pros and cons of the different IRA types.

Traditional IRAs

These work much like 401(k)s. You get to subtract, or "deduct," your contribution from your income—that's the upfront tax break. So if you earn $35,000 and contribute $1,000 to an IRA, you pay tax as though you had earned only $34,000.

Next, the money in your IRA grows without being taxed for many years—that's the long-term break. Come retirement time, you'll pay tax on all the money in your account as you withdraw it. This is called "tax-deferred" growth because you defer (or post-pone) paying tax on that money for many years, which helps your money grow more quickly.

Traditional IRAs like this that offer upfront tax breaks are known as **deductible IRAs.** Unfortunately, deductible IRAs are not available to everyone. Whether or not you're eligible depends on your "adjusted gross income" and whether you participate in an employer-sponsored retirement plan. (For details on calculating your adjusted gross income, see Chapter 9.)

Here are the rules. If your employer does *not* offer a retirement plan such as a 401(k) or a 403(b), you're almost always allowed to deduct your full $5,000 contribution to a traditional IRA. (You don't *have* to contribute $5,000, but you're permitted to.) There is one tricky exception: if you're not eligible for a company retirement plan but are married to someone who *is*. In that case, you can make the full contribution to a deductible IRA only if your combined adjusted gross income is $166,000 or less and you and your spouse file a joint return. So if you drop out of the workplace for a few years to stay home to take care of the kids, for instance, and your spouse has a retirement plan at work, you can still open a deductible IRA as long as your spouse earns $166,000 or less.

But what if your employer *does* offer a retirement plan? In that case, your IRA contribution may not be fully deductible. Here are the rules. If you're eligible for an employer-sponsored retirement plan, you can deduct your *full* $5,000 contribution to a traditional IRA if:

- You're single and your adjusted gross income is $55,000 or less.

- You're married, you file a joint tax return, and together your adjusted gross income is $85,000 or less.

Married people who file separate tax returns, no matter what their incomes, can't claim the full deduction if they participate in retirement plans at work.

If you don't qualify for a fully deductible IRA, you can still put up to $5,000 a year into a **partially deductible IRA** or a **nondeductible IRA**. To find out what part of your contribution may be deductible, consult IRS Publication 590, *Individual Retirement Arrangements*. You can get a copy of this by downloading it from the IRS website (www.irs.gov) or calling the IRS at 800-TAX-FORM.

For years, partially deductible IRAs and nondeductible IRAs were considered too much trouble to be worthwhile. Even though they still allowed your money to grow tax-deferred, they didn't offer the full $5,000 upfront tax break that makes deductible IRAs so appealing. They also require extra paperwork (you'll have to fill out Form 8606 every year when you file your taxes). But now there's a new loophole that can make them more attractive. For details on why nondeductible IRAs are now worth your time, see p. 164.

Roth IRAs

Roth IRAs are a breed unto themselves. Unlike deductible IRAs, Roth IRAs don't give you an up-front tax break on your contributions. (That is, you can't deduct your contribution from your taxable income for that year.) But once your money is in a Roth IRA, it will never be taxed again. Roth IRAs don't just compound tax-free: They stay that way. Forever. When you retire and start taking your money out of a Roth IRA, you won't have to pay federal, state, or local taxes on it as you would with a traditional IRA or a 401(k). In retirement plan lingo, while deductible IRAs offer *tax-deferred* growth (you delay paying tax on your contributions and earnings until you withdraw the money), the Roth IRA grows *tax-free*. For many people—especially young people saving over many years—the Roth IRA is the better deal. (I'll get into the details in a moment.)

One big advantage of Roth IRAs is that you may be able to open one even if you already have a retirement plan at work (which you may not be able to do with a deductible IRA). That's because the eligibility rules for Roth IRAs are simpler than they are for deductible IRAs. It doesn't matter if you and your spouse are eligible for a retirement plan at work—all that matters is your income.

You can make the *full* $5,000 annual contribution to a Roth IRA if:

- You're single and your adjusted gross income is not more than $105,000.

- You're married, file jointly, and your adjusted gross income is not more than $166,000.

You can still get a Roth IRA even if you have a higher income, but the amount you're allowed to contribute is less than $5,000. As long as you earn under $120,000 as a single person or $176,000 as a couple filing jointly, you can make a partial contribution. It's a sliding scale, so if you want to know where you fall, fill out the worksheet in IRS Publication 590 (www.irs.gov). One quirky rule: Married people filing separately can never make the full Roth contribution. There are rare cases—if either has a very low income—where they can make partial contributions.

A WORD ABOUT 529 INVESTMENT PLANS

If you have little kids, you may have heard about these programs that help you save long-term for their college education, and you may wonder if they're something to consider. (You may also wonder why I'm bringing them up here in the retirement chapter.) The reason is that these state-sponsored plans offer tax advantages that are somewhat similar to the benefits you get from 401(k)s and IRAs. My advice, even if you have small children, is to max out your 401(k) plan (up to the amount your company matches) and a Roth IRA before you consider a 529. That's because 529 plans have very strict limits on what you can invest in as well as how you can use the money. If you're one of the rare few who have already maxed out your retirement plans, then you can start investigating 529s at www.savingforcollege.com.

The Choice: Which IRA Is Right for You?

If you want to put money in an IRA, you'll need to decide which kind. Although Roth IRAs are generally considered the better option for younger people, there are a few questions you should ask yourself.

- **Do I qualify for a deductible IRA?** Deductible (traditional) IRAs have relatively low income limits, so you may not qualify for the full $5,000 deduction. No mystery here: If you don't qualify for the full $5,000 deductible IRA, go with the Roth.

- **Can I afford to make the full $5,000 contribution if I go with a Roth?** If not, you may be better off with a traditional IRA. Just be realistic about how much you can manage to tighten your belt. With a Roth IRA, not only are you out $5,000 but you have also paid tax on that money. Here's

A LESSON IN HOW A LITTLE ADDS UP TO A LOT

Although he's never earned more than $40,000 a year, Peter, 40, has more than $200,000 in retirement savings. How did he do it? Peter works at a company that allows him to put 15% of his salary each year into a 401(k). His starting salary in 1991 was just $25,000 a year, but he immediately began contributing the maximum he could to his company plan (even though his company offered no matching program), and has continued to do so ever since. For the three years he lived with his parents after college (he moved out at age 25), Peter also deposited an additional $2,000 into an IRA each year. Although it's true that Peter profited from the fact that stock and bond funds did very well in the 1990s, his real achievement has been his commitment to contributing to his 401(k) and IRA every year. If he continues to save the maximum in his 401(k) plan, gets a 3% cost-of-living salary increase each year, and earns 8% a year on his investments, he will have close to $600,000 by the time he turns 50. Amazing.

what I mean: With a traditional IRA, a $5,000 contribution would result in a $1,250 tax deduction if you're in the 25% tax bracket. In real terms, this means that the full $5,000 contribution would end up costing you just $3,750. But Roth IRAs are not deductible, which means your $5,000 contribution to a Roth would cost you . . . $5,000. If you can afford to put the full $5,000 in a Roth IRA, you'll be doing your future self a big favor. But if you can only afford to put $3,750 in your account either way, the Roth IRA won't provide you with much financial advantage in the long run. In that case, your decision will be based on other considerations, like the ones in the next two points.

- **Will I be in a substantially lower or higher tax bracket when I retire?** When you're in your twenties, you assume you will be richer when you're old, but the fact is many people fall into a lower tax bracket when they retire because they stop receiving regular income from their jobs. (I know this seems a million and a half miles away, but it's important to get the concept.) Of course, it's hard to predict today what your tax situation will look like thirty or forty years from now. But here's the general idea: Roth IRA contributions are taxed today, while deductible IRA contributions are taxed when you take them out. So if you suspect that you will be in a lower tax bracket when you retire than the one you're in today, a deductible IRA makes more sense. I admit that this one is a crapshoot.

- **Will I need to withdraw my IRA money in the next few years?** This is a big one. You can withdraw the money you've put into a Roth IRA at any time without penalty (though you will have to pay a penalty if you withdraw any of the interest on that money). Although this is not advisable— once you've taken out the money, it can't be replaced—it does provide more emergency protection than a traditional IRA, which you can't tap at all under most circumstances without paying tax and penalties. (For details on withdrawing money from IRAs, see p. 153).

LETTING THE BOSS PLAN YOUR RETIREMENT

For years, the theory behind 401(k)s was "you snooze, you lose," meaning that if you didn't take action and invest in one, you'd end up with no money for retirement. In 2006, the rules changed and the Department of Labor told companies they were allowed to automatically enroll employees in their retirement plans—as long as they put the money into low-risk, well-diversified investments. While this is good news for you if you're already signed up, you shouldn't assume that the choices made on your behalf are the best that they can be. Check them out for yourself.

There are two types of mutual funds that the government says fit the bill:

Balanced funds are a pretty basic blend of stocks and bonds. They're hand-picked by the mutual fund manager to create an evenly distributed portfolio. These funds tend to be somewhere between stock and bond funds in terms of both performance and cost.

Target date funds, also called **lifecycle funds,** are a lot

My advice generally is to put as much money as you can in a Roth IRA and leave it there. But if you have reason to believe that a deductible IRA would be better for you, look into the details before you make any decisions. Check out the IRA comparison calculators available at websites like Morningstar (screen.morningstar.com/IRA/IRACalculator.html) and MoneyChimp (www.moneychimp.com/articles/rothira/rothcalc.htm).

more complicated. They also mix various types of investments (usually shares of other mutual funds), but the mix changes depending on how close you are to your prospective retirement date. The way it works is that you pick the date closest to the year you currently expect to retire and you're matched up with investments that the fund company believes will be right for you. In theory, a lifecycle fund designed for people who are several decades from retirement will start by taking greater risks on more speculative investments; it will then evolve into a more bond-heavy portfolio as the investors get closer to retirement and need a more conservative approach.

While these are both reasonable options, you are better off making choices yourself based on my suggestions in the box on p. 154. The defaults may make your retirement savings a breeze, but you pay for that convenience: The average target date fund aimed at young people currently charges 1.25% a year in total expenses and the average balanced fund charges 1.36%. If you just select a no-load stock index fund and a no-load bond index fund, you could pay less than 0.2%, which means your nest egg will grow, on average, an extra 1% every year. That could mean a difference of thousands of dollars for you come retirement.

HOW TO TAP THE MONEY IN YOUR 401(k) OR IRA IF YOU REALLY NEED IT NOW

On the surface, IRAs and 401(k)s have a major downside for young people. Once you put your money into these accounts, you may have to wait until you reach the age of 59½ to be able to withdraw it without paying a penalty. If you try to take the money out before then, you may get hit with a 10% penalty, plus income tax on the amount you withdraw. There's been some talk about allowing people to make early withdrawals without penalties, but even if these plans go through, you'd have access only to a very small portion of your money.

These tough rules are meant to prevent savers from raiding their retirement plans, since withdrawals generally can't be replaced. But if you don't have any other options, you should know that the rules aren't actually as rigid as they seem. Here are the details.

Borrowing from a 401(k)

A 401(k) can be tough to crack. To withdraw money from it, you must prove to your employer that you need it for something urgent, such as paying medical bills, and that you have nowhere else to turn. But many 401(k)s do offer an escape hatch: They allow you to *borrow* the money at rates that are sometimes more favorable than a bank's. When you borrow from your 401(k), you are essentially borrowing money from yourself, and the payments you make— including interest—go right back into your own account.

WHAT TO DO IN A BAD MARKET

It's easy to panic if a large part of your retirement savings suddenly vanishes. But what if so far you've done everything right but the stock market starts plummeting? Should you keep your money in? Pull it out?

Sadly, no one knows. It's hard to time the market. If you feel like you're taking too much risk, you can shift to money market funds. This has its own risk of not keeping up with inflation. And you could miss out when stocks rise again.

One thing is clear: You should not pull your money out of a retirement plan. If you do, you'll have to pay taxes plus a stiff penalty on your withdrawal. And this is never a good thing.

The rules for borrowing vary from company to company, so check the details with your employer. Usually, you can borrow half the amount you contributed to your 401(k) plus earnings. Depending on how long you've worked for the company, you may be able to borrow up to half your employer's contributions too. Some employers do not permit loans of less than $1,000. Loans usually must be paid back within five years, although if you use the money to buy your primary home you may be able to pay it back over a longer period. Although you really don't want to plan to borrow—debt is not something you need—it's good to know the option is there for emergencies.

Even if you can't withdraw or borrow from your retirement plan very easily, it usually still makes sense to invest in a 401(k). The advantage of tax-favored compounding is so great that after about ten years, its benefit could outweigh the 10% penalty you'd have to pay for making unqualified early withdrawals.

Withdrawals from IRAs

The rules for IRA withdrawals differ depending on what kind of IRA you have. With traditional IRAs, you'll have to pay both income tax and a 10% penalty on IRA money you withdraw before the age of 59½.

Roth IRAs have more lenient guidelines: You can withdraw the money you've contributed to them at any time without paying the income tax or the 10% penalty. But that applies only to your *contributions*. You'll have to pay both the penalty and the tax if you withdraw the *interest* on your contributions before you retire. To help you get a better handle on whether you would have to pay taxes and penalties, go to www.irs.gov and search for publication 590.

The government also lets you withdraw money from *any* IRA, without paying the 10% penalty, for any of the following reasons, as long as you've had the IRA open for five years:

- educational expenses for yourself, your spouse, or your children (including tuition, fees, books, and possibly room and board)

DIVIDING YOUR RETIREMENT SAVINGS PIE

Most experts urge young people to put a large part of their retirement money into stocks—and I agree—but there's no magic formula for coming up with a guaranteed successful mix. To get more details about the various investments out there, see Chapter 5.

Many employers offer advice, ranging from sample portfolios for people in a certain age group to face-to-face meetings with a financial advisor, but be careful—these advisors may have a vested interest in selling you an investment that pays them a higher commission. My favorite way for people to divvy up their 401(k) contributions is with the use of the portfolio management tools at Financial Engines (www.financialengines .com). This site helps you determine the best investment mix for your retirement money using a mathematical model developed by Nobel Prize–winning economist Bill Sharpe. (As my grandmother used to say, this man is clearly no dummy.) Financial Engines can help you decide how to allocate the money not only in your company 401(k) plan, but also in your IRA. Your company may provide you with access for free, so ask your employee benefits person. If not, you can get a one-year subscription for $149.95 or a three-month trial for just $39.95. To minimize your costs, consider using the service for just one three-month period every few years.

- unreimbursed medical expenses if they exceed 7.5% of your adjusted gross income (see Chapter 9 to figure out what that means)

- up to $10,000 in home buying costs such as a down payment or closing fees. (This is a *lifetime* cap per person, and the exemption is reserved for people who have not owned a house in at least two years.)

One last tip: If you need your IRA money for a short period of time, you can *borrow* it once a year, without tax or penalty, as long as you pay it all back within 60 days. Of course, this is easier said than done, and should be reserved for a true emergency only.

A WORD ABOUT INFLATION AND TAXATION

Personal finance articles and books often offer dramatic examples of the rewards of saving without ever mentioning inflation. So far in this chapter, I haven't done much better. It's time for me to come clean.

Although saving over a long period of time really is a good idea, the fact is it won't make you as rich as it might seem from the examples given so far. As you may remember from Chapter 5, inflation can drastically reduce the purchasing power of the dollar over time. Consider, for example, the scenario I outlined at the beginning of this chapter—the $126,840 you'd have forty years from now would not buy nearly as much as $126,840 can buy today.*

This doesn't mean you shouldn't save. As the numbers show, you still come out way ahead if you start saving in a retirement account while you're young—even after inflation. When money is allowed to grow for decades without being taxed, the results are extraordinary.

---

* There's a less obvious way inflation comes into play in this example. If you started saving at age 25 rather than 35, each of the $1,000 annual deposits you made during the first ten years would have more "purchasing power" during the year you made it than the $1,000 you deposited each year after that. Although your ten-year head start would leave you with a much larger retirement nest egg, your initial deposits would thus be "more expensive" for you than the ones you made after your 35th birthday. As a result, the benefits of saving early would be offset somewhat by the effects of inflation.

Consider the following example. Suppose you put $5,000 into each of two accounts—a Roth IRA and a taxable account—in 2009. Let's also assume that each account earns 8% a year, the annual inflation rate is 3%, and you're in a 25% federal tax bracket. After 30 years, the $5,000 in the Roth IRA will have grown to approximately $20,728 (in 2009 dollars). The $5,000 in the taxable account, on the other hand, will only have increased to $14,825 (again in 2009 dollars). The bottom line: You will have earned 60% more ($15,728 versus $9,825) by putting your money in a tax-favored account than you would have with a taxable one.

ANSWERS TO SOME COMMON QUESTIONS

Okay. Now you've got the point: You don't want to miss out on the benefits of saving in a retirement plan when you're young. This next section will answer a few questions to help you get started.

The Facts on 401(k)s

Q: Am I eligible for a 401(k)?
A: Ask your employer. You may be required to work for your employer for a year before you can contribute.

Q: One of my 401(k) investment options is stock in my company. Should I bite?
A: Probably not. When you work for a company, you already have a huge "investment" in it. If the business runs into difficult times, you're at risk twice: Not only could you lose your job, but you could also see your retirement portfolio plummet. What's more, as I've mentioned, many employers match employee contributions with shares of company stock, so you may already be heavily invested in your firm. Even if your company puts its match in its own stock, most employers will let you immediately convert those shares into other investment alternatives offered in your 401(k); if yours does,

make sure to take advantage of this option. In any event, by law you have the right to do that once you have three years on the job.

Q: What's the safest thing I can put my 401(k) money in?

A: Money market funds are likely to be your lowest-risk option. They're nearly as safe as bank accounts. The problem—and it's a *big* problem—is that they don't keep up with inflation, so the *value* of your money will decline. Though historically other choices in your 401(k) (like stock and bond mutual funds) have done much better than money market funds, in this climate money market funds are an understandable choice for people who are terrified of losing the money they invested. They're a way to enjoy the benefits of a 401(k)—tax breaks and matching contributions from your employer—without taking on the risk of the market. But this is not a strategy that's likely to provide the long-term growth you'll want in these accounts.

Q: What happens if I get laid off or change jobs?

A: If you move to another company, you can probably transfer your 401(k) money into your new company's 401(k) and you can definitely put it into an IRA. (Transferring to an IRA is also an option if you're laid off.) But there are a few annoying rules regarding how you must handle this. It's important that you tell your old employer that you want a **direct rollover** into your new company's 401(k) or into an IRA.

Although the plan can pay out or "distribute" the money from a 401(k) directly to you, there are several reasons to avoid this method. If you are paid the money directly, the plan must withhold 20% of the amount you are due and send it to the IRS (which will hold on to it until you file your taxes for that year). You are then responsible for replacing that 20% from your other savings when you make the transfer into your new plan. If you can't come up with the money in 60 days, you'll have to pay tax on that 20%, plus a penalty. (I told you these rules are annoying.)

If your account is over $5,000, another option is to leave your 401(k) money with your old company. Once you leave a company, you're no longer eligible to contribute to its 401(k), but your account will continue to grow if your investments do well. If you like the investment options at your old company's 401(k) better than the ones in your new company's plan, this may be a good option for you.

No matter what you do, resist the temptation to simply cash in your 401(k). About half of all people do this when they change jobs, but that's a terrible idea. You will have to pay tax on the money, plus the 10% penalty.

Q: What happens if I have an outstanding loan against my 401(k), and I quit or I'm fired?

A: This is a situation you should try to avoid. Most companies will ask you to pay the entire loan back in one lump sum when you leave the firm. If you can't, the amount you owe may be treated as money withdrawn (instead of borrowed) from the plan, and you may therefore owe taxes plus the 10% penalty. Another reason to avoid borrowing from your 401(k) if at all possible.

Q: What's a Roth 401(k)?

A: Some companies are starting to offer another type of retirement savings plan that you'll want to know about: a sort of hybrid between an IRA and a 401(k) The **Roth 401(k)** provides the automatic tax-free compounding of a Roth IRA. When you contribute to a Roth 401(k), you decide what percentage of your *after-tax* income your employer should subtract from your paycheck and deposit in your retirement account. Because of this, you don't get an upfront tax break, but the money grows *tax free* forever, just like a Roth IRA.

If you leave your job, you can move your Roth 401(k) into a Roth IRA or to your new company's Roth 401(k) if it has one. The rules for rolling over money from a Roth 401(k) are different than they are for traditional 401(k)s, so you'll need to check with your employee benefits office.

Most employers will make you choose one variety of 401(k) and stick with it. Although relatively few companies currently offer Roth 401(k)s, check to see if yours is one of them. If it is, the Roth 401(k) probably makes sense if you expect to be in a higher tax bracket when you retire. Likewise, if you can make the full $16,500 contribution in post-tax dollars, the Roth is probably the winner.

To help you decide, check out the *SmartMoney* calculator at www
.smartmoney.com/retirement.

Q: They tell me I'm vested. What does that mean?

A: To be **vested** is to have a nonforfeitable right to the money
your employer contributed to your retirement plan on your behalf.
Most company retirement plans require you to work for the firm for
a certain number of years before you become fully vested (meaning
entitled to 100% of the money your employer contributed for you).
Typically it takes about five years. Many companies have a gradual
vesting policy. With a gradual schedule, you might be 20% vested
after two years at a company, 40% after three years, and so on.
Once you become vested, however, it doesn't mean you may withdraw your money without paying the 10% penalty and taxes on
your earnings. If you're not vested and you need to get your money
when you leave the firm, you can withdraw the money you contributed (plus earnings on those contributions), but you can't keep any
of the money your employer contributed for you (or the earnings on
those employer contributions). If you're partially vested, you'll get
to keep a portion of the money your employer contributed for you,
plus earnings. Knowing your company's vesting schedule can help
you time a career move. Keep in mind that for vesting purposes,
some companies consider a "year" of service to be less than a full
calendar year (for instance, five months and a day). That's why
you should consult your company's employee benefits or human
resources department to find out the exact date you'll be vested.

Q: Can my employer raid my 401(k) to help himself?

A: If the company you work for is facing rough financial times,
you may worry whether your boss can dip into the 401(k) to pay
his bills. The answer: No. Your employer is not legally allowed
to use the 401(k) money for business purposes. What's more, if
your employer files for bankruptcy, the 401(k) money is protected
and none of the employer's creditors can touch your account. The
person (or company) who is legally responsible for ensuring that
no one tampers with your 401(k) is called the trustee. The trustee
might be, for example, a bank or the president of your company.

And what if your employer decides to end the plan, as unlikely as that may be? You'll still be okay, because you'll receive all the money you put in plus any contributions your employer made on your behalf (as long as you are vested).

The Scoop on IRAs

Q: What's the safest thing I can put my IRA money in?
A: If you're terrified of losing any money, you can open an IRA at a bank and put the money in a CD (certificate of deposit). If you decide to open your IRA at a no-load mutual fund company like I recommend, a money market fund is nearly as safe. Neither of these is likely to keep up with inflation over the long haul, though.

Q: If I'm willing to take a little more risk for the potential of higher earnings, what should I do with my IRA?
A: Historically, the biggest payoff has come from stock mutual funds, followed by bond mutual funds. And although nobody knows for sure, many experts think that this will be the case for the long term.

If you have at least $3,000, you can invest a portion of your IRA money in Vanguard's S&P 500 index fund, which has an expense ratio of an appealingly low 0.15%. If you have only $1,000, you can start with Vanguard's STAR fund (see Chapter 5 for details), which charges 0.32%. (You may want to switch to the S&P 500 fund once you get to $3,000.)

If you're eager to get started with an IRA, another relatively low-minimum company is Dreyfus (www.dreyfus.com; 800-782-6620), which requires just $750 to start—although it does charge 0.5% for its S&P 500 fund. T. Rowe Price (www.troweprice.com; 800-225-5132) lets you start with $1,000 upfront, or $50 a month if you sign up for the automatic investment program. But its S&P 500 fund is slightly more expensive (0.35%).

If you're a teacher or come from a military background, you may qualify to open an IRA at TIAA-CREF (www.tiaa-cref.org; 800-842-2252) or USAA (www.usaa.com), respectively, which offer their

A NEW TYPE OF OLD-FASHIONED PENSION

In your parents' (or grandparents') era, employees stayed with the same company for twenty or thirty years, and many were rewarded at the end of their work lives with pensions paid for by their employers. Today, these old-fashioned pensions, known as defined benefit plans, are virtually extinct.

But not all employers have abandoned pensions altogether. The new trend is toward something called **cash balance plans.** For many younger workers, these plans may actually be an improvement over the old ones, since they're "portable," meaning you can take the money with you if you leave the company before you retire. Traditional pensions rewarded employees for staying with companies for a long time and the benefits increased significantly as these workers neared retirement. But most people today don't plan to spend the rest of their lives at one company. Cash balance plans address that reality.

If you work for a company that offers a cash balance plan, you don't have to sign up; that's done for you. Here's how they work: Your employer simply puts a given amount of money—typically 5% of your salary—toward your pension every year. This isn't money from your earnings; it's money from your employer. Once you're vested, which usually takes about three to five years, you'll be able to keep those benefits even if you leave your job. Contributions don't increase as you get older.

Seniority doesn't enter the picture, and that means two things: Younger workers can accumulate benefits earlier than they used to, and they can move from job to job without worrying about qualifying for pension benefits. If your employer offers you the chance to switch from a "defined benefit" plan —the name for the old fashioned type of pension— to a cash balance plan, take it.

THE RETIREMENT PRIORITY BOX

Now that you know more than you ever wanted to about retirement plans, you may be left with one final question: What do I do first? The reality is, if you're like a lot of people starting out, you'll probably be unable to manage more than the first step below, but that's a great start. If you can do more, here's a quick rundown of the rough priority order of your various retirement savings options—that is to say, what to do if you're able to max out your first retirement option and you still have money you're able to allocate to retirement savings.

1. Contribute to a 401(k) with employer matching. The best deal around and therefore your number one priority. The match alone can generate an immediate 50% to 100% return on your money (once you're vested), and either flavor of 401(k)—regular or Roth—provides years of tax-advantaged growth. Don't put money in any other retirement account until you have reached the limit of what your employer is willing to match.

2. Open an IRA (Roth or fully deductible). After you've reached the match level on your 401(k), the Roth IRA offers

own mix of relatively cheap funds (their S&P 500 funds clock in at 0.32% and 0.19%, respectively) and low minimums (as low as zero at TIAA-CREF, and a one-time initial payment of $250 at USAA).

Finally, for those interested in socially responsible funds, I recommend Vanguard's FTSE Social Index Fund (expense ratio: 0.24%), but again you'll need to have $3,000.

You can open any of these IRAs online by going to the mutual fund company's website.

completely tax-free growth forever. The deductible IRA offers an up-front tax break and then years of tax-deferred growth. IRAs also allow you to withdraw your money penalty-free to buy a home or pay for educational expenses.

3. **Open a partially deductible or nondeductible IRA.** If you have contributed the maximum to your 401(k) that your employer will match and you're not eligible for a deductible or Roth IRA, this is your next best choice. The reason: Starting in 2010, a loophole in the tax code allows you to convert your nondeductible IRA into a Roth. (For details, see p. 166.)

4. **Contribute to a 401(k) without employer matching.** If you've already contributed the maximum to options 1 through 3 above, try to max out your 401(k)—even if it's a stretch on your budget.

5. **Save beyond a 401(k) or IRA.** Once you've exhausted your tax-favored savings options—IRAs and 401(k)s—you'll have to save in bank accounts, money funds, and other types of mutual funds in the regular old taxable way. But if you invest well, you'll be thankful down the road that you did. To get the most from your money, open your account at a no-load, low-expense mutual fund company. (See p. 131 for details.)

Q: What's the timing for getting an IRA?

A: The deadline is April 15 of the *following* year. If, for example, you suddenly realize on January 1, 2011, that you forgot to make your 2010 IRA contribution, you can still contribute and get the tax benefit for 2010. In fact, you have until April 15, 2011, to contribute to a traditional IRA or Roth IRA for tax year 2010 (and in the case of a deductible IRA, deduct it on your 2010 return). Note: you can also put in your contribution for 2011 as early as

January 1, 2011. If you can afford to do so, definitely do it. Your money will have that much more time to grow.

Q: *Can my parents give me the money to open an IRA?*
A: Yes. As long as you (or your spouse) have *earned* at least that same amount during the year it is contributed to the IRA, it doesn't have to be your money that's deposited. (See Chapter 9 for more detail on how the IRS defines "earned" money.)

Q: *Are there any IRA fees I should watch out for?*
A: Yes. One common practice is to tack on an IRA maintenance fee of between $10 and $40 a year. Sometimes the fund company will waive the fee if you maintain a given minimum amount in your account or if you have other accounts at the same institution.

Q: *I want a Roth IRA but earn too much. Should I bother getting a nondeductible IRA?*
A: Yes. Congress recently created a loophole that can help you. Starting in 2010, unless things change, you can open a nondeductible IRA, wait 60 days, and convert it to a Roth IRA. You can do this no matter how much money you earn. After that, you've got a Roth and the money will grow tax-free forever.

You can also take advantage of this if you started out with a traditional IRA because you needed the near-term tax break but now have the cash to pay the taxes and go into the Roth. If you need help deciding, financial software firm CCH Inc. has more detail and a link to a useful calculator at www.finance.cch.com/text/c40s10d330.asp.

IF YOU'RE SELF-EMPLOYED

If you're your own boss—whether you're a full-time freelance writer or have a sideline business selling collectibles on eBay—consider opening one of the three basic types of retirement savings plans for self-employed people. The advantage of these plans is that they allow you to contribute (and deduct) much more than an IRA.

The first type of self-employment retirement plan is called a **SIM-PLE IRA**. As the name suggests, SIMPLE IRAs are the least complicated kind of self-employment retirement plan. They work pretty much like traditional IRAs, except they allow you to set aside (and deduct) more money—up to $11,500 a year—even if that accounts for all your self-employment income. You may be able to contribute even more than that, but the rules are fairly complex, so talk to an accountant before making any decisions. If you don't have employees, a SIMPLE IRA is easy to set up; if you do have people working for you, you may have to contribute for them as well. One catch you should be aware of: If you want to set up a SIMPLE plan, you have to do it before October 1 of the current tax year.

If your self-employment generates a lot more income, you might benefit more from a **simplified employee pension** or **SEP**, sometimes referred to as a **SEP-IRA**. The main difference is the amount of money you can contribute. You can contribute 20% of your first $245,000 in net earnings from self-employment to a SEP, which means that, in theory, you could save up to $49,000 a year toward your retirement and take the tax deduction. (Naturally, you can always set up a much smaller account.) To figure out your net earnings, go to the IRS website at www.irs.gov or consult an accountant. As with SIMPLE IRAs, a SEP may require you to make contributions for any employees you might have. And just like traditional IRAs, you can open a SEP right up to the April 15 tax filing deadline.

A third option, the **Individual 401(k)**, commonly known as a **Solo 401(k)**, works like a 401(k) added to a SEP-IRA. In theory, you can put away as much as $65,500 a year in one of these accounts. The rules are complex, so definitely consult an accountant.

For more details on all of these options, contact a no-load, low-cost mutual fund company. Fidelity (www.fidelity.com; 800-FIDELITY) is a good site for information. And if you do decide to open any of these types of accounts, Financial Engines (see the box on p. 154) can help make sure your investments are on track. Also, IRS Publication 560 (*Retirement Plans for Small Business*) provides comparison charts, examples, and worksheets for all of these types of plans. You can get it online at www.irs.gov/publications/p560 or get a free print copy by calling 1-800-TAX-FORM (829-3676).

BUT I JUST CAN'T AFFORD IT!

There's a little-known but terrific way to get some retirement savings, even if you earn very little. If you're like a lot of people starting out, your salary is just not enough, especially if you spend most of your entry-level paycheck on big-city rent or student loan debt. But something called the "Saver's Credit" provides a means for the government to pay you for contributing to a retirement plan.

Here's how it works. For every $1 you put into a 401(k) or IRA (up to $2,000 a year), the government gives you back 50 cents at tax time. So if, for example, you put in $100, you may qualify for a credit of up to $50. You qualify for the full rebate if your income is under $16,500 as a single person or $33,000 as a married couple. The details vary, but you can still get some money back if you earn less than $27,750 as a single person or $55,500 as a married couple.

To take advantage of this, you'll have to file either Form 1040 or 1040A (not the EZ form) when you do your taxes and fill out IRS Form 8880, which is available at www.irs .gov/pub/irs-pdf/f8880.pdf. The rules are a little complicated, but the IRS has put together a good summary at www.irs .gov/taxtopics/tc610.html.

FINANCIAL CRAMMING

- Enroll in your company retirement savings plan or open an individual retirement account (IRA) at a no-load mutual fund company—right now.

- Looking for easy money? If your company offers a 401(k), contribute at least as much as your employer will match. A fifty-cent match for every dollar you put in is the same as earning a 50% return on your investment.

- Figure out whether a traditional or Roth IRA makes more sense for you. Many younger people have more to gain from Roth IRAs. See p. 147 for details and look at IRA comparison calculators like the ones at www.morningstar.com and www.moneychimp.com.

- Don't cash in your 401(k) when you lose or change jobs. Roll it over instead.

- If you work for yourself, check out SEPs, SIMPLE IRAs, and Solo 401(k)s. These plans may permit you to sock away far more for your retirement than you could with a traditional or Roth IRA.

- Take advantage of the Saver's Credit (see p. 166) if you're eligible. If your income is relatively low, you can get a rebate of up to $1,000 a year from the government by contributing to an IRA or 401(k).

OH, GIVE ME A HOME

The New Rules for
Getting a House or
Apartment of Your Own

B UYING A HOME has always been—
and always should be—treated as a major
commitment. In recent years, though, things got way too casual. All
you needed was to fill out some papers, come up with a tiny down
payment (or maybe none at all), and you were a homeowner. It was
that simple, and it ushered in the biggest housing boom in history.

And then the boom went bust.

Today, lenders are much stricter, so you'll really need to get all
your financial ducks in a row. This chapter explains everything you
need to know to buy a house or apartment of your own. It will
help you figure out how much home you can afford, direct you to
programs that can make things easier, and fill you in on everything
from how to qualify for a mortgage to where to find the best rates.

A 60-SECOND EXPLANATION OF THE MORTGAGE MESS

Before I launch into the nitty-gritty of the steps you need to take, I want to quickly explain some of the factors leading up to the recent home loan crisis—only because it's a great lesson in what *not* to do.

Rewind to 2005. A record number of Americans were buying homes. On the surface this was great news. After all, owning a home has always been considered the holy grail of personal finance and a major element of the American dream. The housing boom, as it was called, kicked into high gear and the new crop of homeowners— as well as lenders, of course—were thrilled.

At the time, few asked the question: Why are so many people who couldn't buy homes before suddenly *able* to buy? The answer was simple. Beginning in 2001—and peaking in late 2005—lenders started relaxing the guidelines for people who wanted a mortgage, which is a loan you take out to pay for a home. Loaded down with lots of credit card debt? No problem, they said. No steady job or salary to realistically keep up with your future mortgage payments? That was okay too. And it didn't matter how much of a down payment you could make. In 2006 the median down payment made by first-time home buyers was just 2% (in the past, they had to put down closer to 20%). In fact, half of all first-time home buyers that year put down nothing at all.

What were lenders thinking?

Most lenders, of course, knew they were making very risky loans. (After all, one of the biggest jobs of a lender is to assess whether a customer can pay back a loan.) But many figured that they could profit by charging borrowers with less than excellent credit (great credit is known as "prime" credit) interest rates that started out low but would go up after a certain amount of time. These were called **subprime loans**. And when interest rates overall started rising, the interest rates on these subprime mortgages shot up, leaving many new homeowners unable to meet their monthly payments. Still, lenders felt that even if the borrowers had trouble making their payments, they could sell their homes at a profit or borrow against their equity as home prices rose. But house prices plummeted, leaving these overextended buyers with no options.

You can guess what happened next. The details varied, but the bottom line was the same: Literally millions of homeowners, starting in 2007, found themselves unable to afford their monthly mortgage payments and the banks took their homes.

So what does this mean for you?

As lenders, financial markets, the government, and individual homeowners continue to sort through this mess—often called "the subprime mortgage crisis"—the lessons learned can actually help you successfully buy (and keep) your first home. But it may be much more challenging for you to qualify, so you'll need to be extremely well prepared.

Of course, if you're like most people starting out, you may be nowhere near the point where you can consider buying a home, so you can benefit from the next section of this chapter, which offers tips on being a smart renter. And you can get an idea of where you're headed and make your goals more concrete.

WHAT EVERY RENTER NEEDS TO KNOW

Even if you're not ready to buy, there are plenty of ways to reduce the cost of renting and eliminate the headaches you're likely to encounter as a tenant. A few strategies to consider:

- **Try to negotiate the rent.** I know a lot of people who feel squeamish about doing this, but you should force yourself. When you find a place you like, tell the landlord you're very interested but hadn't planned to spend as much as he or she is asking for. Ask in a superpolite way if there's any way you can get a break—say, paying $50 or $100 less a month or receiving one month free, depending on what the market is like where you live. If the landlord doesn't agree, nothing is lost. Of course, in cities where there are five renters competing for every apartment, your chances of getting a break are slim to none. So know your market. (You can also check out www.rentometer.com to get a rough idea of what people in that neighborhood are paying.) In some areas, the housing crisis has resulted in a huge supply of rentals. In others, the rental market is more competitive. You'll get a sense of how "hot" the market is by how quickly places get rented or how long they stay vacant. Knowing the details can help you get a better deal.

- **Negotiate the terms of your lease.** Though it isn't exciting, it's important that you carefully scrutinize your lease, which might be several pages long. Look for provisions that seem unfair; they may be illegal. In some states, for example, a landlord can't include clauses banning water beds or demanding excessive penalties for late rent. To find out the rules in your area, call your state or county housing office or office of consumer affairs. These government agencies may be able to provide you with brochures or websites that answer your questions about tenants' rights.

  Also, look for clauses that, although legal, may be a pain. Try to negotiate them out of the lease *before* you sign. Examples are provisions that give your landlord the right to enter your apartment without your permission or the right to raise your rent if his taxes or operating costs increase. Watch out for sections that say no one but you can live in the apartment. Look out for bans on pets; although you might not have one now, you might want to get one in the future. And think twice before agreeing to any unreasonable stipulation the landlord may have added to the standard lease agreement. I know of one couple in San Francisco who had to agree to wash their landlord's plants every week with soap and water! That meant that they couldn't go away for more than a week without getting someone to take over this ridiculous chore.

- **Negotiate with the real estate broker if you're dealing with one.** In most cities, if you use a broker to help you find an apartment to rent, you don't pay him or her a commission. But in a major city like New York, renters are often expected to pay brokers as much as 15% of the year's rent to secure a place. If possible, try to avoid dealing with brokers by searching sites like www.craigslist.org and www.apart ments.com, or going through newspaper ads for apartments rented out directly by owners or an onsite leasing office. If you must use a broker, explain up front that you're a serious customer but are willing to pay a commission of only, say, 10%. If you hunt around, you may find a broker willing to cut a deal.

- **List all your roommates on the lease, and have them all sign it.** Although some landlords won't allow this, it's worth asking about. Having all your roommates listed on the lease ensures that you will all share legal responsibility in case of a problem. It also protects you if one of your roommates suddenly decides to move out before the lease is up. Even if your landlord won't allow you to have all roommates on the lease, you might consider drafting a contract to reflect any agreement you've made among yourselves and getting it signed and notarized. Trouble can happen, and this way if you're left "holding the bag," you have a written document in case you ever need to pursue legal action against your former roommates.

- **Get everything in writing.** Ask for a written lease instead of a verbal agreement. Also, get any additional promises the landlord makes (such as guarantees to paint walls or fix leaky faucets) included in the lease before you sign.

- **Understand how a security deposit works.** A security deposit is money you give to a landlord to protect him in case you damage the apartment or house. If you don't cause any damage, the security deposit will be returned to you when the lease is up. Most states limit the size of a security deposit to one or two months' rent, and many also restrict the ways in which it can be used. In general, the landlord can use the money to fix damages you cause, but not for basic maintenance on the apartment or house.

Get a receipt for the security deposit from the landlord. In some cities, the landlord is required to put your money in an interest-bearing account and pay you the interest at the end of your tenancy. (Even in states that don't require the landlord to pay you interest, some landlords do.) Call your state or local housing office for the rules. When your lease is up and you move out, the landlord must refund your deposit if you haven't caused any damage.

Before you move in, it's a good idea to take pictures of the condition of the apartment and note any issues (no matter how minor they may seem). This will give you a frame of reference for the condition the apartment needs to be in when you leave. Also, be sure to take pictures after you've moved your things out just in case there's a dispute over any damages.

- **If you plan to renew your lease, contact your landlord two months before the lease is up and try to negotiate.** In an area with an abundance of available rentals, your landlord may agree to keep the rent the same or even to lower it. But don't wait too long to bring up the subject. If you wait until the week before your lease ends, the landlord will assume you're bluffing when you say you're thinking of moving out.

- **Know your rights.** The law protects renters in many ways. Here are a few:

  » Federal law prohibits a landlord from refusing to rent to you based on your race, sex, religion, disability, national origin, or familial status (meaning whether you're pregnant or have kids under 18). Some cities and states also prohibit housing discrimination based on age, marital status, or sexual orientation. If you think you've been denied housing for any of these reasons, call the Housing Discrimination Hotline at 800-669-9777.

  » With a fixed lease, such as for one or two years, the landlord is not allowed to raise the rent during the term of the rental contract and must tell you about an impending rent increase before your lease is up. The amount of time within which you must be told of the rent hike varies from state to state. For month-to-month rentals, you must be notified in writing 30 days before the rent is increased.

» In some states, if you disobey a provision in your lease and your landlord knows about it but accepts your rent anyway, the landlord is not allowed to kick you out for violating the provision. For example, if your lease forbids overnight guests, but your landlord knows you have one and accepts your rent check anyway, he cannot evict you later on this basis.

» In most cities, if you provide written notice of major problems such as glitches with heating, electricity, and plumbing, your landlord is required to fix them. Your landlord is not always responsible, however, for taking care of minor problems like leaky faucets or worn-out floors. Check your lease to see what repairs the landlord is responsible for and check the landlord-tenant rules in your city.

» In some states you can withhold rent if there's been negligence on the part of the landlord, but the rules are very specific about how to do this. Again, call or visit the website of your county or state housing office or office of consumer affairs to find out the rules in your area.

For additional information on your rights as a tenant, try contacting local branches of the Legal Aid Society or your state attorney general's office. Nolo.com is a useful website that provides links to renters' rights sites all over the country.

SHOULD YOU RENT OR BUY?

Many people believe that given the choice, renting is a bad idea: They think it's the equivalent of "throwing money away." But when you're young, it's often smarter to rent than to buy. I know many people who purchased a studio apartment soon after college and then two or three years later got married and had to sell their place at a loss.

Unfortunately, making the decision involves a lot more than simply comparing your monthly rent with the monthly mortgage you'd pay as an owner. You also need to take into account how long you plan to own the home, how much you think the home will increase in value (or "appreciate"), the tax break you'll get for buying, the fees you'll have to pay when you buy, and the rate of return you think you could earn by investing the cash you would save by *not* buying (this is called your **opportunity cost**). Of course, plenty of emotional factors go into this decision too, but I'll leave those for you to think about. A great place to start your thinking is with the "buy versus rent" calculators at www.dinkytown.net and www.myfico.com. Also consider these tips:

- **If you can't envision yourself in the same place for the next several years, you should rent.** Like I said, there are many financial issues that determine whether it makes sense for you to buy or rent. One very important factor is the thousands of dollars you'll pay in upfront fees when you purchase a home. These charges are called **closing costs** because they're paid when you close the deal and sign the final paperwork on a new home. Then, when you sell your home, you can expect to pay thousands more to a real estate broker. If you stay in your place for a number of years, these costs won't make much difference, at least in theory. The hope is that your home's selling price will increase enough to cover them and then some. But if you move after a couple of years and your home's value has not appreciated significantly, you may not be able to sell your home for enough of a profit to cover these costs.

- **If you have an amazing deal on a rental, it might make more sense to rent and stash your savings elsewhere.** In some cities there are still low-cost apartment deals to be had. If you're lucky enough to have a **rent-controlled** or **rent-stabilized apartment** (one where the landlord can't charge more than a fixed rent and fixed increases) that's substantially below the going rental rate, you may be better off holding on to it and saving that money in a money fund for a down payment.

- **If you don't have a steady income, keep renting.** It's difficult to get a loan without a regular paycheck. And, of course, it can also be tough to make your mortgage payments. Don't put yourself through the angst of trying to buy if you're not ready.

- **Don't assume you always get a tax break for buying.** Most of us have at least one relative who prattles on about how buying a home is the best tax break around. It's true that the federal government allows homeowners to subtract the interest they pay on their mortgages from their taxable income, and that can make a big difference at tax time.

  Say you paid $10,000 in mortgage interest in a year and had an income of $50,000. You would be able to subtract, or deduct, the $10,000 worth of interest and bring your taxable income down to $40,000. Assuming your tax rate is 25%, that would translate into a savings of $2,500. If you're buying a low-priced home, however, the tax break may be worth very little. That's because all taxpayers (whether they own a home or not) get a tax break known as the **standard deduction,** the amount they can automatically subtract from their taxable income. For 2009, the standard deduction was $5,700 for single taxpayers and $11,400 for married taxpayers filing jointly.

  In general, to reap a tax advantage from buying, the annual interest you pay on your mortgage (plus other deductions you get) must be greater than the standard deduction. If you're buying a low-priced home, this may not be the case. If you don't qualify for a tax break, there's less incentive to buy. (For details on other tax breaks that homeowners can receive, see Chapter 9.)

WHAT LENDERS LOOK FOR

The first question most prospective home buyers ask is "What price home can I afford?" The answer, to a great extent, depends not only on how big a mortgage you can obtain, but on whether you can handle the payments comfortably and the stability of your situation. Your mortgage is said to be "secured by" the property, meaning that if you don't pay it back, the lender can take your home. Recently, with millions of homeowners unable to pay back their home loans, lenders have made the eligibility requirements for getting a loan much tougher. Here is what lenders consider when deciding whether to give you a mortgage and determining your interest rate.

- **Your credit record.** Lenders are concerned about whether you have a history of paying off your debt—especially these days. To find this out, they'll get a copy of your credit reports and credit score, which reveal your financial behavior. (For more details, go to Chapter 3, p. 70). Borrowers with above-average scores can get the best deals, which can save them hundreds of dollars a month and *thousands* of dollars a year compared to someone with bad credit. Borrowers with lower-than-average credit scores will have to look a little harder, and won't get the best deal. And if you have poor credit, it may be hard to find anyone to give you a mortgage. Regardless of your score, lenders also want to see that you haven't defaulted on any loans (that means credit cards, student loans, car loans) or gone bankrupt, especially within the past two years.

- **Your ability to come up with the cash.** Few if any lenders will give you a loan for the full purchase price of a home.

Instead, they require you to contribute some of your own money, called a **down payment**, up front. Lenders tend to want a down payment of 10% or even 20% of the price of the home, depending on both your credit record and the cost of the house. (There are some special programs, which I'll discuss later, that may allow you to make smaller down payments.) Coming up with a down payment is one of the main obstacles for first-time home buyers.

In addition to the down payment, the typical home buyer also has to pay about 1% to 5% of a home's price in so-called closing costs; these include fees for inspections, appraisals, title insurance, credit checks, land surveys, and legal services that can add up to thousands of dollars. Also, some lenders require buyers to have two or three months of mortgage payments saved up in reserve.

- **Your income.** Lenders want to make sure you earn enough to pay the costs of owning a home. To do this they compare your future monthly housing costs (also known as your **PITI**, which stands for Principal, Interest, property Taxes, and Insurance) to your pretax monthly income. The traditional guideline used by lenders is that your PITI should not exceed 28% of your pretax monthly income. During the housing boom, lenders started relaxing that standard, offering mortgages to borrowers whose costs ate up a much higher percentage of their income. Sometimes, they didn't even bother to verify salaries. Those days are long gone. Still, under special circumstances—if you have a spotless credit history or can make a very large down payment— lenders may accept PITI costs of up to 36%.

- **Your debt-to-income ratio.** Lenders also want to make sure you aren't already burdened with lots of loans. That's why they look at your current monthly debt commitments (such as auto loan payments, student loan payments, and minimum credit card payments.) Then they add in your future monthly housing costs and calculate what portion of your monthly income before taxes will go to these expenses. The percentage they come up with is called your debt-to-income ratio. Lenders have traditionally liked to see a debt-to-income ratio that doesn't exceed 36%, but during the housing boom years they became lax, allowing the ratio to rise to as much as 55%. Today, a ratio higher than 36% is the exception—only for applicants making a very high down payment or those with *stellar* credit.

- **Your job history.** Lenders like to see that borrowers have a secure job. In general, if you've worked in the same industry for at least two years, they view you more favorably than if you've switched careers during that time. In the years leading up to the recent mortgage mess, lenders often failed to even check that a borrower actually held the job written on the application! Today they'll also verify your income with your current employer before giving you a loan. If you're self-employed, be prepared to prove what you earn.

THE REAL COSTS OF OWNING A HOME

Owning a home can be great. But the fact is, when you become a homeowner, you'll run up a variety of expenses that you may never even have heard of as a renter. Here's a description of each:

- **Principal and interest.** Your monthly mortgage payment consists of two parts: principal and interest. The amount you borrow from the lender is known as the principal. The fee that the bank charges to lend you money is called interest, and it is expressed as an annual percentage. Suppose you get a mortgage of $100,000 and you're expected to pay it back over 30 years (that's standard). If the lender charges you an interest rate of 7%, after 30 years you would have paid the lender back the $100,000 in principal plus a total of $139,509 in interest. (Shocking, isn't it?) In the early years of your loan, you're paying back mostly interest and very little principal. As time goes on, you start to pay back

the principal. To soften the blow somewhat, you get to deduct your interest payments if you itemize your taxes, which
can save you a lot of money. (For a discussion of what this
means, see Chapter 9.)

To get a feel for what your monthly mortgage payment
would be, check out Figure 7–1.

- **Property tax.** This is a fee you pay to your town, city, or
county. It's based on where you live and the official ap-
praised value of your home, including the land on which it's
built. To get a sense of the property taxes charged for various homes in neighborhoods you're interested in, ask a real
estate broker or go to www.domania.com for recent sales
prices and taxes in the area. They are generally between 1%
and 3% of your home's value per year. You can also call the
town hall or city hall and ask for the tax assessor's office.
One bit of consolation: You may be able to deduct part of
your property taxes. (See Chapter 9 for details.)

- **Insurance.** Most lenders require you to get **homeowners insurance** to make sure that someone will pay the cost of repairing or replacing your home in case of a disaster, such as
a fire. That's because until you pay it off, your home is the
lender's collateral. If it's completely ruined and you walk
away from it (and your loan obligation), the lender needs
to be reimbursed. Depending on where you live, you might
be required to buy flood insurance also. (For tips on buying
insurance, including renters coverage, see Chapter 8).

If you make a down payment of less than 20% there's
another type of insurance you'll be required to buy. It's
called **private mortgage insurance (PMI).** PMI protects the
lender if you default on your mortgage. Once you've reached
20% of your home's **equity** (the value of your house minus
what you owe), you can ask your lender to discontinue PMI
coverage. They're legally required to do so once you've paid
off 22% of the purchase price, as long as you've made all of
your payments on time in the prior two years. (At the height
of the housing boom, lenders became less stringent about re-

quiring PMI, and homeowners were able to avoid it. Today, though, so many lenders have been burned by borrowers who defaulted on their home loans that most won't give you a loan unless you have mortgage insurance.)

You can pay PMI in monthly or annual installments. PMI amounts to roughly 0.5% to 0.75% of your total annual mortgage cost; ask your lender what your payment options are and decide which makes more sense, depending on your budget. The good news is that you may be able to subtract the premiums you pay on PMI from your taxable income. (For more details, see Chapter 9, p. 275.)

Many people who take out thirty-year mortgages do not actually expect to keep their homes for that long. That's why you should ask your lender about **lender-paid mortgage insurance (LPMI)**. With LPMI, the lender takes care of the insurance premium, and you pay it back slowly with a somewhat higher interest rate (about one quarter of one percentage point) over the length of the loan. The advantage is less of a cash outlay month to month. The downside is that you'll keep paying for your insurance even after the 22% mark. But if you are planning to leave your home in fewer than ten years, that probably won't matter. Ask your lender to run the figures on both scenarios—PMI and LPMI—to see which one is better for you.

- **Condominium and cooperative fees. Condos** and **co-ops** are housing units (usually apartment buildings) that are jointly owned. Each resident owns his or her own unit or apartment, while the common spaces (stairwells, elevators, hallways, lobbies) are owned collectively by all the residents. To pay for the upkeep of these common spaces, residents pay extra fees, known as **maintenance fees** or **common charges**.

   The primary difference between a co-op and a condo is the way in which the units are owned. In a co-op, residents do not technically own the apartments; instead they own **shares**, or units of ownership, in the cooperative. The cooperative owns all the units in the building. In order to buy or sell units in a co-op, residents usually must get approval

FIGURE 7-1

GETTING A HANDLE ON YOUR MONTHLY MORTGAGE PAYMENTS

First, locate the price of the home you're thinking about buying in the lefthand column. Now look to the far right and find the approximate interest rate a lender would charge you for a thirty-year fixed-rate mortgage. As you can see, regardless of the interest rate on your mortgage, you'd have a lower monthly payment with a 20% down payment than with 5% down.

Keep in mind that this table includes only principal and interest payments, *not* property taxes, homeowners insurance, or PMI. The following rules of thumb will help (roughly) estimate these costs: Annual property taxes are typically between 1% and 3% of the cost of a home; PMI amounts to about 0.5% to 0.75% of your total annual mortgage costs, and homeowners insurance can range from $400 to $1,000 a year. These extra costs can vary dramatically, depending on where you live and the amount of your mortgage. For more precise estimates, ask a lender or a local real estate agent.

Cost of Home	Down Payment %	Down Payment $	Monthly Mortgage Payment with Interest Rates of: 4%	6%	8%	10%
$100,000	5%	$ 5,000	$ 454	$ 570	$ 697	$ 834
	10%	10,000	429	540	660	790
	20%	20,000	382	480	587	702
$150,000	5%	7,500	680	855	1,046	1,251
	10%	15,000	645	810	991	1,185
	20%	30,000	573	719	881	1,053
$200,000	5%	10,000	907	1,139	1,394	1,667
	10%	20,000	859	1,079	1,321	1,580
	20%	40,000	764	959	1,174	1,404
$300,000	5%	15,000	1,360	1,709	2,091	2,501
	10%	30,000	1,289	1,619	1,981	2,369
	20%	60,000	1,146	1,439	1,761	2,106
$400,000	5%	20,000	1,814	2,278	2,788	3,335
	10%	40,000	1,719	2,158	2,642	3,159
	20%	80,000	1,528	1,919	2,348	2,808
$600,000	5%	30,000	2,721	3,417	4,182	5,002
	10%	60,000	2,578	3,238	3,962	4,739
	20%	120,000	2,292	2,878	3,522	4,212

Source: Fannie Mae

from the **co-op board,** which is a group of co-op residents. With a condo, residents have more autonomy; they own the apartment and can usually buy and sell the place without getting permission from any board.

It's good to ask questions such as whether you're allowed to rent out your apartment or whether it's permitted to join two smaller apartments into one. These issues may not seem relevant to you now, but in the future they could matter. Co-ops often have more stringent rules than condos. You should consider asking for a copy of your condo or co-op association's bylaws, which regulate everything from outdoor gas grills to when you can put out your garbage.

LOANS TO DISCUSS WITH YOUR LENDER

There are several mortgage options out there. Lenders might not tell you about all of them, so it's up to you to find out what you qualify for. Here are some of the choices:

- **Get a Federal Housing Administration (FHA) loan.** As a first-time home buyer, you may want to consider an FHA mortgage, which is a loan made by banks and mortgage companies but insured by the federal government. The main appeal: The program allows you to make a low down payment of just 3.5%. In some cases, borrowers can have slightly lower-than-average credit scores, although they'll most likely have to pay higher interest rates.

  One drawback to FHA loans is that sometimes they can be a bit costlier than others because you also have to buy federal mortgage insurance (about 1.75% of the loan amount paid up front, plus annual fees of about 0.5% of the loan amount), which is more expensive than private mortgage insurance (usually about 0.5% to 0.75% of the loan amount). But if an FHA loan is the only kind of mortgage you can get, the additional cost may be worth it.

There are no income limits on FHA borrowers, and you can get a loan for up to $625,500 if you live in a high-cost area. For more information, try the FHA (www.fha.gov: 800-225-5342).

• **Get a "Fannie Mae" or "Freddie Mac" loan.** Fannie Mae and Freddie Mac are two companies that were created by the federal government decades ago to help banks and mortgage companies give loans to lower-income borrowers who wouldn't otherwise be able to buy. They don't make the loans directly; instead, they create and fund mortgage programs that are offered to the public by thousands of lenders across the country.

You may have seen a lot of bad press about Fannie and Freddie in recent years, after they took a huge hit during the housing crisis. If you are about to buy a home, all that matters to you is finding a bank that offers these programs and deciding whether they're a good deal for you. In some cases, you may be able to make a down payment of as little as 3%. Also, you can sometimes use gifts from friends and relatives to help come up with part of the down payment. But no matter what, you'll need good credit to get one of these loans.

Some Fannie and Freddie programs have income limits, so if you earn an above-average salary by the standards of the area where you want to buy, you may not qualify for certain loans. For the latest about these programs and what they currently offer, ask a lender or go to www.fanniemae.com (800-732-6643) and www.freddie mac.com (800-FREDDIE).

• **Get state or local housing agency assistance.** One of the best-kept secrets of home buying is the special mortgage deals offered by state and local housing agencies to first-time home buyers. The reason you've probably never heard of these programs is that they're not advertised much. The interest rates on the mortgages they offer tend to be lower than bank rates, saving you hundreds of dollars a month on your mortgage payments. They may also be able to help you with your down payment.

Details vary from state to state—some housing agencies have income limits, dollar limits, or geographic restrictions, for example. Typically, you can participate in the program if your income is no more than the county or state's median household income and the home you want to purchase costs slightly less than the area's average price. But some states will accommodate you with a different program if your income (or house price) is too high to qualify. And certain states have special programs to assist people in particular professions. California, for example, has a program called "Extra Credit" to help eligible teachers buy homes.

For more information about your own state housing agency, check out the site of the National Council of State Housing Agencies at www.ncsha.org or call 202-624-7710. There's also a chart on the following pages listing state agency contact information. When you call, say that you're a first-time home buyer looking for a mortgage and ask for a list of lenders that participate in state programs.

- **Get a loan under the Community Reinvestment Act (CRA).** It pays to check with banks in the area in which you want to live and ask if they offer mortgages under the Community Reinvestment Act. The CRA was created by Congress to help people with relatively low incomes to buy homes. Depending upon how much you make, it may have a good deal for you. Be sure to ask, since banks usually don't advertise this program.

- **Get assistance from the Department of Veterans Affairs.** If you've ever been in active duty in the U.S. military for at least 181 continuous days, or have served at least six years in the Selected Reserves or the National Guard, you may be eligible for a Veterans Affairs (VA) mortgage. Requirements vary depending upon when you served and if it was during wartime. You can get these VA mortgages from regular lenders.

STATE HOUSING AGENCIES

State	Website	Phone Number
Alabama	ahfa.com	800-325-2432
Alaska	www.ahfc.state.ak.us	800-478-2432
Arizona	www.housingaz.com	602-771-1000
Arkansas	arkansas.gov/adfa	501-682-5900
California	www.calhfa.ca.gov	877-922-5433
Colorado	chfainfo.com	303-297-2432
Connecticut	chfa.org	800-877-2432
Delaware	www.destatehousing.com	302-739-4263
District of Columbia	dchfa.org	888-363-8808
Florida	www.floridahousing.org	904-488-4197
Georgia	www.dca.state.ga.us	800-359-4663
Hawaii	hawaii.gov/dbedt/hhfdc	808-587-0641
Idaho	www.ihfa.org	208-331-4882
Illinois	ihda.org	312-836-5200
Indiana	indianahousing.org	800-457-8283
Iowa	ifahome.com	877-622-4866
Kansas	kshousingcorp.org	785-296-5865
Kentucky	www.kyhousing.org	502-564-7630
Louisiana	lhfa.state.la.us	888-454-2001
Maine	www.mainehousing.org	800-452-4668
Maryland	mdhousing.org	410-514-7001
Massachusetts	masshousing.com	888-843-6432
Michigan	michigan.gov/mshda	517-373-8370
Minnesota	mnhousing.gov	800-657-3769
Mississippi	mshomecorp.com	800-544-5960
Missouri	www.mhdc.com	816-759-6600

Montana	housing.mt.gov	800-761-6264
Nebraska	nifa.org	800-204-6432
Nevada	nvhousing.state.nv.us	702-486-7220
New Hampshire	www.nhhfa.org	800-649-0470
New Jersey	nj-hmfa.com	609-278-7400
New Mexico	housingnm.org	800-444-6880
New York	nyhomes.org	800-382-4663
North Carolina	www.nchfa.com	800-393-0988
North Dakota	ndhfa.org	800-292-8621
Ohio	www.ohiohome.org	888-362-6432
Oklahoma	ohfa.org	800-256-1489
Oregon	www.ohcs.oregon.gov	877-788-2663
Pennsylvania	phfa.org	800-342-2397
Puerto Rico	gdb-pur.com	787-765-7577
Rhode Island	rhodeislandhousing.org	401-457-1234
South Carolina	www.schousing.com	803-896-9001
South Dakota	sdhda.org	605-773-3181
Tennessee	thda.org	615-815-2200
Texas	tdhca.state.tx.us	800-792-1119
Utah	www.utahhousingcorp.org	801-902-8200
Vermont	www.vhfa.org	802-864-5743
Virginia	vhda.com	877-843-2123
Washington	www.wshfc.org	206-464-7139
West Virginia	wvhdf.com	800-933-9843
Wisconsin	wheda.com	800-334-6873
Wyoming	www.wyomingcda.com	307-265-0603

Source: National Council of State Housing Agencies

VA loans generally do not require any down payment at all if your loan doesn't exceed $417,000 (although this figure varies in different parts of the country), but in some cases the individual lender that supplies the VA loan may require one. The way it works: You pay a one-time charge called a **funding fee**, which is basically an upfront payment of your mortgage insurance. As of 2009, the funding fee ranged from 1.25% to 3.3% of the mortgage, depending on the terms of your loan. If you *are* able to come up with a down payment, the funding fee will be lower. There are no maximum income limits for applicants. For more information go to www.homeloans .va.gov or call 800-827-3702.

IF YOU DON'T QUALIFY FOR A MORTGAGE

As you know by now, lenders are really cracking down on who gets a mortgage. If you don't qualify because you have a poor credit score, I recommend that you wait a year or two. Focus on improving your score (pay your student loan and credit card bills on time for at least a year), and apply for a mortgage when it's better. One warning: Steer clear of mortgage brokers who promise to get you a loan despite your credit history. If they can do it at all, the interest will be astronomical.

But if credit isn't the problem and you're set on purchasing right now, here are some tips to help you get your mortgage.

- **Get the down payment (or part of it) as a gift.** About one in four first-time home buyers receives money from friends or relatives to cover the down payment. Some lenders require that your down payment consist at least partially of your own money. Others permit the entire down payment to come from a gift. Some lenders require that the gift come from a relative; others allow it to come from friends. In most cases, lenders require a letter from the generous friend or relative stating that the down payment money is a gift, not a loan. (To aid in this effort, I've heard of newlyweds who ask for cash toward a down payment rather than register for china.)

Some lenders will review your bank records before granting your loan. If they see that a large sum of money was deposited in your account a few months before you tried to get a mortgage, they'll ask you to prove that the money is not a loan. So keep careful records of cash gifts and make copies of any large checks you receive (like wedding gifts, for instance). Also, if you sell something valuable (like a car), keep a receipt of the transaction.

- **Try to find seller financing.** When a homeowner who is trying to sell his house helps you to buy it, it's through a lending process called seller financing. The homeowner, because he or she is highly motivated to sell, gives you a loan (either with little or no interest due) to help you come up with a down payment. This has become more popular in recent years. Regardless of the seller's reasons, this can be a great deal for the buyer. Make sure that you get the best interest rate possible by comparing terms at a number of banks. Be sure to get everything in writing and have a lawyer look over the loan agreement before you sign.

- **Tap into your IRA.** You can withdraw up to $10,000 from your IRA to pay for a first-time home purchase without paying the usual 10% penalty. But "first time," in the case of IRAs, is a very loose term. To qualify as a "first-time" home buyer, you don't actually have to be buying your first home; you just can't have owned a home within the prior two years. Also, the $10,000 IRA withdrawal represents a lifetime limit. You don't have to use it all up at once, though. You can take, say, $5,000 now and $5,000 later for a future home purchase.

  But there are serious disadvantages to making this kind of withdrawal. With a traditional IRA, you'll have to pay tax on the money you withdraw, though not if you have a Roth IRA that's at least five years old. More seriously, IRA withdrawals—unlike loans from a 401(k)—can never be paid back. Because of the miracle of compounding, money in your retirement account is worth much more than any other savings you accrue. Think twice before you use this money for a home purchase.

THE SLIPPERY SLOPE OF LOW DOWN PAYMENTS

If you don't have a lot of cash, you might think a low down payment would be a life saver. But as too many homeowners learned the hard way, it can be hazardous because it allows you to buy a more expensive home than you can really afford.

Take the case of a buyer with $20,000 to put down on a home. If she put 20% down, she could buy a $100,000 home. But if she put down only 5%, she might be able to get a $400,000 home.

Of course, that more costly home would also come with much higher monthly payments. With a thirty-year mortgage and a 7% interest rate, the $100,000 home would cost her about $532 a month, whereas payments on the $400,000 home would be $2,528 a month. And if she ran into any sort of financial trouble along the way, she would most likely have a problem making those hefty monthly payments.

And if home prices started to plummet (as they did drastically in recent years), borrowers like this would have an added

SHOPPING FOR A MORTGAGE

If you were shopping for a car or even a digital camera, you probably wouldn't dream of buying the first one you saw. This should be true when you shop for a mortgage as well. If you're able to find an interest rate just half a percentage point lower, you'll save thousands of dollars over the life of the loan. The good news is that it's easy. The best place to start your search is online so you can get a

---

complication. Take the case of that $100,000 home. If real estate prices dropped by 6%, the home would be worth $94,000. Since the buyer made a $20,000 down payment, she would have an $80,000 mortgage. If she couldn't make the mortgage payments and was forced to sell the house for $94,000, she could pay off the $80,000 mortgage and walk away with $14,000 of the original down payment—a $6,000 loss. Bad news, but not devastating.

But what if she owned the $400,000 home? If she made a $20,000 down payment, she would have a $380,000 mortgage. After a 6% drop in real estate prices, that home would be worth $376,000. In other words, she would actually owe the bank $4,000 more than the actual value of her home. And if she was forced to sell the house at that value to pay off her debts, she would suffer a loss of $24,000—the entire down payment plus an additional $4,000.

If you owe more than your house is worth, you have what is known as an **upside-down mortgage**—a situation that has ensnared millions of homeowners. You do not want to be one of them.

sense of what various rates are. The websites www.hsh.com, www
.freeratesearch.com, www.zillow.com, and www.bankrate.com can
help you sort through the offerings of dozens of major lenders.
Next, see if your bank or credit union can top the best rate you
find online. Sometimes, the best deals are in your own backyard. At
your own bank, ask if you can get a better rate than what's advertised because you're already a customer.

Fixed Rates versus Adjustable Rates

All lenders offer two basic types of mortgages. The most common type
is a **fixed-rate** mortgage, which is usually paid back over thirty years.
This is a mortgage whose interest rate stays the same over the life of
the loan. One of the key benefits is the peace of mind that comes from
knowing your monthly payments will remain steady forever.

The other general type of mortgage is the **adjustable-rate mortgage (ARM)**, sometimes known as a variable-rate mortgage. In theory, the interest rate on an ARM changes based on what happens to
interest rates in the economy. If rates go down, your ARM interest
rate should drop, and so would your monthly payment. If rates go
up, your interest rate and monthly payments will rise. With most
ARMs, the lender raises or lowers the interest rate only once a year,
called the **adjustment period.**

ARMs have been tempting to first-time home buyers because
their *initial* interest rate is lower than the rates on fixed-rate mortgages. This lower initial rate means lower monthly payments for the
first couple of years of the ARM. And because ARMs have lower
monthly payments at the beginning, they can be easier to qualify for
than fixed-rate mortgages. But you are taking a gamble; the ARM
ultimately could cost you much more than a fixed-rate loan. (See
the box on pp. 196–97.)

ARMS have been disastrous for literally millions of homeowners, but they can make sense for certain borrowers. If, for example,
you're absolutely sure that you'll move in a few years, an ARM
could save you money in the short term. This is tricky and things
could change, so be careful. Read all the provisions and know the
worst-case scenario.

Interest Rates and Mortgage "Points"

As you've figured out by now, the most important factor contributing to the cost of a mortgage is the interest rate; that's what the
bank charges you to borrow money, and it's expressed as a percentage of your loan. But this rate can be reduced if you choose (and
have the cash) to pay **points,** up-front fees that you pay when you
buy the home.

Here's how it works: One point equals 1% of the loan. So one
point on a $100,000 loan equals $1,000. If you pay more points
to the bank, you'll get a lower interest rate, which is why they're
sometimes called "discount points." If you pay fewer points, you'll
get a higher interest rate.

If you're going to be in your home for many years, it makes
sense to pay more points and get a lower interest rate. The lower
payments you'll have with a lower rate will more than make up for
the few thousand dollars you paid in points. Also, points are sometimes tax deductible; check on www.irs.gov for more information.
If you don't plan to stay in your new home for very long, it's better
to pay fewer points. If you want to calculate whether you would
save or lose money by paying points, there are some free calculators
at the HSH website (www.hsh.com) and at the Mortgage Professor's website (www.mtgprofessor.com/calculators.htm).

No matter which rate/point combination you choose, you'll want
to go with the lender that offers you the most attractive deal. To
make it easier for you to shop, the federal government requires lenders to tell you a mortgage's **annual percentage rate (APR).** The APR is
what you'd get if you took most of the charges you're paying on the
mortgage (including the interest, points, private mortgage insurance,
and certain fees) and expressed them as one annual rate.

This makes comparison shopping much easier. You can just
compare APRs of the same types of loans (say, a thirty-year fixed-
rate mortgage). It's not an exact science, though. The APR doesn't
take into account certain charges like appraisal and document preparation fees. Plus, the APR can be affected by a lender's specific
policies. For example, *refundable* application fees are taken into
account when calculating the APR, but *nonrefundable* application

fees are not. So in addition to asking for the APR, ask each lender for a list of fees that are not included in the APR. Also, if you're interested in an adjustable-rate mortgage, don't rely on the APR alone since other factors come into play. (See the box on pp. 196–97 for further explanation.)

Fifteen-Year versus Thirty-Year Mortgages

By far the most common type of mortgage is a fixed-rate loan that lasts for thirty years. Another type of mortgage you may consider is a **fifteen-year fixed-rate mortgage.** This type of loan is more difficult to qualify for than a thirty-year mortgage, and it often has a lower interest rate than a thirty-year fixed-rate loan. Since you pay it off in fifteen years rather than thirty, you're able to build up **equity,** or ownership, in the home sooner.

Although some people view a fifteen-year mortgage as a disciplined way to pay off their home loans faster, it's not always the best choice. The monthly payments on a fifteen-year mortgage are higher than those on a thirty-year loan. Depending on your situation, it may make more sense to go with the lower monthly payments on a thirty-year loan and use the cash you're not pouring into your home for other investments. For example, you may be better off putting the money into a 401(k) in which your employer matches your contributions.

Also, instead of locking yourself into the higher monthly payments on a fifteen-year mortgage, know that if you have a thirty-year loan you can always pay it off faster. Be sure you get a mortgage without prepayment penalties (which are fees for paying off your loan early) so you have this option.

A Mortgage to Avoid

One type of mortgage to stay away from is a **balloon mortgage.** The way it works is that you make small monthly payments for a fixed number of years—from five to seven—and then you're required to pay off the remainder of the loan in one lump sum. People sometimes opt for balloon mortgages if they plan to sell their home in a few years or if they anticipate that they'll be getting a chunk of cash—such as an inheritance—before the loan comes due. But if something goes wrong and you can't make the final massive payment, you could lose your home.

MAKING THE PROCESS GO SMOOTHLY

If you've gotten this far in the chapter, you have a good basic understanding of what you need to know to get a mortgage. When you're actually ready to begin your search, though, you're likely to encounter some hassles. Here are some tips to make the search as painless as possible:

- **Before you do anything, get a copy of your credit report and credit score from all three bureaus.** Even if you've never been late on a payment, you should do this. (See Chapter 3 for details on how.) Credit reporting agencies are notorious for making mistakes.

- **Before you start house hunting, call your bank or a mortgage company and say you want to get "prequalified" for a mortgage.** Prequalification is a way for lenders to give prospective buyers a sense of whether they can qualify for a mortgage, and, if so, how large a mortgage they can get. It's something you can do very quickly online or by phone. Although prequalification doesn't mean you have a guaranteed mortgage from the lender, it is a way to get a rough idea of what kind of mortgage you *might* be able to get. Once you have a ballpark figure, you can use it when shopping around as long as you are comparing similar loan products.

THE PROBLEM WITH ADJUSTABLE-RATE MORTGAGES

When my friends Nicole and Jimmy found their dream house, they were thrilled to find a lender offering an adjustable-rate mortgage (ARM) with an introductory (sometimes called a "teaser") rate of 5%. They assumed that if interest rates in the economy held steady, their rate would remain the same. Unfortunately, that's not the way it always works. Even if the interest rates in the economy *fell* slightly, their ARM rate could increase to 7% the next year.

Nicole and Jimmy aren't the only ones who didn't understand how their ARMs worked. In fact, millions of homeowners in recent years were stunned to see their monthly payments shoot up after their ARMs adjusted. This, indeed, was one of the primary contributors to the mortgage crisis. That's not to say that ARMs are pure evil. They can make sense if you need to keep mortgage payments down for a year or two, for example. But you absolutely need to be aware of the worst-case scenario and see if you could handle it. Here is what Nicole, Jimmy, and all prospective ARM customers need to know:

- **The benchmark the ARM rate is pegged to.** Your ARM's rate fluctuates based on ridiculously named benchmarks like "LIBOR" or the "One-Year Treasury Constant Maturity." Know which one your ARM is tied to.

- **The introductory or "teaser" rate.** Sometimes a lender will offer you a low initial interest rate for the first year or two. Don't let this rate fool you. In the case of Nicole and Jimmy, 5% was the initial rate. Their ARM was pegged to the LIBOR, which was 5.5% when they got their loan. So when their ARM adjusts for the first time, the new rate they pay will be based on the current rate of the LIBOR plus a fixed number of percentage points (typically two to three), called a margin. Nicole and Jimmy's margin is three percentage points.

- **The cap.** With an ARM you will need to be sure you can afford the worst-case scenario. Most ARMs have an annual cap, which is the maximum amount the rate can increase in any one year. Nicole and Jimmy's ARM has an annual cap of two percentage points. Here's why the cap protects them somewhat. If LIBOR falls to 5.25% at adjustment time, the lender would ordinarily add three percentage points (the margin) to it, resulting in a new rate of 8.25%. But since Nicole and Jimmy's ARM has an annual cap of two percentage points, the lender will increase their rate to just 7% (their current 5% teaser rate plus the two percentage point cap). It's also smart to look for an ARM with a lifetime cap of five or six percentage points. That way you'll know exactly how bad it can get.

A word of warning: Even in today's more cautious lending environment, banks have a vested interest in getting you into the largest loan you qualify for because they make more money in interest on them. Just because a bank tells you that you can afford a certain loan doesn't mean you should take it. Many new homeowners believe the old adage that you should try to get the most expensive home you can afford. Don't do it. You need to take a realistic look at what payments your current lifestyle can handle and whether you're willing to scale back in other ways to make them on time.

- **If you find a lender offering a good deal, consider getting a "preapproved" mortgage.** Although "prequalify" and "preapproved" sound similar, their meanings are very different. While prequalification is a quick exchange with no guarantee, **preapproval** is serious. It's a process by which the lender does a thorough analysis of your financial situation and commits to offering you a mortgage before you find a home you want to buy. You may be able to fill out the preapproval application online, but you'll still have to submit all the necessary paperwork in person or by mail (including verification of employment, bank statements, and tax paperwork). The lender will also look at your credit report and credit score. If everything checks out, the lender will give you a letter of commitment that says you're entitled to a loan. For a list of the info you need to have handy when you apply for preapproval, see Figure 7–2.

  Lenders sometimes charge as much as $100 for this service, but if they do you should try to dispute it. Once you've done your homework and you're convinced a lender is offering a good mortgage deal, get preapproved. A preapproved loan can even be used as a bargaining chip with a homeowner who is anxious to sell. The seller may be willing to knock the price down a bit when he or she discovers that you have a mortgage commitment, because that means the deal can take place immediately.

- **Consider enlisting the help of a mortgage broker.** Mortgage brokers are people who shop for a mortgage for you. Because they played a key role in the mortgage mess, with shady operators getting people into subprime loans and collecting big fees, they earned the industry a bad reputation. Despite the horror stories, though, some brokers can find you a better deal on a mortgage than you might find on your own because of their relationships with certain lenders. Before you sign up, find out exactly what you'll be charged for the service. The broker may charge you (or the lender) a fee—often 1% to 2% of the loan amount. So use a broker only if the mortgage he or she finds you, minus any fee you have to pay, is a better deal than the best mortgage you could get directly from a lender. And don't pay anything upfront.

- **Find out if you can lock in a rate.** Some lenders will allow you to lock in an interest rate when you "go to contract," which means you sign an official document with the seller agreeing to transfer ownership of the property. Before you pay extra for a lock-in loan, find out all the details. Some lenders charge as much as $350 to lock in a rate and won't refund the fee; others don't charge at all. These programs protect you if rates soar. If rates fall, however, many lenders will not allow you to renegotiate, so be sure you understand what you're committing to. Try to find a lender that offers this flexibility.

  Before you lock in a rate, you should get preapproved by the lender so that you are sure you can get the loan you've paid to lock in. Also, ask how long the lock is good for. A month could go by between the time you sign the contract and the closing date (when you officially own the property), so to be safe try to get a minimum 60-day lock. It's a gamble, but if rates rise by the time you sign the papers, it could be worth it. A few hundred dollars upfront can save you thousands over the life of a loan.

- **Avoid excessive fees.** Some lenders try to boost their profits by charging for ridiculous services like "document preparation," which is essentially just printing and can cost as much as $150. Even more annoying is that you may not find out about the extra fees until you're signing the papers to close the deal. Even though lenders are required to give you an estimate of fees in advance, they often tack on these

FIGURE 7-2

PAPERWORK YOU WILL NEED IN ORDER TO APPLY FOR MORTGAGE PREAPPROVAL

GENERAL INFORMATION

Name and co-borrowers' names
Age
Marital status
Social Security number
Landlord info

Number of children
Address
Telephone number
Residence history
    (last two years)

INCOME

Employer's name and address
Job title
Date hired
Federal tax information
Salary

Bonuses
Average overtime or
    commissions
Employment history
    (last two years)

ASSETS

Total sums in:

Bank (including savings,
    checking, money market
    accounts)
CDs
Mutual funds
Stocks
Bonds

Other investments, including
    real estate
Retirement accounts
Cash-value life insurance
Automobile, including year
    bought and current value
Gifts expected from friends
    or relatives

DEBTS AND EXPENSES

Current balances and monthly payments on:

Credit cards
Student loans
Rent

Car loans
Other loans

additional charges at the last minute. If that happens, all you can do is try to negotiate a better deal (you may be surprised at how successful this can be). This will, however, be less of an issue in 2010 when new regulations issued by the Department of Housing and Urban Development (HUD) go into effect. Lenders will have to fill out a standard form, a Good Faith Estimate, with a detailed estimate of your costs. They will then have to show you a direct comparison at the closing of estimated costs and actual final costs, which are not to be more than 10% higher.

- **Cozy up to your loan processor.** You can't just fill out your application and keep your fingers crossed. You have to stay on top of it. Stay in touch with whoever is overseeing your loan. This person, your **loan processor,** will be able to tell you if your paperwork is complete and how long the process should take. He or she will know the status of your application. If you've filled out a mortgage application online, the advice is still the same: Call and find out the name of your loan processor. Then be assertive but polite. Call once a week to see how the process is going and if there's anything you can do to move it along.

- **Don't always trust your real estate agent.** First-time buyers tend to put too much faith in real estate agents (also known as real estate brokers). An agent's goal is to get you to buy the house or apartment he or she shows you, not to get you the best deal or to find you the perfect home. He or she gets a commission of about 3% to 5% of the home's price from the seller. On a $200,000 house, the agent can make as much as $10,000. And the more you pay, the more he or she gets.

    If you live in a state that requires an attorney to be present during the closing, use a lawyer you find on your own— not one who's recommended by the agent. Get a referral from friends or family. If you don't have any luck that way, try your regional Better Business Bureau; go to www.bbb.org. And when you're looking for a mortgage, don't ask the advice of your real estate agent; many mortgage companies offer incentives to real estate brokers who steer business to them.

One final suggestion: Comb your local newspaper's real estate listings and check online real estate sites for places that are being sold directly by the owner. If you don't use a broker, you may be able to get the seller to accept a lower price.

IF YOU CAN'T PAY YOUR MORTGAGE

Millions of homeowners have been unable to make their payments in recent years. If you're in danger of losing your home, there are steps that you can take to avoid disaster:

- **Talk to your lender as soon as you realize you might have trouble making payments.** Don't avoid your bank or mortgage company if you can't pay. Often, your lender is the first place you should go and the only one who can help. The bank wants its money, not your home, so it may be receptive to working out a new deal. At least half of the people who faced foreclosure during the recent housing crisis never spoke to or responded to their lender, and most didn't even know they had other financing options available.

  When you speak with someone on the phone, be direct and honest. Say that you're concerned about being unable to make payments and would like to know what options are available to you. Lenders will be much less likely to take legal action if they know you are serious about trying to find a solution to the problem and repaying. Be sure to write down the date, the full name of the person you speak with, and the relevant details of your conversation. The Federal Trade Commission website (www.ftc.gov) has a useful list of things you need to prepare for this conversation; start out by searching for "Mortgage Payments Sending You Reeling?"

- **Look into FHA, Fannie Mae, or other means of refinancing.** When one lender issues you a new loan and pays off your remaining mortgage debt, it's called **refinancing.**

  See if you are eligible to refinance your troubled loan with the FHA (www.fha.gov) or with Fannie Mae (www.fanniemae.com). It's also a good idea to consult your state housing authority, as many have special programs to help homeowners in trouble.

  Also, if you're in the military, banks are required by law to give you an extra nine months after you complete your service before they can foreclose on your property. Beyond that, you might also qualify for refinancing programs through the Veterans Administration (www.va.gov).

- **Try loan modification.** In rare cases, you can modify your loan by getting your lender to lower the interest rate or reduce the payments. Banks don't want to foreclose on your home—it takes a lot of time, expense, and paperwork for them. Lenders evaluate requests for loan modification on a case-by-case basis, so you'll have to apply to your lender and see if anything can be arranged.

- **Don't walk away from your home or trash it.** If you're feeling desperate, it may seem logical to just walk away. Don't! It is almost always better to try to sell your home at a loss, however big, than to give it up. Be wary of companies that will take your money in order to help you walk away— sometimes all they provide is financial counseling that you could get elsewhere for free. If you do walk away or ruin the property, not only will you destroy your credit, you will also give up any chance of returning. The lender may also come after you for the damages, even after a foreclosure.

- **Reach out for help.** The Homeownership Preservation Foundation (www.995hope.org) is a federally supported effort to help distressed homeowners. You can learn more about avoiding foreclosure and about government-sponsored programs to help homeowners by calling the Homeowners'

HOPE hotline, 888-995-HOPE. HUD has also revamped its website (www.hud.gov) with a link to its new *Guide to Avoiding Foreclosure,* which provides details about the agency's latest housing information and resources to help home buyers in trouble. You can also reach out to the National Foundation for Credit Counseling (www.nfcc.org) to find a credit counselor. If you work at a university or a school, or belong to a credit union, see if there are people there who can advise you financially. Sometimes they offer free counseling to people in the community too.

- **Be skeptical of for-profit companies offering assistance.** Be leery of anyone offering unsolicited "loan approvals," and don't sign anything you don't understand. Although some of these companies can help, often they will only do what you could yourself for free. There is helpful advice on how to avoid traps at the Freddie Mac website (www.freddiemac .com) and the HUD website (www.hud.gov/foreclosure).

    There are also plenty of scam artists. You need to be on your guard against scammers trying to capitalize on people's vulnerable financial state. They offer everything from seminars to new high-risk mortgages to foreclosure "protection"—which is anything but.

FINANCIAL CRAMMING

- If you're about to rent an apartment, read the lease carefully. There may be conditions you don't like. Try to have unwanted provisions taken out of the lease before you sign.

- When shopping for a mortgage, be sure to research all the loans available to you. Check online and with several banks and mortgage companies. Websites like www.hsh.com and www.freeratesearch.com are great places to start. Also consult local newspapers, which often print weekly listings of mortgage rates. Try your state's housing agency (see pp. 186–87 for a list of phone numbers). And ask your local lender about FHA, Fannie Mae, and Freddie Mac mortgages. Careful shopping can save you thousands of dollars in the long run.

- If you're thinking about buying a home, try to boost your credit score as much as you can in advance. For a free copy of your credit reports, go to www.annualcreditreport.com. To get all of your scores, try www.myfico.com. See p. 71 for details.

- Be wary of adjustable rate mortgages (ARMs). Make sure you know how high your interest rate could rise in the future—and how high your monthly payments could go. In most cases, it's best to get a fixed-rate mortgage instead. See pp. 196–97 for details.

- Before you go hunting for a home, get "prequalified" for a mortgage. Prequalification will not guarantee you a home loan, but it will give you an idea of how big a mortgage you can afford. It's also a good idea to get "preapproved." This way, if you do find your dream home, you'll be absolutely sure you'll get a loan in time to buy it.

- If you've bought a home and you're having trouble making the payments, contact a free counseling service for help working out a repayment plan or possibly postponing payments until you get your finances in order. See p. 78 for details.

8

INSURANCE: WHAT YOU NEED AND WHAT YOU DON'T

Finding the Right Policies and Skipping Coverage You Can Do Without

F OR MOST OF US, there are two classes of insurance: insurance we have too much of and insurance we have too little of. Into the first category goes the life insurance policy you were talked into buying when you graduated from college and the credit protection you signed up for when you got your Visa or MasterCard. Into the second group goes the renters insurance you never even thought about purchasing and the health insurance you figure is too expensive and can get by without. This chapter will help you decide how much protection you should have, if any, in each of the basic categories: health, auto, disability, home, and life. It will alert you to types of policies to avoid, show you how to maximize insurance-related benefits from your employer, and offer you advice on how to find the least expensive comprehensive policies.

No matter what type of insurance you think you need, read the first three sections—"Getting the Best Deal," "Shopping for Insurance," and "Making the Most of Your Employer's Plans." Then you can skip around and read about only the type of insurance you need.

GETTING THE BEST DEAL

The point of insurance is to protect you and your family from financial loss due to illness, accident, or natural disaster. The charge you pay for all types of insurance is called the **premium**. Remember this term. You'll hear it a lot.

Premiums can vary tremendously from one insurance company to the next. Take the case of car insurance. Studies have shown that insurers in the same city often sell the same exact policies for radically different rates. A 20-year-old guy living on the West Side of Chicago, for example, could pay as little as $808 or as much as $3,441 for the same amount of auto liability protection! The point is clear: You might be able to save yourself thousands of dollars if you shop around.

Before I get into the details of the various types of coverage, here are some general tips that will help you save money when you buy insurance:

- **Compare quotes online.** There are several sites that will scan their multicompany databases and send you a free list of the least expensive policies. If you buy a policy through one of these outfits, you pay no more than you would have had you bought it directly from an insurance agent. (Insurance is generally sold by specialized salespeople called **agents.**) Some of these services make their money by keeping the commission the agent would have received. Others point you to the best deals sold by outside agents; they make their money directly from these agents. One advantage to these Web-based search firms is that they have access to many more policies than an individual insurance agent would.

- **Check with a couple of insurance agents.** While the Web makes it a lot easier to *compare* products from different insurance companies without meeting directly with an insurance agent, you'll often find you still have to go through an agent if you want to *buy* a particular policy. Since you might have to end up working with an agent anyway, mention other offers you're seeing online to see if you can get a better deal.

Insurance agents usually make their money by commission, so they're understandably eager to sell you something, but they do have some flexibility in pricing a premium in order to get your business. If the first agent you talk to is less than accommodating (impatient or not forthcoming with answers), don't be shy about finding another one. (Ask relatives and friends for recommendations.) And don't feel obliged to buy from an agent just because he or she did some research for you. That's the agent's job. *Your* job is to go with whoever gives you the best deal.

- **Contact insurance companies that sell directly to consumers.** Some companies don't sell through agents. These firms often charge less because they don't have to pay the salaries of a sales force. The service reps who answer the phones at these companies may not be able to advise you on what to buy, but they can answer basic questions. If you're confident about being able to choose a policy (and you should be after you read this chapter), then get a price quote from such a firm, typically known as a **low-load** company. For names and numbers, see the sections on specific types of insurance later in this chapter.

- **Get the highest deductible you can afford.** With certain types of coverage—health insurance, home insurance, and some auto insurance—you must pay a certain amount of the costs out of your own pocket before the insurance pays for anything. This fixed amount is known as a **deductible.** For example, on a health insurance policy with a $500 annual deductible, you have to pay for the first $500 worth of medical bills you incur each year with your own money. Expenses beyond $500 will be paid, at least in part, by the insurance company.

One way to get a lower premium (there's that word again) is to get a policy with a higher deductible. Say you're a 30-year-old single L.A. resident purchasing a health insurance policy from Blue Shield of California. If you opt for a $500 deductible, you'll pay a premium of $445 a month. If you choose a $2,000 deductible, you'll pay just $157 a month—65% less. The same principle applies to renters insurance, homeowners insurance, and auto insurance.

This rule isn't right for everyone, of course. It makes sense to choose a lower premium only if you have enough savings to cover the higher deductible. Also, with policies that have higher deductibles, you'll end up regularly covering certain costs yourself—for example, routine physicals or minor car and home repairs. But pay attention to your

CAR INSURANCE: YOU'D BETTER SHOP AROUND

Lainie, 24, was about to move from New York City to Washington, D.C., and had to purchase auto insurance for her 2004 Ford Taurus. With just three phone calls to insurance companies, she was able to reap the rewards of shopping around. She gave each company representative the same information: She wanted a $500 deductible, had a spotless driving record, wouldn't be using the car to commute to work, and would be driving only about 2,000 miles a year. One firm quoted Lainie an annual rate of $2,192. Another firm said it charged $3,110 a year. The third firm quoted her an annual rate of just $1,322. An added bonus: When Lainie mentioned that she was turning 25 in a few months, the agent at the third firm said she should call back a month before her twenty-fifth birthday and she'd get a $194 discount. (The other two also offered discounts for turning 25, although they were smaller.) The bottom line: In just 20 minutes Lainie saved almost $2,000 by comparison shopping.

individual situation. If you tend to go to the doctor a lot or you're prone to car accidents, a lower deductible might make more sense. Otherwise, a higher deductible is probably a smart option.

CHECKING OUT CREDENTIALS

You're not going to spend your life (or even several days of your life) investigating every detail of a particular insurance company or agent, but it does pay to do some legwork. The following tips can help you avoid disaster:

- **Check on the insurer's financial health.** It's a good idea to do business with a financially sound insurance company. Even though states have "guaranty funds," which are supposed to protect consumers (up to certain limits) if insurance companies go bankrupt, the rules and level of protection vary by state. (The National Organization of Life & Health Insurance Guaranty Associations has all the details at www .nolhga.com.) You could wait a long time before you collect on a claim—and even then, you may not get all that you had hoped for. It's uncommon for an insurance company to go belly up, but it does happen.

    There are four major rating agencies that judge the financial security and soundness of insurance companies: A.M. Best, Fitch Ratings, Moody's, and Standard & Poor's. Stick with an insurer that gets high grades from at least two of these firms. But even then, you won't be guaranteed that a company is sound. For instance, A.M. Best gave one insurer an A+ rating just a week before it failed, while Standard & Poor's and Moody's both gave it an A. Nevertheless, make sure the company you're interested in hasn't received a really low grade from one of these agencies.

    You can get free information online from most of the agencies. Fitch is the easiest. Just go to its website (www .fitchratings.com) and look up "insurers." The only info you want is the corporate finance rating; don't worry about any reports you have to pay to read. A.M. Best will let you check its ratings on its website (www3.ambest.com/ratings/default.asp) for free once you register. So will Moody's (www.moodys.com). Standard & Poor's will let you browse through all of its insurance ratings online, but the list is a bit tricky to find. Go to www.standardpoors.com, select "United States," then "Ratings," then "Insurance," and then, at last, you can click on the "Credit Ratings List."

As you do your research, it's essential to know what each rating means. For example, a company that gets a "B" from Moody's is considered to be "weak." Consult each company's ratings definitions to make sure you're interpreting them correctly.

- **If you use an agent, ask about qualifications.** When you're buying life, health, or disability insurance, look for an agent who has the letters "CLU" after his or her name. This stands for Chartered Life Underwriter. If you're looking for car, homeowners, or renters coverage, the designation to look for is "CPCU" (Chartered Property Casualty Underwriter). Although these credentials offer no guarantee that you'll get good service, they do tell you that the agent has taken tough insurance courses and has a certain amount of basic knowledge. For a list of individuals with a CLU, try the Society of Financial Service Professionals (www.financialpro.org/consumer/find.cfm). To verify that an agent is a CPCU, go to www.aicpcu.org/about.htm, then click on "Search for a Certificate/Designation Holder."

- **Run a check with your state insurance department.** Figure 8–1 lists the websites and phone numbers of every state insurance department. Send an email or call to make sure the agent you're dealing with is licensed in your state. Some state insurance departments will tell you whether there have been any complaints filed against an agent. You can also call to see if there have been any complaints filed against the insurance company you're considering.

MAKING THE MOST OF YOUR EMPLOYER'S PLANS

If you work for a big company, your employer might be paying for the bulk of your health insurance premiums and may supply you with a fixed amount of life and disability insurance. The type and amount of insurance employees get varies widely. The best way to learn about your plan is to read the information your employer provides, whether it's online or in the handouts you got when you were hired. (I know, I know—this is about as much fun as doing your taxes. But the time you spend will be worth it.) Then make an appointment with whoever is in charge of benefits at your company so you can ask questions about your coverage.

In the health, disability, and life insurance sections below, I've listed specific steps that will help you evaluate your employer's offerings. Meanwhile, here are some general rules to keep in mind:

- **If your company has a "flexible benefits plan," make the most of it.** A flexible benefits plan (also known as a flex plan or a **cafeteria plan**) is a program that gives employees the opportunity to choose among a variety of benefits. Options often include health insurance, life insurance, and disability insurance. With some flex plans you may also be given a choice of noninsurance benefits, such as paid time off, legal services, or additional employer contributions to a 401(k) plan.

  Under a flex plan the employer gives you a fixed number of "credits" to spend on benefits. You get to decide how to use the credits. For instance, you may opt for a top-of-the-line health insurance plan but forgo life insurance, because, if you don't have kids, you probably don't need it yet. Or if your spouse has a terrific employer sponsored health insurance plan that covers you, you could forgo your own company's health insurance and opt for extra disability insurance. These plans can be extremely beneficial if you study your choices carefully and spend your credits wisely.

FIGURE 8-1
STATE INSURANCE DEPARTMENTS

State	Phone Number	Website
Alabama	334-269-3550	aldoi.gov
Alaska	907-269-7900	www.dced.state.ak.us/insurance
Arizona	602-364-3100	www.id.state.az.us
Arkansas	501-371-2600	insurance.arkansas.gov
California	213-897-8921	insurance.ca.gov
Colorado	303-894-7499	www.dora.state.co.us/insurance
Connecticut	860-297-3900	ct.gov/cid
Delaware	302-674-7300	delawareinsurance.gov
D.C.	202-727-8000	disr.dc.gov
Florida	850-413-3140	floir.com
Georgia	404-656-2070	www.gainsurance.org
Hawaii	808-586-2790	insurance.hawaii.gov
Idaho	208-334-4250	doi.idaho.gov
Illinois	217-782-4515	idfpr.com/doi/default2.asp
Indiana	317-232-2385	ai.org/idoi
Iowa	515-281-5705	www.iid.state.ia.us
Kansas	785-296-3071	ksinsurance.org
Kentucky	800-595-6053	doi.ppr.ky.gov
Louisiana	225-342-5900	idi.la.gov
Maine	207-624-8475	maine.gov/insurance
Maryland	410-468-2000	www.mdinsurance.state.md.us
Massachusetts	617-521-7794	mass.gov/doi
Michigan	517-373-0200	michigan.gov/ofis

Minnesota	651-296-4026	www.commerce.state.mn.us
Mississippi	601 359-3569	www.mid.state.ms.us
Missouri	573-751-4126	insurance.missouri.gov
Montana	406-444-2040	sao.state.mt.us
Nebraska	402-471-2201	www.doi.ne.gov
Nevada	775-687-4270	doi.state.nv.us
New Hampshire	603-271-2261	nh.gov/insurance
New Jersey	800-446-7467	www.state.nj.us/dobi
New Mexico	505-827-4601	nmprc.state.nm.us/id.htm
New York	800-342-3736	ins.state.ny.us
North Carolina	919-807-6750	www.ncdoi.com
North Dakota	701-328-2440	nd.gov/ndins
Ohio	614-644-2658	ohioinsurance.gov
Oklahoma	405-521-2828	oid.state.ok.us
Oregon	503-947-7980	oregoninsurance.org
Pennsylvania	717-787-2317	www.ins.state.pa.us
Rhode Island	401-462-9520	www.dbr.state.ri.us
South Carolina	803-737-6160	doi.sc.gov
South Dakota	605-773-3563	state.sd.us/drr2/reg/insurance
Tennessee	615-741-2241	state.tn.us/commerce/insurance
Texas	512-463-6169	tdi.state.tx.us
Utah	801-538-3800	insurance.utah.gov
Vermont	802-828-3301	www.bishca.state.vt.us
Virginia	804-371-9741	scc.virginia.gov/division/boi
Washington	360-725-7080	www.insurance.wa.gov
West Virginia	304-558-3386	wvinsurance.gov
Wisconsin	608-266-3585	oci.wi.gov
Wyoming	307-777-7401	insurance.state.wy.us

- **If possible, purchase health insurance on a before-tax basis.**
  If your employer offers this option, it means you won't have
  to pay taxes on the portion of your salary that goes toward
  your premium. Some companies also let you set pretax dollars aside to pay for commuting or day care. Any of these
  little perks can save you hundreds of dollars a year.

- **If your company offers a flexible spending account (FSA),
  use it.** An FSA is a special tax-favored account offered by
  most large employers. Don't confuse a flexible spending
  account with a flexible benefits *plan*. (Clearly, employee
  benefits personnel could use a little help coming up with
  more creative names.) An FSA is an account in which you
  can set aside a fixed amount of your own money—typically
  anywhere from $60 to $5,000, taken from your paycheck
  during the year—to pay for specific medical expenses that
  aren't covered by health insurance. (Many FSAs will also
  cover day care expenses.)

  One thing that makes an FSA different from a savings account is that you can put the money into the FSA on a before-
  tax basis, and that money will never be taxed. FSA money is
  commonly used to pay for eyeglasses, contact lenses, allergy
  shots, dental care, prescription drugs, chiropractic sessions,
  and transportation to or from the hospital or doctor's office.
  You can also use the money to pay the deductibles on your
  medical and dental plans. You can't use FSA money to pay
  for things like cosmetic surgery, electrolysis, or a health club
  membership. (Although if you need a weight loss program
  or some other activity to help with a medical condition, it
  may qualify, so check.) While the IRS is very clear on a few
  things that are and aren't allowed (look at Publication 502 at
  www.irs.gov for details), rules on other expenses vary from
  company to company. Educate yourself before you sign up,
  and always ask the plan administrator before you assume a
  health-related expense is *not* covered.

  An added perk: You don't actually have to wait to build up
  the money in your FSA to have access to it. They're **prefunded**,
  which means the entire amount you've agreed to contribute

over the next 12 months is automatically available to you when the new year starts (even though it's siphoned from your paycheck month by month). This means you don't have to put off a medical expense until your account balance builds up.

There is one drawback to an FSA: If you don't use the money you put into the account, you'll lose it. Some employers will take back your unused FSA dollars on December 31, while others will let you file claims on qualified medical expenses as late as March 15 of the next year. But after that, the unused money is theirs. That's why you should put in only an amount you're sure you'll spend. And if you do find yourself nearing the deadline with cash in your account, use it before it's too late.

HEALTH INSURANCE

Everyone needs health insurance. There's now huge political will to make sure everyone has coverage, but don't hold your breath. (Never a good idea, but especially if you don't have insurance.) It could take several years for universal health care to become a reality. Meanwhile, it's up to you to make sure you're covered. If you're lucky, you're insured through your job. Although you probably have to pay for some portion of the annual cost, the amount you pay is much less than what you'd pay if you had to purchase insurance on your own. If neither you nor your spouse has an employer who provides coverage for you—if you freelance, run your own business, work for a small company that doesn't offer insurance, or are unemployed, for example—you're responsible for your own health insurance.

Because individual coverage is so expensive, it may be tempting to go without it. (About one in three people in their early twenties do just that.) Don't. If you get into an accident and you're hit with thousands of dollars in medical bills, you could lose every penny you have and find yourself deep in debt. This section will help you find the right coverage for you, whether your employer offers it or you're shopping for health insurance on your own.

Cracking the Health Code

The jargon used in the health insurance industry is so confusing, it's enough to make anyone feel sick. But you need to learn the essential terms, even if you have group coverage through your employer.

Many health insurance policies require you to pay an annual deductible (the average is around $650). Once your medical bills exceed that annual deductible, the insurer will start chipping in, usually paying 70% to 100% of the costs. You're responsible for the rest. The percentage you pay is what's often known as the **co-insurance rate.** (One warning: Annoyingly, some companies call the part the *insurer* pays "coinsurance," so if you're comparing your policy and your spouse's, for example, make sure you're comparing apples to apples.) Whichever way you see this term quoted, you want to make sure the insurer picks up most of the bill. After all, that's what you're paying for.

In most cases, instead of paying coinsurance you make a **co-payment,** which is a fixed sum of money that's usually less than $25. For example, you might have to pay $20 per doctor's office visit or $15 for a prescription drug refill—always, even after you've already met the deductible. (Sometimes you'll have to make a co-payment and pay coinsurance, as well as meet a deductible!)

But many policies have a ceiling (usually $2,000 to $4,000) on the total amount you will have to shell out in any given year. This is called the **out-of-pocket limit.** If your medical bills get truly enormous, you have the comfort of knowing that the insurance company will pay for everything beyond the out-of-pocket limit. However, many insurers have another limit that protects *them.* It's a **maximum lifetime benefit,** which is the total amount they're obligated to pay over the life of your policy. This tends to be $1 million or higher, an amount that will likely be enough to take care of your needs even if you get seriously ill.

The Basic Types of Health Insurance

There are so many different health insurance plans out there, truly understanding your own plan will take some effort. The truth is, even if two medical plans have the same deductible, co-payment structure, coinsurance rate, and benefit limits, they may be different. Some exclude certain costs while accepting others, are stricter about allowing you to see a specialist, or simply have a different list of participating doctors. The details of your company's health insurance options will probably vary somewhat from what I'm going to lay out here, but you can use these descriptions to decode anything in your own plan and make an informed choice if your company offers multiple options.

By far the most common health insurance offering these days is known as **managed care,** which gives you a list of doctors called a **network.** If you stick with doctors in your network, your costs will be much lower than if you use doctors outside the network. No matter what, know how the process works so you can get properly reimbursed for all out-of-pocket costs the insurance company should cover.

There are three main types of managed care programs. The most restrictive is the **health maintenance organization (HMO).** In an HMO you usually have to get permission from your primary doctor—your "gatekeeper"—if you want to see a specialist like a dermatologist or ophthalmologist. (Most HMOs, though, allow you to see in-network OB/GYNs without getting a referral.) Also, your choice of physicians is limited to your HMO's network. If you prefer to see a specialist outside the network, you'll usually have to foot the whole bill yourself, although most plans will let you apply for reimbursement afterward. The benefit of HMOs is their low cost: Most plans won't make you pay any deductible, so your total cost per doctor's visit is usually limited to your $15 or $20 co-payment.

With a newer, more common type of managed care plan, called a **preferred provider organization (PPO),** you don't need permission from your primary doctor in order to see a specialist in your network. But this freedom will cost you. Most PPOs require you to pay an out-of-pocket deductible, typically $500 to $600, before

BEFORE YOU LEAVE YOUR JOB,
ASK ABOUT YOUR HEALTH COVERAGE

If you work for an employer with twenty or more employees, in most cases your company must offer you the option of continuing your health coverage for 18 months—whether you're fired or you quit. (Actually, if you're fired for doing something truly heinous, like embezzling company funds, you probably won't be eligible.) Under the Consolidated Omnibus Budget Reconciliation Act of 1985 (COBRA), your employer must offer you the same health insurance you had as an employee, but you'll have to pay for the coverage. The law says the employer can charge you 102% of the cost. (If your employer pays $350 a month to cover you, you'll pay $357 a month, plus whatever share of the premium you were paying beforehand.) Still, this may be less expensive than the rate you would pay for a policy of your own with the same type of coverage. After you've signed up for COBRA, you may want to switch to a lower-cost offering from your old company. You can do this during its open enrollment season.

More important, it means there's no lapse in your coverage. So even if you intend to shop around for a cheaper plan, taking advantage of COBRA for a month or two is a good idea while you make the transition. And even if you worked for a smaller company, you still might be eligible for continued coverage under state law. Check with your employee benefits office for details, or take a look at the Labor Department's list of frequently asked COBRA questions (www.dol.gov/ebsa/faqs/faq_consumer_cobra.html).

your coverage kicks in. (Many PPOs, however, do cover certain basic medical needs—like a routine checkup, an office visit when you're sick, or prescription drugs—without forcing you to pay your deductible first. You'll probably have a co-payment of about $20 in this case.) PPOs also offer you the option of seeking treatment outside your network, but it will be more expensive than sticking to the list. Instead of the flat $20 you'd pay for a visit inside the network, you'll have to pay 30% to 35% of the total cost of your treatment up to an established maximum (usually $2,000). But not all PPOs work this way. In fact, some require you to pick up 20% to 25% of the bill even for in-network doctors. So read carefully all the details your company gives you.

Another managed care plan, a **point-of-service (POS) plan,** is usually described as a hybrid between an HMO and a PPO. (I know. This is kind of absurd, but bear with me.) With point-of-service plans, you have plenty of options. You can save money by staying within your network and going through your primary care physician when you need special treatment; as with an HMO, you will pay a flat fee of $15 or $20. Or you can go outside the network and pay 30% or 35% coinsurance (up to a preset ceiling of about $2,000), as with a PPO. Either way, like PPO plans, about half of all POS plans require you to pay a deductible (usually $500 or $750), before they start to pay your medical costs.

While most companies have some sort of managed care plan, a few employers offer an old-fashioned type of insurance once known as an **indemnity plan** but now more frequently called a **conventional plan.** (Most of your parents or grandparents had this type of health coverage.) Under an indemnity plan, there's no network and you're free to go to any doctor or specialist you choose. That freedom may be welcome, but it's also made these plans so expensive that over the past two decades they've become a rarity. Only about 10% of all companies now even offer this type of coverage.

If you're in an indemnity plan, the rules are pretty simple. Once you meet the annual deductible, the insurer will pay 70% to 100% of your medical expenses. As with managed care plans, out-of-pocket limits put a ceiling on how much money you'll have to pay for health care in any given year, and maximum lifetime benefits put a ceiling on how much money the insurer will pay over the life of your policy.

If Your Employer Offers Health Insurance

Whether your employer lets you choose your health plan or not, you'll need to be smart about your coverage. Here are some suggestions:

- **Evaluate your managed care options carefully.** Some companies allow employees to choose between an HMO and a PPO or POS plan. (They might even offer an indemnity plan.) Though it might be tempting to go with the cheapest plan, there are some serious trade-offs to consider. Depending on which network you sign up for, you may have to wait several days, if not weeks, to see a specialist. You may find that your doctor is less apt to prescribe expensive lab tests than doctors you have visited in the past. As I mentioned earlier, you may have to get permission from your primary physician before you can see a specialist, such as an allergist or a cardiologist. In the case of HMOs, if you want to see an out-of-network physician, you will have to cover all or much of the cost yourself. And in the case of a high-deductible plan, you'll have to pay at least $1,000 up front before the insurance kicks in at all. That gives you an incentive to avoid going to the doctor, which could cost you (and your health) more in the long run. (For more details on these plans, see the box on the following pages.)

  If your company offers different plans, speak to a few of your coworkers about their experiences before you make a decision. If you already have a regular doctor, find out if he or she belongs to any of the networks your company offers. If not, ask him or her to join.

  Finally, with premiums and expenses rising, don't assume the plan you used last year is still the best choice. Reevaluate annually.

- **Know what's covered by your plan.** Some cover everything from prescription drugs to physical therapy sessions to chiropractic adjustments, while others cover a limited range of services. All are required to treat physical and mental health care the same. If you want to know the details, check your insurance company's website. For about six months on my first job, I didn't know that all I had to do was show my company insurance card at the drugstore to get my prescription medication for just $5. Not too swift.

You'll also need to understand your plan's reimbursement policies. Many plans cover 70% to 80% of what they consider "usual, customary, and reasonable" out-of-network charges. If your doctor charges $100 for a checkup but your plan specifies that $60 is the reasonable and customary charge for a doctor in your area, the plan will reimburse you for $48 (80% of $60), leaving you to pay the remaining $52 yourself. If you know this in advance, you can explain the situation to your doctor and ask for a discount. Some doctors are surprisingly flexible.

- **See if you can get a higher deductible and pay a lower premium.** Some companies have a fixed deductible for all employees. A few base your deductible on your income, while others let you pick from two or more options. No matter how your employer sets your deductible, you should find out if you can raise it to keep your premium costs down. Again, you need to make sure you have enough savings to cover that deductible.

- **Ask about waiting periods or exclusions when you start a new job.** If you have any chronic medical problems, known in the insurance world as **preexisting conditions,** find out if your company insurance plan will cover you for these ailments immediately. Some plans will have a delay of up to 12 months, but most HMOs don't have any waiting period. And if you're transferring directly from a job where you had health insurance (or coming directly off of your parents' coverage), any waiting periods probably will not apply to you, thanks to the Health Insurance Portability and Accountability Act of 1996 (HIPAA). The Department of Labor has created a good overview of how this works; take a look at www.dol.gov/ebsa/faqs/faq_consumer_hipaa .html.

- **Find out the cost of covering pregnancy.** If you're considering having a baby within the next couple of years, find out about maternity benefits and pediatric care. Many managed care plans offer attractive deals. There is usually no deductible with an HMO as long as you stay in the network. Every doctor visit, the full cost of delivery, the hospital stay, and well-baby care are almost completely covered. (I know

THE HEALTH CARE OPTION THAT'S GREAT FOR YOUR BOSS (BUT RISKY FOR YOU)

In order to cut costs, some employers have started offering what are called **high-deductible health plans,** which generally offer low premiums but require you to pay more than $2,000 a year on your own medical bills. At its core, this is just a version of old-fashioned "catastrophic" health insurance that gives you a way to pay the biggest medical bills, but leaves you on your own for everything else. The way it works: You'll have to pay full price for all your basic health care—generally including visits to the doctor or prescription drugs—until you meet that high deductible. Insurance firms save a huge amount of money because they're not picking up these frequent, everyday costs, and they pass on some of the savings to your company. That's why high-deductible plans are enticing to employers.

Should you sign up? For most people, it's difficult to come up with that $2,000 plus deductible. To help ease the burden if you do choose a high-deductible option, your employer may give you a chunk of money (from several hundred dollars to around $1,000) every year in an account called a **Health Reimbursement Arrangement (HRA).** You can draw on

someone who paid just $5 for all her pregnancy care needs!)
Because PPOs tend to have a deductible and will make you
pay coinsurance on top of that, you'll probably end up paying quite a bit more. On the flip side, if there are any com-
plications that require specialists or a longer hospital stay, a
PPO can get pricey, but you may be glad to have a broader
range of specialists to choose from.

that money for a wide range of medical costs. Any funds you
don't use will stay there from year to year.

Some employers now offer another type of account, known
as a **Health Savings Account (HSA).** Like an HRA, an HSA
provides you with money you can draw on for medical expenses, but with a key difference: With an HSA, you can contribute
your own money as well as whatever your employer provides.
(As of 2009, the contribution limit was $3,000 for single people
and $5,950 for families.)

Even if your employer doesn't offer an HRA or an HSA, if
you opt for one of the high-deductible health plans that meet
the government's requirements you can open an HSA yourself
at any bank or credit union and contribute to it every year.
HSAs have three tax benefits: Contributions you make are tax-
deductible, withdrawals for qualified medical expenses are tax-
free, and the interest on these accounts grows tax-free as long
as you withdraw the money for a qualified medical expense. You
can even tap these accounts for nonmedical purposes, but you'll
have to pay taxes and a 10% fee if you do.

Be sure to study all the plans your employer offers. If you
unexpectedly get sick, this system may not be a good choice.
But if it's the only coverage you can afford (or the only one your
job offers), take it.

What to Look For in an Individual Health Policy

If you don't have coverage through a group plan, you'll have to buy insurance on your own. An individual policy is often expensive, but if you know what you're looking for and you do some research, you can find a decent deal. Your goal is to find coverage that will help you pay for a major medical problem. Policies that cover anything more may be prohibitively expensive, depending on where you live. You may find it necessary to pay for routine medical services with your own money and to rely on your health insurance to protect you only in case of a medical catastrophe.

If you've developed an illness or condition that would otherwise make you uninsurable, you're probably entitled to individual coverage if you had insurance at your last job within the last couple of months. That's because your right to be insured is protected by HIPAA. The gist: Once you've exhausted your 18 months of COBRA coverage, you are entitled to **guaranteed-issue individual coverage (GIIC)**. The premiums for GIIC can be very high, but some states will subsidize them, making them somewhat more affordable. Call or email your state insurance agency (Figure 8–1) for more information.

For a good brochure that spells out your rights, get a copy of the Department of Labor's publication *Your Health Plan and HIPAA . . . Making the Law Work for You* (www.dol.gov/ebsa/publications/yhphipaa.html).

No matter where you get a policy, make sure it doesn't offer such skimpy protection that it's worthless. Try to find a policy that meets these conditions:

- **It covers at least 80% of your hospital, surgery, and in-hospital doctor bills once you meet the deductible.** Ideally, you'd be able to find a policy that covers 100%, but this type of coverage can be prohibitively expensive. With a policy that covers 80%, you'll have to pay the remaining 20% out of your own pocket. To avoid getting hit with tremendous medical expenses, look for a policy that caps your annual out-of-pocket costs at around $3,000 (or whatever you can comfortably afford after paying the deductible).

- **It has a maximum lifetime benefit of at least $1 million.** A lifetime cap is the dollar limit the insurance company will pay over the course of the policy. While a given health condition might not cost that much to treat, remember that you'll probably need medical treatment more than once during your lifetime. Anything substantially less than $1 million isn't enough, and if you plan to keep the policy for a while (for example, if you're more or less permanently self-employed), think hard before settling for less than $2 million.

- **It doesn't have unreasonable exclusions and limits.** Some individual policies will not cover preexisting conditions like asthma or recurring knee problems. Others won't cover these problems for the first year or so of the policy, or they will charge astronomically high premiums.

- **It pays for any prescriptions you need.** Medicine for a condition like high blood pressure, asthma, or diabetes can be expensive. Even if you're currently healthy, think twice before signing up for any policy that looks cheap but won't help you with your ongoing pharmacy bills if you do get sick.

Before You Buy an Individual Health Policy

Depending on your current situation, you may have some alternatives to buying an expensive individual policy. Here are a few to consider:

- **A state-run option.** A few states have created programs to provide low-cost health insurance to people who otherwise might not be able to afford it. To find out if your state offers such a program, call your state insurance department (Figure 8-1).

- **Your parents' plan.** Several states allow children to be covered until age 26; New Jersey will give you until age 30. (For a list, check out statecoverage.net/matrix/dependent-coverage.htm.) Otherwise, if you're not in school, chances are your coverage has already stopped. If it hasn't, there's a way to extend it. Under federal law, you can continue to receive your parents' coverage for 18 months if your parents make the request within 60 days after they're notified that your coverage is about to lapse. You will have to pay for this coverage, but the price will probably be less than the price of a similar policy you could get on your own.

- **A group plan.** Groups get better deals than individuals. See if there's a professional association, religious organization, or any other group that will offer you coverage. The Freelancers Union (www.freelancersunion.org) offers group health insurance in New York State and individual plans in thirty other states. If you're a lawyer, try your local bar association. If you're a real estate or travel agent, call your local trade association. If you're an artist, contact a community artists league. If you're currently doing temp work, look for a temp agency that offers health benefits. (Some agencies offer employees the chance to buy group coverage.)

- **Temporary coverage.** If you're out of work but seriously hunting for a job, look into a temporary insurance policy. This type of policy lasts up to a year and can be renewed once; the rules vary from state to state. After twelve months you will hopefully have found a job with health benefits. The advantage of these policies is that they're cheap. The disadvantage is that you probably won't be covered for any preexisting conditions. You should also consider a temporary policy if you start a new job and your employer requires you to be with the firm for several months before your health insurance kicks in.

Keep in mind that many insurers will take your medical condition into account when determining your premium, and they might even deny you coverage outright. (The only exceptions: New York, New Jersey, Massachusetts, Maine, and Vermont.) The healthier your lifestyle, the lower your insurance rates will be; for example, quitting smoking can cut your premiums by 10% to 15% a year. (Not to mention save your life.)

How to Find an Affordable Individual Health Policy

Unfortunately, locating a reasonably priced individual health insurance policy isn't easy. Here are some tips that may help you in your search.

- **Search online for quotes.** Start shopping for online health insurance quotes at eHealthInsurance (www.ehealthinsur ance.com), which lets you compare policies from many insurance companies. If you find a policy that's a good fit, you can then apply right on the site. But before you sign up, visit NetQuote (www.netquote.com), which can put you in touch with agents affiliated with some of the nation's largest health insurers. Tell them about the best deal you found online and ask if they can beat it.

- **Try Blue Cross and Blue Shield.** They're the largest managed care and indemnity providers in the United States but they don't accept everyone who applies. You can contact your local Blue Cross and Blue Shield company or visit the website (www.bcbs.com) to find out about eligibility requirements and rates.

- **Contact your state insurance department.** If you have a pre-existing condition that makes it difficult for you to get insurance, get in touch with your state insurance department and ask if it sponsors any "high-risk" insurance policies. Most do. If yours doesn't, ask if it may be able to point you toward a private insurer that does. And even if you're healthy, check the website of your state's insurance department to see if you're eligible for any special deals.

- **Ask about special deals for people in good health.** Some insurers and HMOs (as well as your state's insurance department) offer discounts to people who can show they're in great shape. If that sounds like you, ask the agent whether you can get one.

- **As a last resort, consider catastrophic (also known as "high-deductible") coverage.** If you have very little money to spend on health insurance, look into catastrophic coverage. This kind of policy charges low monthly premiums in exchange for very high deductibles (often $2,000 or more) and fairly high out-of-pocket limits. While this kind of coverage won't pay for routine checkups and sick visits, it will protect you from financial ruin if you develop a major illness or get into a serious accident. And that's the main thing you need to insure yourself against anyway. If a high-deductible plan is your only option, be sure to open a Health Savings Account (see p. 224) at your bank or credit union so you can save up for your medical bills in the most tax-advantaged way.

CAR INSURANCE

Auto insurance covers harm done to you, your car, other people, and other people's property. The total amount of coverage you need depends on the amount of health insurance you have, the condition of your car, the value of the assets you must protect in case you're held responsible for an accident, and the rules in your state.

Many auto insurers have been raising their rates, sometimes by a large amount, in recent years. This coverage is especially expensive for people in their twenties, because statistically they have more accidents.

Three Basic Types of Auto Coverage

Car insurance consists of three separate kinds of protection: auto liability coverage, medical payments coverage, and collision and comprehensive coverage. Here's a rundown of each:

- **Auto liability coverage.** If you cause an accident with your car and injure someone or damage something, auto liability insurance will pay your legal expenses as well as the medical and repair expenses for whoever got hurt. Of the three major components of auto insurance, auto liability—which is technically known as **bodily injury liability** and **property damage liability**—can make up more than half of your auto premiums.

  Some states, known as **no-fault states,** require drivers (and their insurance companies) to pay for their own medical costs after a car accident, regardless of who was responsible. But even if you live in a no-fault state, you still need liability protection. That's because each no-fault state has a threshold above which a person who causes an accident can be sued. For example, in some no-fault states a driver can be sued if he causes severe physical injury to another driver.

  Most states require car owners to purchase at least some liability protection, but you should probably buy more than that amount. Even if you don't have many assets, you need liability protection in case a court decides to garnish your future wages. Insurance analysts are hesitant to say what the "right" amount of liability protection is, but when pressed, they suggest that the following guideline is reasonable: If you don't have much savings and you don't own a home, get coverage of at least $100,000 per person, $300,000 per accident, and $100,000 for property. If you own a home and have some money saved, consider purchasing an umbrella liability policy, which is coverage above and beyond any auto or homeowner's liability protection you have. (For details, see the home insurance section.)

- **Medical payments coverage.** This insurance covers your medical and hospital bills (up to a certain dollar amount) if you're injured in a car accident. It also covers the medical and hospital bills (again, up to specific limits) of any passengers in your car. If you live in a no-fault state, you'll be required to buy a minimum amount of medical payments coverage, typically called **personal injury protection** or **no-fault insurance.** Personal injury protection insurance covers your medical and hospital bills (and in some states, your loss of income if you're disabled) regardless of who's to blame for an accident.

  If you live in a "fault" state, you're usually not required to purchase medical payments coverage, but you may want to anyway. Accidents in which no one can be proven negligent won't be covered by liability insurance, and liability insurance will not cover your own injuries in accidents that you've caused. If you already have good general health insurance, you won't need medical payments insurance to cover your own medical bills, but you may still want to consider purchasing it if you often have passengers in your car.

- **Collision and comprehensive coverage.** Collision insurance pays for damage to your car if you bang it into something, like a tree, your garage door, or another car. Comprehensive insurance covers damage caused by fire, flood, theft, tornado, and just about any other physical damage that's not covered by collision. In all states, both these types of coverage are optional. However, if you took out a loan to buy your car or if you're leasing, the lender or leasing company will require that you purchase collision and comprehensive coverage.

  The maximum amount an insurance company will pay under a collision or comprehensive policy is, at least in theory, the cost of replacing the car with a comparable used one. (Unfortunately, some insurers aren't this generous.) After your car is about five years old or you've paid off your loan, you may want to consider dropping your collision and comprehensive coverage. To decide whether it

BABY, YOU CAN'T DRIVE MY CAR

It may seem like no big deal, but when someone asks to borrow your car you should think twice before saying yes. If you allow someone to drive your car and he or she has an accident, *your* insurer is likely to pay for the damage (less any deductible you have to pay). That means your insurance company may raise your premium just as if you had caused the accident.

makes sense to continue this coverage, figure out the value of your car (at the Kelley Blue Book website: www.kbb .com) minus the deductible. Compare that number to your annual premium.

An additional type of insurance required in some states is **uninsured motorists coverage.** This protects you if an uninsured driver crashes into your car and you're injured. You may also want to consider getting **under*insured* motorists coverage,** which will protect you if the driver who crashes into your car has some, but not enough, insurance to cover your costs. If you have really good health insurance, you can probably skip it.

If You Rent a Car, Cover Your Assets

One type of coverage you'll want to have when you rent a car is liability protection. If you also own a car, your standard auto liability and collision damage coverage should insure you when you rent a car—unless, for example, you're traveling on business or you're renting for more than a couple of days. Check with your insurer to get the rules on your policy.

If you don't own a car, some credit card companies will give you automatic collision coverage (or even comprehensive coverage) as a perk if you use their cards to pay for rental cars. (Lately, Master-Card has been providing collision and comprehensive coverage, but check your card agreement to be sure.) If you don't have coverage, buy it at the car rental counter. Frequent renters may find it cheaper to get something called a "nonowner" policy from an insurance company.

How to Reduce Your Auto Insurance Costs

Your premiums are based on factors such as your age, where you live, the type of car you drive, your gender, marital status, credit rating, driving record, and how much driving you do. The following suggestions can substantially reduce your premiums:

- **Shop around.** Plenty of websites let you compare car insurance quotes from various companies. The trick is finding out whether the quotes they give you really are the best available. Try both www.carinsurance.com and www.netquote.com; between them they cover nearly all of the bigger (and smaller) names in the industry. Some companies that offer competitive prices include Esurance, Progressive, Amica, Allstate, The Hartford, and GEICO. You can also try State Farm (www.statefarm.com), which doesn't provide quotes to either of the sites mentioned above. If you've been in the military or a family member has, USAA (www.usaa.com; 800-531-8080) also offers auto insurance.

- **Plan ahead.** If your policy is due to expire in a month or two, start shopping for a new one now. Insurance companies will often give you a discount of around 10% if you sign up with them before your old coverage ends.

- **Drive safely.** Insurance companies charge less for drivers who have no violations or accidents. If you have a clean record, point it out when you're pricing policies.

- **Cut down on your driving time.** Some insurance companies charge you less if you spend less time on the road. For instance, one major insurer charges lower premiums for customers who drive fewer than 10,000 miles a year. If you join a car pool or start taking public transportation, alert your agent.

- **Choose your car carefully.** Certain types of cars are harder to damage, less expensive to repair, and less likely to be stolen than others. Insurers use this information when setting rates. You can reduce your collision and comprehensive coverage by as much as 45% if you buy a new or used car that's considered low-risk, such as a Volkswagen Beetle. Ask your agent for a list of such cars, or look at the car safety ratings from the Insurance Institute for Highway Safety (www.highwaysafety.org).

- **Get good grades.** If you're currently a student with a B average or better, on the Dean's List, or in the top 20% of your class, tell the insurance agent. Good grades can reduce your premium by up to 25%. In some cases college graduates are eligible for these discounts until they either reach age 25 or get married.

- **Grow up.** Most insurers will give you a lower rate when you hit a certain age, but their policies vary. Some will simply award you a 5% to 10% discount on every birthday until age 28 as long as you maintain a good driving record. Others will knock 10% off your premiums at age 25 (for a single man) or 23 (for a single woman). Your birthday is a good time to make sure you're getting the best deal out there. Call your insurer with a reminder.

- **Get domestic.** Insurance companies also view married couples as safer than singles. Married men can usually expect to pay 5% to 10% lower rates than single guys; the discount for married women is usually around 15%. A growing number of companies are extending this break to same-sex couples as well.

- **See if you're entitled to a household, or "multicar," discount.**
  If you're married and you and your spouse both have cars,
  see if you can save money by getting auto coverage from the
  same company. Insurers often offer discounts of up to 20%
  if both of your cars are insured on the same policy or by the
  same company. If you live with your parents, you might be
  able to get a similar discount if your car is insured under your
  folks' policy.

BAD CREDIT BOOSTS YOUR INSURANCE BILLS

Insurers, like creditors, look at your credit history when calculating your home and auto premiums. People who are in
poor financial shape are considered more of a risk, so the
credit rating agency Fair Isaac Corp. (see Chapter 3) has created special insurance scores to help insurance companies
assess applicants. These work a lot like general credit scores
and take into account all the same factors your credit report
does. At the time of this writing, there's no way for you to
see your Fair Isaac insurance score.

To further complicate the situation, there are specialized
firms out there that keep track of the claims you file on your
house or car. Virtually all car or home insurers look at your
claims history whenever you apply for new coverage; if you
have a lot of claims on your record, they may think you're
likely to cost them a lot of money down the road.

You're entitled to a free copy of your auto and home claim
reports every year. Go to www.choicetrust.com to get yours.

- **Consider getting your home and auto insurance from the same company.** Some auto insurers will give you a better deal if you insure the rest of your earthly possessions with them. (Renters insurance usually counts.)

- **Take a class.** Many auto insurers will offer discounts of 10% to 15% if you take a defensive driving class, which can cost about $30 to $40. Some will let you take the course online or watch a DVD.

- **Get insured through an "affinity group."** As with other kinds of insurance, you can sometimes get a break on car insurance by belonging to a certain group, such as an alumni association or a trade union. Some insurers even offer discounts to people who buy hybrid cars. (The reason: Hybrid owners tend to be safer, more conscientious drivers.) Your employer may also offer group auto insurance.

- **Stay close to your parents.** Find out what insurance company your parents use; some insurers will give you a break if your parents are customers. In fact, I know of one insurer that gives the kids of existing policy holders up to a 50% discount until they turn 27.

- **Check with your state's insurance department.** Some state insurance departments publish lists of companies and prices. (See Figure 8–1 for websites and phone numbers.)

DISABILITY INSURANCE

What would happen if you had a horrible skiing accident and you couldn't work for ten months?

At the time of this writing, only Puerto Rico and five states—California, Hawaii, New Jersey, New York, and Rhode Island—require employers to provide any income to disabled employees who get hurt off the job. And federal disability benefits from Social Security are extremely difficult to get; the majority of people who apply are rejected.

Your only real protection, therefore, is likely to be private disability insurance. Although you may never have heard of it, it's something you should have. Ideally, you should have coverage that would pay you 60% to 70% of your income following an accident that left you unable to work. For many young people, disability coverage is more important than life insurance.

If you work for a large company, you may already have some disability insurance under a group policy—and that may be all you need. If you don't work for a company that offers disability protection, consider buying an individual disability policy. This insurance can be very expensive for people who have physical jobs like carpentry or driving a truck.

If Your Employer Offers Disability Insurance

Disability protection is different from workers compensation. **Workers comp,** as it's known, protects you if you're injured while performing your job. Disability insurance, sometimes known as **income protection,** covers you for any injury or illness, whether it happens at home, on vacation, or on the job. (Pregnancy, oddly, can count as a short-term disability here, which is why disability insurance can be especially expensive—and valuable—for women.) If you're lucky enough to work for an employer who provides you with disability insurance, assess exactly how much protection it gives you. Here are some tips to help you understand your coverage and figure out if you need more:

- **Find out what percentage of your income you'll receive if you're disabled.** Large companies with more than 500 employees often provide disability insurance that will pay 60% of your income—usually up to $5,000 a month—if you suffer a long-term disability. If you earn more than $100,000 a year, consider supplementing your employer's coverage with an individual policy. (More on that later.)

- **Ask about waiting periods and benefit periods.** You'll typically start receiving benefits three to six months after becoming disabled. This period is known as the waiting period or **elimination period.** (I guess that's because during it, any savings you have are eliminated!) Most employers who offer disability coverage also offer short-term benefits that cover the elimination period; at the low end of the scale, these benefits are called "sick leave." The period of time during which you receive disability payouts is known as the **benefit period.** During this time, you don't have to pay premiums. Many companies offer policies that pay disability benefits until the employee reaches age 65.

- **Take advantage of your flexible benefits plan.** Sometimes you're given a choice between disability insurance and life insurance. If you're single with no kids, pick disability. On average, 20-year-olds are twice as likely to become disabled before retirement as they are to die.

What to Look For in an Individual Disability Policy

Insurance companies offer all kinds of confusing extras attached to their disability policies. Below are the basics you will need:

- **A policy that's non-cancelable.** This means the insurer generally can't cancel your current policy or raise your premium for any reason.

- **A policy that's guaranteed renewable.** This means you can renew each year without taking a medical exam, and the insurer can't single you out for a rate increase just because you've made a lot of claims. Only general rate increases will affect you.

- **A policy that offers residual benefit protection.** If you're partially disabled, some policies will pay you a portion of your disability benefits, known as "residual benefits." This is extremely important coverage in case you're in a situation where an injury or illness allows you to work only part time.

- **A policy that offers inflation protection.** You don't want your benefits to shrink over time, especially if they're the only income you have to live on. Some policies will give you a "cost-of-living allowance," which means they adjust with the rate of inflation year to year.

How to Reduce Your Disability Insurance Costs

The problem with individual disability coverage is that it's not cheap. A 27-year-old paralegal who earns an annual salary of $40,000 might pay about $1,000 a year for a top-of-the-line policy (one that provides 70% of his salary if he becomes unable to work). Here are ways to keep your costs down:

- **Compare quotes.** Only a handful of insurance companies specialize in disability coverage. Two of the largest are Unum (www.unum.com; 877-322-7222), which sells only through agents, and Northwestern Mutual Life Insurance (northwesternmutual.com; 800-388-8123). Also, check with Financial Solutions Group (www.affordableinsurance protection.com) to find the best quotes from twelve disability insurers.

- **Consider a step-up, or gradual-payment, policy.** This allows you to pay lower premiums when you're young and— gradually—higher ones when you're older. With this plan, the paralegal might pay only about $721 a year for the first year, $723 in the next year, and so on. The advantage here is that those early payments (during what you hope will be your leanest years) are a lot lower than what you'd pay on a standard policy; however, after about a decade, the step-up policy would be charging you more per year than you'd pay otherwise.

- **Buy through your employer.** Not all employers will pay for disability coverage. But a growing number of employers now have systems in place to let employees *buy* individual coverage on a voluntary basis. These arrangements can cost significantly less than what you might pay for a policy on your own, especially if you're a woman. Believe it or not, women can generally expect to pay up to 40% more than men for individual disability insurance. (Again, it's because insurers characterize pregnancy as a disability.) But if you buy a policy through your job, you're protected by workplace equality laws. Check with your human resources department to see whether you have this option.

- **Decrease your benefit period.** Relatively few disabilities last more than five years. In fact, most last less than two years. If you're willing to accept the risk, you can save up to 35% of your premium by accepting a benefit period of only five years, instead of being insured until you retire.

- **Limit yourself to emergency coverage.** If you can't afford a full scale disability policy, look into coverage that will kick in only in a worst-case scenario, such as a debilitating accident or a catastrophic illness like a heart attack or a stroke. These no-frills disability policies have very short benefit periods (they'll typically pay for just one or two years) and generally cost about $200 to $300 a year.

- **Find less-extreme hobbies.** Remember, disability insurance differs from workers comp by covering you if you have an accident off the job. As a result, someone who does a lot of kiteboarding or rock climbing, for example, should expect to pay higher premiums than someone who doesn't (or be prepared to have the insurer include a clause that says

you're not covered if you hurt yourself while chasing your
thrills). I know this one may sound annoying, but it's true.

HOME INSURANCE

If you own a home, you probably have some homeowners insurance. But if you're like a lot of homeowners, you don't have enough
coverage—or you're paying too much. And if you rent, you may
never even have thought about buying any coverage.

Three Basic Types of Coverage
If You Own a Home

Homeowners insurance covers the cost of rebuilding or repairing
your home (and surrounding structures such as a detached garage)
if it's destroyed or damaged by disasters such as fire, lightning, snow,
or windstorm. It also covers the *contents* of your home up to a fixed
dollar amount in the event of many of these same disasters—as well
as theft. And it can also protect you if you're held responsible (also
known as "liable") for injuring people or damaging property, even
when you're away from home. Here's a more detailed rundown of
each type of protection.

- **Your home's structure.** You need to buy enough insurance
  to cover the full cost of rebuilding your home. To figure out
  approximately how much it would cost to rebuild, contact
  a local builders association or insurance agent and find out
  the "building cost per square foot" in your area. (These professionals won't charge you for this information. A real estate appraiser can also answer the question but may charge
  a fee.) Multiply the number of square feet in your home by
  the local square foot building cost. This will give you an
  idea of how much it would cost to rebuild your home.

- **The contents of your home.** Standard homeowners policies usually cover your personal property for 50% to 70% of the amount you insured your home's structure for. So if you insured the structure for $200,000, your home's contents would automatically be insured for $100,000 to $140,000. You can increase the amount of coverage you have for a fee. Make sure your **personal property insurance** covers you for **replacement cost,** not **actual cash value,** of your home's contents. Coverage for replacement cost gives you enough money to buy new comparable items to replace your belongings. Coverage for actual cash value pays you the amount of money you could get to repair or replace the items, *minus* the depreciation on the items. That amounts to a whole lot less.

To figure out how much personal property insurance you need, make a list of everything you own and estimate how much it would cost you to replace these items. This is a hassle, but it's worth doing (just rough figures are fine) and there's free software out there to make the job a little easier. (One program is Know Your Stuff, which you can download from the Insurance Information Institute at www.know yourstuff.org.) Write down the approximate purchase date and purchase price of all your belongings, including furniture, rugs, electronics, computers, dishes, pots and pans, artwork, and major appliances. Also list your suits, dresses, shoes, and coats. (Don't forget the expensive stuff, like your wedding dress or tuxedo.)

Gather as many receipts as you can to back up your list. Write down the serial or model numbers for appliances. When you make major purchases, save the receipts. Take pictures of your more valuable belongings. This inventory will come in handy if you ever need to file a claim. Keep a copy of the list, along with the receipts and photos, in a safe place (perhaps at work). Also give a copy to a trusted friend or relative. (Don't leave a copy lying around your apartment. It's a great road map for a burglar. For the same reason, don't give the list a revealing file name on your home computer.) Most people never get around to doing this exhaustive inventory, but at the very least take pictures or a video of your valuables and store the photos or video in a safe place.

- **Damage you do to other people and other people's property.** Homeowners policies include liability protection that covers you for damage you accidentally cause inside or outside your home. If you leave a pair of boots in the middle of your kitchen floor and your neighbor trips on them and breaks her leg, your liability insurance will probably cover your legal costs, as well as her medical bills and other costs, assuming you're held responsible for the injury. If you run a shopping cart over someone's foot in a supermarket, your liability coverage may pay for his or her medical expenses if you're found liable. If you have a pet, your policy will often cover you for damage the pet does to people or their property as well.

  Many homeowners policies come with a standard amount of liability insurance: a minimum of $100,000 per accident. In these litigious times, this may not be enough. There's no perfect way to figure out how much you need. To get a rough idea, tally up all your major assets including your home, your car, your possessions, and your investments (including retirement savings). The amount of liability coverage you get should exceed this amount. Sometimes the additional cost of coverage up to $500,000 is only a dollar or two per month.

What's Covered and What's Not

Your insurance options here are vaguely reminiscent of high school chemistry—in most states, you can choose HO-2 or HO-3. Insurance agents sometimes refer to these two classifications as broad (HO-2) and special (HO-3) coverage. If you can afford it, buy HO-3. It doesn't cost much more than HO-2, and it covers a much wider range of perils. But certain situations, such as earthquakes and floods, aren't covered by either of the standard homeowners policies. (See the box on p. 246 for more on disaster insurance.)

There are other limits on what most homeowners policies cover. For example, many policies provide only $1,000 to $2,000 of theft coverage for valuables like jewelry. If this isn't enough to replace what you own, purchase extra protection by adding an endorsement, sometimes referred to as a floater. This is simply an amendment to your insurance policy to protect a specific item. With an endorsement, you can, for example, increase the coverage on your valuables—such as Grandma's silver tea set—from $2,000 to $10,000 if they are worth that much. The cost for this increase in coverage would range from $15 to $100 per year.

Many homeowners policies include **off-premises** protection, which covers your possessions outside your home—whether you're mugged while on vacation or your bike is stolen on the sidewalk. If, for example, your portable computer or luggage is lost or taken when you're trekking around Europe, your homeowners insurance should cover the loss. Check your policy carefully. If you live in a high-crime area, you may have to pay extra for it.

Most policies include some **loss of use** protection. If your home is damaged and you're forced to live elsewhere for a while, this coverage will pay the cost of your hotel bills, meals, and other basic living expenses as long as they are reasonable. Don't expect the policy to pay for lavish hotels or restaurants. Typical coverage is 20% of the total amount of insurance you bought for your home's structure.

If you work at home, your home office equipment is usually not covered by your homeowners policy. If the business is small, you can get additional coverage by purchasing an endorsement. For larger businesses, you'll have to purchase a separate policy. Ask an insurance agent for details.

If you live in a co-op or condo, you'll need to purchase a special policy known as HO-6 to protect your personal property and the unit you own, but not the common property owned by the association.

PLANNING FOR THE WORST:
CATASTROPHE INSURANCE

After Hurricane Katrina devastated the Gulf Coast in 2005, a relatively obscure area of home insurance—flood overage—became a central issue for millions of Americans living in areas the federal government classifies as flood-prone. Because normal homeowners and renters policies won't pay to repair water damage caused by storms or other natural disasters, you need separate flood insurance to collect if a hurricane swamps your house.

Most companies don't cover flood damage. Instead, the federal government offers flood insurance at a low cost in an effort to protect people and their homes. (But unfortunately, many people weren't paying attention. Only 66% of the homeowners in New Orleans' Orleans Parish had flood insurance before Katrina because many thought their basic coverage would protect them. The lawsuits were still going on years later.)

Look up your home's flood risk (and find out how to buy a policy if you need one) on the National Flood Insurance Program's website (www.floodsmart.gov). There are high-risk areas in surprising places; for example, towns in the hilly region of New England are susceptible to runoffs from melting snow in spring. (Who knew?) Even if you're not in a high-risk area, look into it. It's relatively inexpensive and could protect you from losing everything in a total disaster.

There's also specialized insurance for other natural disasters. Normal homeowners policies won't cover earthquake damage, so people in California in particular should buy earthquake insurance through the state's Earthquake Authority (www.earthquakeauthority.com).

If You Rent, Get Insurance

If you rent an apartment or house, the idea of buying **renters insurance**, also known as **tenants insurance** (or in insurance industry lingo, an HO-4 policy), may not have crossed your mind. You may figure that because you have few valuables and little or no savings, you don't need it. But you're wrong. The first and most obvious reason to buy it is to protect your personal property. If all your possessions were stolen or ruined in a fire, including your clothes, jewelry, stereo equipment, television, DVD player, computer, camera, sofa, and bike, a renters policy would cover you up to a fixed dollar amount.

In addition to protecting your possessions, a renters policy will offer you some liability protection inside and outside your home. If someone slips and falls in your apartment, your renters policy could cover that person's medical bills if you're held liable. If you accidentally leave the tap running when you go to work, ruin the floor and are held responsible, your renters insurance may pay for the cost of repairs. (For more general types of water damage, you'll probably need separate flood insurance. See the box on p. 246.) And if you knock over a sculpture in an art gallery, your renters policy may protect you, up to a set maximum.

How to Reduce Your Homeowners or Renters Insurance Costs

The first step (as with health insurance) is to get a high deductible so you can keep your annual premiums low. Remember, this makes sense only if you have enough savings to cover the higher deductible. Here are four other suggestions that apply whether you own a home or rent.

- **Compare quotes.** Netquote.com and insweb.com will poll agents representing some of the biggest home insurance companies to see which has the best deals. You can also go to companies that sell directly to consumers, such as Amica (www.amica.com; 800-242-6422). Also contact State Farm (www.statefarm.com), which is one of the largest home insurance providers and sells through so-called captive agents (meaning they work only for State Farm). Active duty or retired military personnel and their families can go to USAA (www.usaa.com; 800-531-8080).

- **Ask if you're eligible for any discounts.** If you have deadbolt locks on your doors or live in an apartment building with a doorman, you may be able to get a discount of as much as 10% on your premium. If you have a security alarm, a fire extinguisher, and a smoke detector, you can often get a discount of as much as 20%, depending on the type of system you have.

- **Consider moving your car coverage to the same insurance company as your homeowners or renters coverage.** Some companies will offer you a dual-policy discount of up to 15%.

- **Check with your state's insurance department.** It may publish a list of companies and the premiums they charge for

CONSIDER AN UMBRELLA LIABILITY POLICY

If you have a lot of assets—or you have the potential to earn a lot—you should consider getting an **umbrella liability policy.** This special type of policy expands the liability protection provided by your car and homeowners coverage. It also may protect you in case you're sued for something unrelated to your car or home, such as slander. The price of a $1 million umbrella liability policy in 2008 was about $150 to $300. Umbrella policies are usually a better deal than more auto liability and home liability coverage.

homeowners insurance. (See Figure 8–1 for websites.) This can help you shop around.

LIFE INSURANCE

If you've never received a friendly letter from a life insurance agent, just wait. In the next few years, you'll probably get at least half a dozen trying to sell you life insurance. Throw them out. There's a good chance you don't need life insurance.

The purpose of life insurance is simple: If you die, it protects the people who rely on your income. So if you have kids (or anyone else financially dependent on you), you need it. If you're married without kids, and your spouse could handle the basic housing and living expenses without you, you don't need it. If you're single and you aren't financially responsible for anyone but yourself, you don't need it. (Of course, there are always exceptions, but these are good guidelines.)

Two Types of Life Insurance

The most basic form of life insurance is **term life insurance.** It's called that because it protects you for a specific period of time (a term), typically up to thirty years. When the term runs out, you can usually renew the policy and begin another term. If you die, the insurance company will pay out a specified amount of money to your beneficiaries. This payment is called the **death benefit.**

When you're young, the premium you pay for term insurance is very low. For a death benefit of $100,000, a 25-year-old nonsmoker would pay about $150 a year. Your premium may stay the same for many years or increase slightly from year to year, depending on which type of term policy you get.

Term life insurance gives you the most coverage for your money when you're young. But don't be surprised if insurance agents discourage you from buying it. Agents don't like to sell term insurance because the commissions on such policies are low. It's pure self-interest on their part.

Most life insurance agents will instead urge you to buy what they may call a "permanent" insurance policy or a **cash value policy.** (For a sampling of some of their most common pitches, see the box on pp. 252–53.) With a cash value policy, the insurance company takes your annual premium and deducts sales and administrative charges, the actual insurance part, and a margin for profit. The remainder goes into a kind of savings account for you, generally called your cash value. The most common forms of cash value policies are **whole life, universal life,** and **variable life.** With whole life and universal life policies, the insurance company invests your cash value in bonds and various bond-like investments. With variable life policies, the insurance company offers you a choice of mutual fund–like investments to choose from, and you decide how to invest the cash value. Because of quirky rules in the tax law, the money in the savings account of a cash value life insurance policy grows tax-deferred and is tax-free (to your heirs, naturally) if held until death.

The cost of a cash value policy is usually much higher than that of a term policy for a young person. Even if you can afford it, it almost always makes sense to avoid cash value policies and buy term if you need life insurance. That's because the commissions and other expenses on most cash value policies are very high; they can be more than 150% of your first year's premium, and renewal commissions in subsequent years can be 5% to 8%. You're better off buying term insurance and investing the money you save in a tax-favored retirement savings plan like an IRA or a 401(k). In any case, many term policies can easily be converted into cash value policies down the line if you change your mind.

There's one set of circumstances, though, under which it's smart to buy a cash value life insurance policy. If you need life insurance and you're already putting the maximum allowable amount into tax-favored retirement savings plans, such as IRAs and 401(k)s, you may want to consider a **low-load** cash value policy, which has relatively low commissions and expenses. Low-load companies that sell cash value life policies include Ameritas (www.ameritas.com; 800-745-1112) and Columbus Life (www.columbuslife.com; 800-677-9595); if you or a parent has a military background, you might also explore USAA (www.usaa.com; 800-531-8722). Keep in mind that not all of these insurers sell policies in all states.

Because cash value life insurance can be both expensive and confusing, it's an area where expert advice might help. "Fee-only" insurance consultants are considered unbiased because they don't get commissions from the insurance or investments they recommend. Glenn Daily, one of the pioneers in this field, keeps a short list of fee-only consultants on his website, www.glenndaily.com/glenndaily.htm.

How to Shop for Term Insurance

Okay. So you get that you're best off purchasing a term policy, but there are still two basic types of policies to choose from. (It's never simple, is it?) **Annual renewable term** is coverage that doesn't require you to take a medical exam each year to renew it, though each year your premium will usually increase somewhat. A **level premium policy** lasts for a fixed number of years (commonly ten or twenty) and allows you to lock in a premium for that period of time. Some level premium deals will guarantee you twenty years at the same premium; others may guarantee the coverage for twenty years but only guarantee the same premium for five or ten years. After your coverage period ends, you usually have to pass a medical exam in order to renew at attractive rates; otherwise, your premium will increase dramatically.

Although annual renewable policies may cost less at the beginning, level premium policies may be less expensive in the long run. You should definitely consider a level premium policy if you're able to afford it. Look for a policy that guarantees the premium for at least ten years, and compare the cost to that of an annual renewable term policy.

One final tip: Look for a term policy that you are able to convert to a low-cost cash value policy at any time, regardless of your health. As mentioned above, you may decide when you're older (and contributing the maximum to your retirement plans) that you want to purchase a cash value policy.

You have many options when shopping for term insurance. Try contacting individual firms that sell low-load policies, like TIAA-CREF (www.tiaa-cref.org; 800-531-8000) and Ameritas (www

.ameritas.com; 800-745-1112) In addition to getting quotes from agents, check out sites that will let you compare quotes from different firms side by side. One highly regarded site is Term4Sale (www .term4sale.com). Other good sites include www.selectquote.com, www.accuterm.com, and www.insure.com.

WHY THE PITCHES DON'T MAKE SENSE

Perhaps you've heard the saying that life insurance isn't bought, it's sold. That sentiment comes from the fact that life insurance agents can be very aggressive and extremely persuasive. Who can blame them? The commission an agent gets from selling a cash value policy is substantial. If you've ever met with a life insurance salesperson, you've probably heard one of the following pitches.

The pitch: "*Maybe you don't need life insurance now, but you should buy today when you're young and healthy to protect your insurability in the future.*"

The reality: The chances of your developing a health problem that renders you unable to qualify for life insurance before you reach age 35 are very slim. Since you have limited funds now, why spend your money on insurance you don't need?

The pitch: "*Even though you're single, you need life insurance to pay your funeral costs and your debts.*"

The reality: Your parents, other relatives, or friends will probably be willing to pay for your funeral in the unlikely event you die with no assets. As for your debts, unless you cosigned a loan with parents, partners, or friends, no one else will be re-

How Much Coverage Do You Need?

You need enough life insurance to provide for your dependents (spouse and kids) so that they can carry on a decent lifestyle if you die prematurely. If you have young children, that means you need to figure out how much they would need to live for at least the next fifteen to twenty years. One rough rule of thumb says you should

sponsible for paying them. If you have any assets, the creditors will sell them to pay your debts. Otherwise, the creditors will simply take the loss.

The pitch: "*If you have a child, you should buy a policy to cover his or her life.*"

The reality: A child is the last person who needs a life insurance policy. Parents need life insurance. Buying coverage on your child's life is a waste of money despite what late-night infomercials may claim.

The pitch: "*Cash value life insurance offers tax-favored growth and is a great forced-savings plan.*"

The reality: This is true, but you can get the same tax-favored growth by putting money in a 401(k) or IRA, without paying a commission to an agent. And with retirement plans, you also get a tax deduction. (For details, see Chapter 6.)

The pitch: "*Buying term insurance is like renting. Buying cash value insurance is like buying. When the term is up, you don't have anything to show for it. But look how much money you'll have in twenty years if you buy a cash value life insurance policy.*"

The reality: Life insurance companies are notorious for using extremely attractive, overly optimistic future rates of return when selling cash value policies. There's no guarantee that your returns will be as good as an agent says.

buy a policy that will pay seven to ten times your annual before-tax income if you die, but many people need more than that—especially if they have many kids or if they're single parents. If you have high aspirations for your kids—for example, if you want to send them to expensive private schools—or if your spouse doesn't work, you will certainly need more. The calculator on personal finance firm Myvesta's site (www.myvesta.org/calculators/LifeInsurance.html) will help you crunch all the numbers.

If Your Employer Offers Life Insurance

Many large employers provide some life insurance for employees. Your company might pay for a term policy with a death benefit of $50,000—more than enough if you're single and have no dependents. If you need more, you might be better off buying directly from an insurance company rather than through your employer. Policies you get through work may be hard (or at least expensive) to convert if you switch jobs. Plus, some employers charge all employees the same rate on life insurance, regardless of age. If that's the case with your employer, you would be paying the same premium as a 45-year-old, for example, which would be much higher than what you'd pay elsewhere. Find out about your employer's offerings and also price several term policies on your own.

INSURANCE YOU PROBABLY DON'T NEED

It's very tempting to buy quickie insurance on impulse. After all, it seems so cheap—just $10 a day to get collision coverage at the rental car counter, or $25 for $50,000 worth of life insurance at the airport. But before you throw money at this kind of coverage, evaluate it carefully. In most cases, you don't need it.

- **Rental car collision protection.** If you've ever rented a car, you were probably asked if you wanted to buy the **loss** damage waiver, which is just a fancy name for collision insurance. Next time, do a little research in advance. Review your credit card agreements to see if you're automatically protected when you charge a car rental on the card. And if you already have collision and comprehensive insurance on your own car, find out if your policy extends to rented cars. (See p. 233 for more on the ins and outs of insuring rental cars.)

- **Flight accident insurance.** If you need to insure your life, the cheapest way to do it when you're young is to buy a term life insurance policy. Don't waste money buying life insurance at a vending machine in the airport. Sure it's tempting (this type of insurance plays on our fear of flying) and it also seems cheap, but it doesn't make sense. Your chances of slipping and killing yourself on the ground are much greater than your chances of dying in a plane crash. Besides, you may already be covered if you have life insurance, for example. Many credit card companies give you automatic flight insurance if you charge your tickets on their card, so be sure to check.

- **Travel insurance.** Policies promising to protect your vacation against flight cancellation, delays, or even lost luggage have proliferated, but as long as it's a short domestic trip you're booking yourself, you're unlikely to need any of it. For one thing, cancellation and baggage insurance is a very common credit card benefit—as long as you charged the tickets on your card, you're probably already covered. For another, you can probably just pay a fee and rebook a hotel or reschedule a flight.

  The exception is if you're going abroad, in which case travel medical protection may be a good idea. (Few if any U.S. health plans will cover you if you get sick overseas.) Here too, many credit cards, especially those with an international or airline focus, come with some travel medical coverage. Check with your issuer and at www.insuremytrip.com to make sure you've got what you need.

- **Long-term care insurance.** Some insurance companies aggressively pitch long-term care insurance—which will pay the costs if you have to spend time in a nursing home—to younger people. Their argument goes that people should buy this type of policy while they're young and healthy and hang on to it. But in fact, most young people end up paying premiums for a while and then letting their coverage lapse. At your age, you should consider disability insurance instead.

- **Credit protection insurance.** Credit card and mortgage companies have been stuffing their envelopes with invitations to buy "credit insurance," which is supposed to cover your credit card bills or housing payments in the event that you become unemployed, disabled, or dead. Supposedly, this insurance will protect your credit from damage during periods when you can't make ends meet. In reality, it mainly protects the lenders—you're shelling out extra money to make sure they keep getting their payments on time. This insurance costs much more than it tends to give back, and for most people offers little or no protection that would not already be provided by regular life and disability insurance.

WHY YOU MAY NEED A WILL

Since we're on the topic of life insurance, this is as good a time as any to discuss the subject of wills. The truth is, I don't know anyone in his or her twenties who has a will. But that doesn't mean you don't need one.

If you're single, for example, you may want to leave all your possessions (even if that's just a car and a small savings account) to a friend or sibling. But according to state law, without a will, your property will be distributed to your closest relatives. If you're married, you may assume that your spouse will get everything in the event of your death. But depending on the state you live in, your parents may be entitled to a share of what you leave behind. If you're a parent, you may not want to think about what would happen to your children if you're no longer around. But without a will, a probate court will select a guardian for them. You get the picture.

The easiest way to tackle this task is to get a lawyer to draw up a will for you. If you don't have much in the way of assets and your situation is straightforward, this should cost about $350 or less. For a list of local lawyers specializing in wills, take a look at the American Bar Association's Lawyer Locator (www.abanet.org). If you can't afford the lawyer's fee, your situation is uncomplicated, and you're willing to spend the time, you can write your own will. One book that can help is Nolo's Simple Will Book (Nolo Press, about $25). You may also want to check out Nolo's Online Will, which costs about $70 when you order it directly from the website (www.nolo .com). Keep in mind that once you start earning more money and accumulating more assets, you're going to need to update your will. But having one today is a precaution worth taking.

FINANCIAL CRAMMING

- If you work for a company that offers a flexible benefits plan, evaluate your options carefully. If you're single without any dependents, for instance, it probably makes sense to skip the life insurance offered by your employer and opt instead for better health insurance or more disability coverage.

- Don't go without health insurance, even if you're healthy. To find affordable coverage, see if there's a group you can join, such as a trade association or religious organization, that gives you access to a group policy. If you're between jobs, buy low-cost temporary coverage. (For general tips on shopping for an individual policy, see p. 226.)

- For car insurance, check online with companies that sell directly to consumers (see p. 234). And think twice before allowing a friend to drive your car. If there's an accident, *your* insurance record will be tainted, not your friend's.

- Get disability insurance to protect yourself in case you can't work due to injury or illness. Ideally, you should have coverage that would pay you 60% to 70% of your income if you become disabled. (For advice on reducing the cost of your coverage, see p. 238.)

- Buy renters insurance if you rent a house or an apartment. It protects your possessions if they're ruined in a fire or stolen, and it also offers you some liability coverage inside and away from your home.

- If you have kids or anyone else dependent on your income, buy term life insurance for yourself and write up a will. If you don't have dependents, you probably don't need any life insurance at all, but you probably still need a will.

HOW TO MAKE YOUR LIFE LESS TAXING

Put More Money in Your Pocket and Less in Uncle Sam's

YOU CAN RUN from many financial subjects, but you can't hide from taxes. Still, if you're like most people, you find the tax rules complex, the forms confusing, and the Internal Revenue Service (IRS) intimidating. But whether you're a highly paid professional or a hardly paid grad student, this is one area where knowing the rules can save you money.

My goal in this chapter is to help you get over your fear of filing. It describes exactly what kind of taxes you pay, explains how to figure out which tax bracket you're in, offers tips on filing your taxes online and off, and, most important, outlines specific strategies that can save you money. Although exploring the intricacies of the tax code isn't anyone's idea of a good time (except for an accountant I once dated), taking the time to understand the basics could save you hundreds of dollars each year. Whether you do your own taxes—something I recommend you try at least once—or you hire someone to do them, knowing the rules ensures that you won't miss out on any money-saving breaks.

One quick note: Although this chapter will give you a good

overview of what you need to know about taxes, you should keep in mind that tax law is constantly changing. And while I've made every effort to provide accurate, up-to-date information on the tax code's latest twists and turns, you'll need to check the current rules when you fill out your tax return. The instructions for the tax forms as well as the free IRS publications available online are a great starting point.

WHY IS YOUR PAYCHECK SO SMALL?

When you received your first paycheck, it became painfully clear that your before-tax salary was an illusion. Your take-home pay, or **net wages,** was much smaller, thanks to all those deductions: Social Security tax, Medicare tax, federal income tax, and maybe state and local income tax.

Your employer subtracts or "withholds" tax because the U.S. tax system uses a "pay-as-you-go" method, meaning we pay tax on the money we earn as we earn it rather than paying it all in a lump sum at the end of the year. If you're a freelancer or self-employed, you're responsible for making sure you pay the correct taxes each quarter (every three months). If you're an employee, your employer withholds income tax from each paycheck based on salary and the information on the **Form W-4** that you filled out when you were hired. On a worksheet attached to the W-4, you answered some basic questions to help you calculate the number of **withholding allowances** you're entitled to. A withholding allowance represents an estimate of the exemptions and deductions you are likely to be entitled to in the coming year. (You'll learn all about exemptions and deductions later on.) The more withholding allowances you take, the less income tax your employer withholds from your paycheck; the fewer allowances you take, the more tax is withheld. The number of allowances you're eligible for can depend on a variety of factors, including whether you're single or married, whether you have kids, and whether you own a home.

THE TAXES YOU PAY

Here's a list of the major ones:

- **Income tax.** The federal government, and some state and local governments, require you to pay tax on your **earned income,** which is the income you receive for work you do. The federal government and certain state and local governments also require you to pay tax on income you receive from investments. Such **unearned income** includes the interest you get from your savings account and the dividends or capital gains you receive from mutual funds, stocks, and bonds. (Not to mention any lottery money you may be lucky enough to win!) The total of your earned and unearned income is known as your **gross income.**

- **Social Security and Medicare payroll tax (FICA).** Everyone who works must contribute a portion of his or her wages to a fund that provides retirement income for people 65 and older, as well as disability benefits for those who can't work (that's Social Security) and health insurance for this same crowd (that's the Medicare part). Together, these two contributions make up your FICA tax, named for the Federal Insurance Contributions Act. In 2009, if you're an employee of a company, the Social Security tax you pay is 6.2% of your income, up to a maximum income of $106,800. The Medicare tax is 1.45%, with no maximum. Your total employee contribution to Medicare and Social Security is 7.65% of your income, and your employer matches that amount, meaning all together the contribution is 15.3%.

    If you work for yourself, you have to cover the full 15.3% yourself; this is also referred to as the **self-employment tax.** Many states also impose state unemployment and disability insurance taxes.

- **Property tax.** Some state and local governments require residents to pay tax on certain types of property that they own. In Virginia, Kentucky, and Connecticut, for example, residents must pay **personal property tax** on the value of their cars each year. And in most states, if you own a home, you have to pay real estate tax, also known as **real property tax,** to your municipality and/or county. This figure is based on the value of your home and the land on which it is built.

- **Sales tax.** Most states and many cities and counties impose tax on the items you buy (sofas, potato chips, sneakers) and the services you use (dry cleaning, haircuts, lawn care).

- **Capital gains tax.** Your profit or gain when you sell an investment (even something as small as one share of stock) is subject to something called capital gains tax. Money you make from financial assets (like stock mutual funds) that you've had for a year or less is taxed at your regular income tax rate. (I will show you how to figure out your tax rate in the next section.) But gains from investments that you've held for more than one year are considered **long-term capital gains,** and are generally taxed at a lower rate. And if you are in the 10% or 15% tax bracket for ordinary income, you don't have to pay any taxes on long-term capital gains.

FIGURING OUT YOUR TAX RATE

When people talk about their tax bracket or tax rate, they're usually referring to their federal income tax bracket or rate. Federal income taxes probably make up the largest share of your total tax bill. Your federal income tax rate depends on how much income—including wages, bonuses, tips, and earnings from investments—you received over the course of the year. (It also depends on the tax breaks you're eligible for, but I'll tell you more about those later on.)

The federal government has a "graduated" tax system that requires people with higher incomes to pay a higher percentage of

TAXES AND INHERITANCE

When Jacob's uncle Al died, he received $13,000 in cash from his estate, which he put in his bank savings account in January. He was thrilled by this windfall, but he worried about whether or not he would owe tax on the money. Here's how it generally works: You do not owe income tax on money you receive as an inheritance. Instead, the executor—the person in charge of sorting through a will and distributing the money to beneficiaries—is responsible for making sure the applicable inheritance taxes are paid. But if you put that money in a bank account, you will have to pay tax on the interest. So Jacob had to pay tax on the $520 that his uncle's money earned him in interest.

their incomes in taxes. A range of income levels is grouped together in what is called a **tax bracket.** A **tax rate** is assigned to each tax bracket. To figure out your tax bracket, you first need to calculate your **taxable income,** which you can do by following the step-by-step instructions on your tax return. For example, if you were single and your taxable income was between $0 and $8,350 in 2009, you would be in the 10% tax bracket. The dollar amounts that fall within each bracket are adjusted for inflation every year. Every few years, the president, with the help of Congress, changes the number of brackets and adjusts the range of incomes in each bracket in order to win friends and influence people. As of this writing, there are six brackets and therefore six rates: 10%, 15%, 25%, 28%, 33%, and 35%. But figuring out the tax you owe involves more than finding out which rate corresponds to your income.

Take a look at the tables in Figure 9–1. If you're single and have a taxable income of $8,000 (maybe you're a part-time student), that would put you in the 10% tax bracket. Simple. But say your income was $32,000. Here's where it gets complicated. Not all your income will fall into the same bracket. The first $8,350 will be taxed at the

10% rate, but the remaining $23,650 will be taxed at the 15% rate. In this example, 15% is known as your **marginal tax rate,** the rate at which the "last dollar you earn" gets taxed. The marginal rate is the highest rate at which any of your money is taxed. Knowing your marginal rate will help you evaluate the merits of making certain investments.

Depending on where you live, you may have to pay state and

Figure 9-1
2009 TAX RATES

Filing Status	For taxable income that is:	Marginal rate is:
Single	Not over $8,350	10%
	Over $8,350 but not over $33,950	15%
	Over $33,950 but not over $82,250	25%
	Over $82,250 but not over $171,550	28%
	Over $171,550 but not over $372,950	33%
	Over $372,950	35%
Married couples filing jointly	Not over $16,700	10%
	Over $16,700 but not over $67,900	15%
	Over $67,900 but not over $137,050	25%
	Over $137,050 but not over $190,200	28%
	Over $190,200 but not over $372,950	33%
	Over $372,950	35%
Married couples filing separately	Not over $8,350	10%
	Over $8,350 but not over $33,950	15%
	Over $33,950 but not over $68,525	25%
	Over $68,525 but not over $104,425	28%
	Over $104,425 but not over $186,475	33%
	Over $186,475	35%

local income taxes too. On average, you can expect your state and local tax to be roughly 5% to 10%. (Some states charge no state income tax at all, however, and others impose a tax only on certain types of income like interest and dividends.) Add about 5% to your federal marginal rate to get a rough idea of your combined federal, state, and local marginal rate. To calculate your federal, state, and local marginal income tax rate more precisely, consult your state's tax booklet to find out your true state and local marginal rate. You can get a copy by calling your state's department of taxation (or reaching it online via www.taxsites.com). Inside you'll find tables to help you figure out your state and local rates.

Remember, your marginal rate does not indicate what percentage of your income will go toward tax. In the example above, if your annual taxable income was $35,000, most of your money would be taxed at a rate of either 10% or 15% rather than at the marginal rate of 25%. Your overall rate, known as your **effective tax rate,** is a blended, or weighted, average of the tax rates that apply to your income. In this case it's a weighted average of 10%, 15%, and 25% that results in an effective tax rate of about 14%.

FILING YOUR TAX RETURN

The term **filing** simply means filling out your tax forms and sending them to the IRS, the government agency responsible for collecting taxes. Although your employer subtracts money for taxes from your paycheck during the year, the amount withheld is generally an estimate, not the exact amount of tax you actually owe. By filling out tax forms, you learn whether you still owe the IRS some money or whether the IRS owes you a refund, and then you (or the IRS) write the appropriate check.

April 15 is the last day you can file a tax return and pay tax for the previous calendar year without having to pay interest or a penalty. (In years when that date falls on a Saturday or Sunday, the IRS allows you to file up until the following Monday.) If you owe the IRS money and miss the April 15 deadline, you may have to pay interest and a penalty on the money you owe.

Start getting your paperwork together early in the year. By the end of January, your employer will have sent you a **W-2** form that shows your gross wages and the amount of tax that was withheld from your paycheck over the course of the previous year. Your bank, mutual fund company, and/or brokerage will each send you a **1099** form, which lists the interest, dividends, or capital gains you earned during the year. If you've done freelance work, you'll prob-

PAPER-FREE FILING

You don't have to wait in long lines at the post office on April 15. Most people now find it easiest to fill out and file their returns online. If you decide to **e-file**, you have a few options. First you can go to www.irs.gov and search for "e-file for Business Partners." The IRS has teamed up with a number of private companies that provide online forms you can use to file your returns electronically.

You can also choose to use the forms available on sites like H&R Block's TaxCut (www.taxcut.com) or Intuit's TurboTax (www.turbotax.com). Costs for using any of these options range from about $19.95 to $59.99 per return.

You may have another possibility. If your adjusted gross income was $54,000 or less in 2009, the IRS's Free File program allows you to fill out and e-file your tax forms online at no cost. Go to www.irs.gov and search for "Free File."

If you e-file and discover that you owe the IRS money, you'll be able to pay it electronically or by check or money order. If the IRS owes you a refund, you can click a box indicating you want the money deposited directly in your checking or savings account, and it will appear there within about a week of e-filing. With paper tax returns, refunds can take up to eight weeks.

ably receive a 1099 from each of the companies you did the work for. Compare your pay stubs or direct deposit records and financial statements to your W-2 and 1099s to make sure the figures are accurate. Save these forms in a folder marked "Tax Returns," and create a new folder for each tax year. When it's time to fill out your tax return, you'll be ready to do it.

Although this chapter deals mostly with federal taxes, don't forget that your state and local taxes are also due on April 15.

Who Has to File a Tax Return?

If you're single and your parents are not claiming you as a dependent on their tax return, you must file a tax return as long as your gross income is $8,750 (as of 2009) or more. For married couples who file a joint return, the 2009 minimum income for filing is $17,500.

If you're a full-time student and you're under 24, your parents can claim you as a dependent. But if your income exceeds certain limitations you might still have to file. The rules for these limits can be found at the IRS website (www.irs.gov); search for Publication 17, *Your Federal Income Tax.* They're incredibly convoluted, so it would probably take longer for you to sort through them than to fill out a simple tax form. My advice: File a tax return, even if you're not entirely sure you need to. It can't hurt.

When Should You File?

If you're expecting a refund, send in your tax forms to the IRS as soon after January 1 as possible so that you can get your refund fast. If you owe money, though, and you want to hang on to your cash as long as possible (the idea being you'll get more interest), wait until close to the deadline. Your return will still be on time if you either file electronically by April 15 or if your paper tax return and check are postmarked by that date.

If you are in fact going the paper route and simply can't get it together in time, you can file for an automatic six-month extension

A NOTE TO STUDENTS

Scholarships that pay for tuition, course-related fees, books, and supplies are not considered taxable income if you're working toward a degree. But if you received a scholarship to, say, study abroad for a year, and the course work is not related to your getting a degree, you must count the money you receive as income. And whether you're working toward a degree or not, the portion of a scholarship used to pay for room and board, travel, and research is considered taxable income. For details go to www.irs.gov and search for either Tax Topic 421, *Scholarship and Fellowship* Grants, or Publication 970, *Tax Benefits for Education.*

by filling out Form 4868 and submitting your full tax forms later. But if you think you owe money, you must estimate how much you owe and still send in a check to the IRS by April 15. If you haven't sent all that you owe by April 15, the IRS might charge you interest on the unpaid amount, plus a penalty if you've paid less than 90% of the amount due.

If You Can't Pay

Even if you don't have enough money to pay the IRS the tax you owe, you should file your return by April 15. If you don't, you'll be charged a monthly penalty of 4% of the amount of tax you owe, up to a maximum penalty of 25% of your total IRS debt. You'll also have to pay interest. You can request to pay in installments, however, so go to www.irs.gov and find Form 9465. You can print it and send it in with your completed return, or you can do it online. Within 30 days, the IRS will tell you if you've been accepted for the installment plan. The IRS will still charge you a monthly late payment charge of 0.5% of the balance due, up to 25%, plus interest and a one-time charge of $52.

If You Need Help

If you have questions about how to complete your tax return or how the tax laws apply to you, go to www.irs.gov and click on "Contact IRS" to find your nearest Taxpayer Assistance Center, where you can meet with an IRS representative in person.

Once you've filed your return, if you have a dispute and need help with a problem, such as a missing refund or a penalty you believe was unfair, go to www.irs.gov/advocate to find your local

PAYING YOUR TAXES WITH PLASTIC?

Paying your taxes with your credit card may seem like a good idea, especially if your credit card has a rewards program that gives you say, airline mileage or cash back. But before you reach for your credit card to pay your tax bill, think it through: It's rarely a good deal.

First of all, the IRS charges you a "convenience fee" for using cards. This can range anywhere from 2.5% to 3% of your tax bill and this is likely to negate any rewards you are able to accrue. For example, say you owe $2,000. If you get a reward of one mile for every dollar you spend, that's 2,000 miles, but those miles will cost you up to $60 in convenience fees. Probably not worth it if it'll take you 25,000 miles to earn a free flight that would otherwise cost $400. A better option is to use your debit card. The convenience fee in this case is usually $2.95, and you might still earn miles. The IRS will walk you through the payment process on its website, www.irs.gov.

Taxpayer Advocate Service office. You can also search for Publication 1546, *The Taxpayer Advocate Service of the IRS—How to Get Help with Unresolved Tax Problems.*

If You're Single

If you're not married but have children or dependent relatives living with you, you may be able to file as a **head of household.** This status generally allows you to pay less tax than an ordinary single person. To see if you qualify, check the instruction booklet that comes with your tax forms, or go to www.irs.gov and consult Publication 501, *Exemptions, Standard Deduction, and Filing Information.*

MAXIMIZING YOUR TAX BREAKS

Although the government wants citizens to pay their fair share of taxes, it does offer taxpayers ways to reduce the amount of their

IF YOU CHANGE YOUR NAME, TELL SOCIAL SECURITY

If you get married (or divorced) and change your last name, contact the Social Security Administration. The IRS checks in with Social Security to make sure that the name you use matches for both. If you change your name without alerting the Social Security Administration, the IRS may delay sending you the refund check you are due. What's more, you might not get credit for the money your employer deducts from your paycheck and sends to Social Security. Go to www.ssa .gov or call 800-772-1213 to get a copy of Form SS-5, which you'll have to fill out to register your new name.

income that's subject to tax. This section will discuss the various tax breaks for which you may be eligible.

Exemptions and Deductions

One type of tax break available to most taxpayers is an **exemption**, a specific amount ($3,650 in 2009) that can be subtracted from your taxable income. If you're single and have no children (and are not being claimed as a dependent on someone else's tax return), you are allowed one personal exemption. If you're married and you file a joint return, you and your spouse are each entitled to a personal exemption. You also get an additional exemption for each child you have. If you earn a very high income, however, you may not be entitled to any exemptions.

The other type of tax break is a **deduction**. Deductions are specific expenses that the government allows you to subtract from your taxable income, thus reducing the amount of tax you pay. (For an example of how this works, see the box on p. 272). Uncle Sam offers deductions for certain expenditures. For instance, to encourage people to buy homes (which has been seen as a good thing for the economy), the government allows taxpayers to deduct the interest they pay on their mortgages.

There are two distinct ways to take advantage of deductions. The simpler way is to take the **standard deduction**, which is a fixed dollar amount that Congress allows all taxpayers to subtract from their income. Even if you don't participate in activities that are deemed deductible by the government, you still get to take the standard deduction—everyone gets it. (Technically, you subtract your standard deduction from a figure known as your **adjusted gross income,** or **AGI.** Your AGI is basically your gross income minus special deductions known as "adjustments." Don't get bogged down in the technical details of how to determine your AGI now. When you fill out your tax form you'll be able to calculate it.) In 2009, the standard deduction for a single person was $5,700. For a married couple filing a joint return, the standard deduction was $11,400. These figures are adjusted each year for inflation.

A more complicated but potentially more rewarding method

is to **itemize** your deductions. Itemizing means listing the specific "items" that are deductible according to current tax rules and then subtracting their cost from your AGI. If you choose to itemize your deductions, you cannot take the standard deduction. It's one or the other.

Whether you should itemize or take the standard deduction depends on the specifics of your financial life. The following two sections describe some potential itemized deductions. Once you read through them, make your own list of the itemized deductions that are relevant to your life. If the total of your itemized expenses is greater than the standard deduction, you should itemize. If the standard deduction is greater, you should take the standard deduction. It's that simple. In the event you *do* itemize, make sure you can substantiate the amounts you claim with receipts. This is the part of your return that the IRS is likely to scrutinize.

But before you read the following lists of possible deductions, I should add a disclaimer. The rules concerning deductions, even those that seem straightforward, can be very tricky. They also change frequently. Use this list only as a starting point. Consult a

FIGURING OUT THE VALUE OF A DEDUCTION

Your tax bracket plays a major role in determining just how much a deduction is worth. Suppose you got a mortgage to buy a home. Assume in the first year the interest payments you made on the mortgage totaled $10,000. You would be able to subtract, or deduct, that $10,000 from your adjusted gross income for that year. If you're in the 15% tax bracket, that would mean saving yourself $1,500 (15% of $10,000). But if you're in the 28% tax bracket, the $10,000 tax deduction would be worth $2,800 (28% of $10,000). Compare the cash value of your deduction with the standard deduction to figure out whether it's worth itemizing.

current tax guide or go to www.irs.gov to make sure specific deductions are still valid. Also, if you earn more than $166,800 in 2009 (whether you're single or married filing jointly), you may be subject to a limit on some of the itemized deductions. Check your Form 1040 instructions for more details.

Some Straightforward Itemized Deductions

To see whether it makes sense for you to itemize, read the following list of possible deductions:

- **State and local income tax.** On your federal tax form you can deduct the state and local taxes you paid (including amounts withheld from your paycheck) over the course of the year. Because most people pay these taxes automatically out of their paycheck, you're likely to be eligible for this tax break.

- **Sales tax.** If you itemize, you have the option of deducting either state and local income tax *or* state and local sales tax on your federal return (not both). For people who aren't subject to state income tax, such as Texans, it's a no-brainer: Deduct the sales tax and save money. You either deduct a set amount, which is determined by your income, or you can save all your receipts and add up the sales tax. If you buy a big ticket item, such as a car, it might be better to deduct the actual amount you paid. To figure out whether it makes more sense to deduct income tax or sales tax, go to www.irs.gov and search for the sales tax deduction calculator.

- **Property tax.** If you own a home, you can deduct the property taxes (also known as real estate taxes) you pay from your taxable income. If you live in a co-op, it pays property taxes for you as part of your monthly maintenance fee; find out what your share of these taxes is so that you can deduct them.

- **Donations to charity.** If you make a contribution to a group that's considered a "qualified tax-exempt organization" by the IRS, you can deduct it, but you'll need to have the proper paperwork to support your deduction. Qualified organizations include most churches, synagogues, charities, and educational organizations. If you're unsure whether a particular organization qualifies, ask before you make a donation. Contributions you make to your college's alumni association, for example, might be deductible.

  If instead of cash you donate clothes, furniture, or household items to the Salvation Army, for instance, you get to deduct their current market value as long as they are in decent condition. Write down a description of each item you donate and how much each is worth (basically that means how much you estimate you could get if you sold it at a garage sale). You'll need a receipt from the charity—they do this all the time. For noncash donations worth more than $500 (like clothing or books), you'll have to fill out a special form (Form 8283) when you file your tax return. If your noncash donation is worth more than $5,000, you'll need to get a professional appraisal.

  You can also deduct some of the expenses you incur when you do volunteer work. If you volunteer at a senior center on weekends, for example, you can deduct some of your transportation costs as long as there's no significant element of recreation or vacation in the travel.

  If you get any "benefit" (theater tickets, a tote bag, a meal) in exchange for a contribution, you can deduct only the amount of your donation that exceeds the value of the benefit. Say you pay $200 to attend a fund-raising dinner for the Save the Lizards Foundation and the actual value of the dinner is $50; you can deduct $150 on your tax return. The receipt you get from your charity should specify any such "benefits" you have received.

- **Housing costs.** If you own a home, you can deduct the interest you pay on your mortgage. (You cannot deduct the portion of your mortgage payment that goes toward paying off the principal.) You are also allowed to fully or partially deduct the premiums on your private mortgage insurance, provided you earn less than $109,000 a year and you bought your home in 2007 or 2008 (but not before).

Also, in the year you buy a home, you may be able to deduct the points, even if these points were actually paid by the seller of the home. (See Chapter 7 for an explanation of points.) If you live in a co-op building, the co-op might pay interest on a mortgage for the building. If it does, find out what your share of this interest is; you may be able to deduct it.

Some Trickier Itemized Deductions

Certain expenses are deductible only in specific situations. Here are some of those deductions. Again, remember that some are not available to taxpayers with very high incomes. Check a current tax guide for details.

- **Job-related expenses and other miscellaneous deductions.** These are costs related to producing income. Clear so far, but the rule is annoyingly complex: You can deduct the combined total of these expenses that exceeds 2% of your adjusted gross income (AGI)—in other words, you can't deduct that first 2%. Here's how that works. Suppose your AGI is $30,000. You could not deduct the first $600 (2% of $30,000), but you *could* deduct anything beyond that point. Below are examples of job-related expenses. For more details visit www.irs.gov and find Publication 529, *Miscellaneous Deductions*.

  » *Work-related home computers, cell phones, and other equipment.* You can deduct these costs if your employer requires you to purchase any equipment. But you must be able to prove that you use the equipment more than 50% of the time for business, and that your employer told you the item was necessary for your job. Ask your

boss to write a letter or email to that effect, and file it
away in case you need to show it to the IRS some day.

» *Job-search expenses.* The IRS allows you to deduct
costs related to a job search as long as you're looking
for a position in your *present* occupation. If you're trying to change careers—say, you're a lifeguard looking
to break into investment banking—you don't get the
deduction. If you're currently out of work, the kind of
job you did most recently is considered your occupation. Those looking for their first job don't get the tax
break. The expenses you can deduct if you qualify include the fees of career counseling and employment or
placement agencies; the cost of prepping, printing, and
mailing your résumé; phone calls; and transportation
costs (and 50% of the cost of meals while traveling) for
a long-distance job search. Items like clothes and shoes
for interviews are not deductible.

» *Work-related educational expenses.* If you take a course
that helps you maintain or improve the skills you use
to perform your current job, you may be able to deduct
your expenses. Also, if a course is required either by
your employer or by law in order for you to keep your
job (and, of course, the company doesn't cover the tuition), you may be able to deduct its cost. But if you take
a course to help train you for a new line of work or that
enables you to meet the minimum educational requirements of your profession, you can't deduct the tuition.
So a financial analyst taking a cooking course can't deduct the cost of the class, and a paralegal can't deduct
the tuition costs of law school. But a teacher who takes
a course to learn how to operate new technology in the
classroom may be able to deduct tuition expenses.

» *Mandatory uniforms for work.* Suits and ties aren't
deductible, but nurses' uniforms, firefighter uniforms,

postal uniforms, safety shoes and glasses, hard hats, and work gloves are. (If you're a computer programmer who wears a hard hat to work for kicks, it doesn't count.) If your employer reimburses you for these expenses, you can't deduct them.

» *Unreimbursed business travel and entertainment expenses.* If you pay these costs yourself, there are very specific rules about how much you're allowed to deduct. In general, you must keep a detailed log of your trips and be prepared to prove the business purpose of each expense.

» *Union dues and initiation fees, professional and business association dues, and job-related subscriptions to trade magazines and professional journals.* Make sure to deduct these expenses if you are not reimbursed for them by your employer.

» *Tax preparation fees.* Even though these aren't directly related to work, you can deduct the cost of tax-related software and tax publications. You can also deduct money you pay to a tax preparer.

• **Medical expenses.** You can deduct out-of-pocket medical and dental expenses, for yourself or any dependent, that are greater than 7.5% of your adjusted gross income. Include premiums you pay for medical insurance, co-payments for doctor visits, the cost of birth control pills or cigarette-quitting programs, prescription medicines not covered by your health plan, and transportation needed for medical care.

• **Losses due to theft and disasters.** You're allowed to deduct the cost of items you lose in a burglary, fire, or other disaster that exceed 10% of your adjusted gross income. The first $100 of losses above the 10% threshold is not deductible.

Deductions You Can Take
Without Itemizing

Most deductions have to be itemized, and their total must be bigger than the standard deduction for them to be of any use. But there are exceptions to that rule. Here are four of the most important deductions you can take even if you don't itemize:

- **Contributions to a traditional IRA.** If you aren't eligible for an employer-sponsored retirement plan or if your income falls below a certain level, the money you contribute to a traditional IRA—though not a Roth IRA—may be deductible. (See Chapter 6.) If you're in the 25% tax bracket, a deductible $2,000 IRA contribution will save you $500 on your tax bill. (The math: $2,000 times 25% equals $500.) There's a place on the tax form that will prompt you for this. One nice feature about the IRA deduction is that you technically don't have to make your contribution during the tax year in question: The deadline for contributing to an IRA is the same as the deadline for filing your taxes that year. So, for example, you can deduct an IRA contribution for tax year 2010 as long as you make the contribution before April 15, 2011.

  An aside about 401(k)s: You don't list 401(k) contributions on your tax return because your employer has already subtracted your contribution from your gross salary. The net salary on the W-2 you receive in January from your company already reflects your contribution.

- **Student loan interest payments.** You are entitled to deduct the *interest* payments you make on your student loans, up to a maximum of $2,500 in interest per year. You can't deduct money that goes toward repaying the principal. If you make $75,000 as a single person or $150,000 as a married couple, you're not eligible for this deduction. For more information, contact the IRS at 800-TAX-FORM (www.irs .gov) for Publication 970, *Tax Benefits for Education*.

- **Alimony payments.** If you're divorced and pay alimony to your former spouse, you might be able to deduct it. But certain conditions apply. You can deduct only money that you are legally required to pay your ex-spouse by the divorce or separation agreement. You can deduct only payments that you make in cash (including checks and money orders), not in property. And child support is *not* deductible. For details, check Publication 504, *Divorced or Separated Individuals*.

- **Tuition and fees.** The IRS may let you deduct up to $4,000 a year in higher education tuition and fees (including graduate school), provided your income is within certain limits. You have to choose between this deduction and one of the education credits available (see the next section)—you can switch between them from year to year, but you can't take both at one time. Do the math to see which way saves you the most money. Obviously, if your income is too high to be eligible for the credits, the deduction is better than nothing at all. Once again, Publication 970, *Tax Benefits for Education*, has all the details.

MAKING THE MOST OF YOUR TAX CREDITS

Tax credits are special breaks that are subtracted directly from the tax you owe. (That's different from a deduction, which reduces the amount of your income that's subject to taxation.) For that reason, a tax credit could be worth a lot. Here are some that you should take advantage of:

- **Hope Scholarship Credit.** If you're paying your way through college, you may be eligible for a tax credit of up to $1,800 in each of the first two years of school. A full 100% of the first $1,200 you spend on tuition can be claimed for the Hope credit, plus 50% of the next $1,200. You're not eligible for the full credit if you make more than $50,000 (single) or $100,000 (married filing jointly). To find out more,

contact the IRS at 800-TAX-FORM (www.irs.gov) and get
a copy of *Tax Benefits for Education,* Publication 970.

- **Lifetime Learning Credit.** If you haven't claimed the Hope
  credit in a given year, a "lifetime learning credit" worth up
  to $2,000 a year may be available. Unlike the Hope credits,
  a lifetime learning credit can be taken in any year of college
  or graduate school. The credit covers up to 20% of the first
  $10,000 of eligible tuition and related expenses, which be-
  gin at the same income levels as the Hope credit. For details,
  check out IRS Publication 970, *Tax Benefits for Education.*
  There's no limit to the number of times this credit can be
  claimed, making it a real boon to perpetual grad student
  types.

- **Child Tax Credit.** You can take a tax credit of up to $1,000
  in 2009 for each dependent child who's under 17 at the end
  of the tax year, including stepchildren and foster children.
  The credit begins to phase out for singles with incomes over
  $75,000 and married couples earning more than $110,000.
  You can find more about this in IRS Publication 17, *Your
  Federal Income Tax.*

- **Earned Income Credit.** In 2009, if you're at least 25 and
  earn less than $13,440 (and no one can claim you as a
  dependent) you may be eligible for this special tax break.
  If you have a child, you must earn less than $35,463 to
  qualify; if you have two or more children, you must earn
  less than $37,783. To find out if you're eligible, see the in-
  struction booklet that comes with your tax forms, Schedule
  EIC, or go to the IRS website (www.irs.gov) and search for
  "Earned Income Tax Credit."

- **Child Care Credit.** If you pay someone to take care of your
  child while you (and your spouse, if you're married) work,
  the IRS allows you to subtract as much as 35% of your
  child care expenses (up to $3,000 for one child, or $6,000
  for two or more) from your tax debt. For details, go to www

.irs.gov and search for Publication 503, *Child and Dependent Care Expenses*. In order to get the credit, you will have to pay your sitter totally by the book—that means you have to pay the required employment taxes, such as Medicare and Social Security, for your child care worker. For details, contact 800-TAX-FORM (www.irs.gov) and get a copy of Publication 926, *Household Employer's Tax Guide*.

- **Adoption Credit.** If you adopt a child, you're allowed a credit for up to $12,150 of specified adoption expenses.

- **Saver's Credit.** This special credit is to encourage people with somewhat lower incomes to save for retirement. If you make less than $27,750 as a single person or $55,000 as a married couple filing jointly in 2009, a little known but potentially helpful benefit is that you can get a credit of up to $1,000 per person for contributing to a 401(k), IRA, or other retirement account. This is in addition to any other tax break you get from your 401(k) or IRA. For more details, see p. 164 in Chapter 6.

- **Alternative Home Energy Credit.** Put solar panels on your roof and you could earn a credit for 30% of the cost. So if you install a typical $10,000 system, you could get a credit of more than $3,000. You can also get a 30% credit for installing a small wind turbine on your property.

- **Hybrid Car Credits.** If you're a supporter of all things green or just want to reduce your high gas costs (who doesn't?), you may have taken the plunge and bought an alternative fuel vehicle, or hybrid—and you're due a tax credit for it. The dollar amount varies depending on the type of car. To find out more, check out www.fueleconomy.gov or search www.irs.gov for "hybrid cars."

TEN TAX MOVES THAT COULD SAVE YOU MONEY

Here are some additional ideas that might work for you:

1. **Bunch your deductions into one year.** If you don't have enough deductible expenses to make it worth your while to itemize this year or if you don't meet the minimums for certain deductions, take the standard deduction now and put off additional deductible expenditures until next year. For example, make your charitable contributions next January rather than this December.

2. **See if you can deduct your moving costs.** If you relocated to a new place for a full-time job, you may be able to deduct the cost of your move, including transportation, packing, and shipping costs. You don't have to itemize in order to get this deduction. But rules governing who gets this deduction are tricky, so read the following description slowly. The distance between your *new job* and your *old house* must be at least 50 miles more than the distance between your *old job* and your *old house.* (I know. It's outrageously complicated.) You must also stay in your new job at least 39 weeks. (If you take this deduction and do not stay in your new job at least 39 weeks, you either have to go back and file an amended return for that year or report the tax savings from that deduction as "other income" the next year.) Special rules apply if you're self-employed. If you recently graduated and didn't have a job at school, your moving expenses may be deductible if your new job is at least 50 miles from your college residence (on or off campus). You'll need to fill out and attach Form 3903 to your tax return to deduct these costs. For a specific explanation of eligibility, go to www.irs.gov and consult *Moving Expenses,* IRS Publication 521.

3. **Figure out if you'd save money by filing jointly or separately.** If you work and your spouse doesn't, it generally pays to file a joint return. Of course, there are few young married couples who fit this description. If you and your spouse both work, you should figure your tax on both a joint return and on separate married returns to see which way saves you money. (Sorry, but it could save you a lot of money.) Filing separate married returns may make sense if you have many deductible expenses that are subject to an "adjusted gross income threshold." Say you and your spouse each earns about the same amount of money but you have exceptionally high medical bills. If you file a joint return, your medical bills would have to exceed 7.5% of your *combined* adjusted gross income in order to be deductible. If you file separately, you can deduct medical costs that exceed 7.5% of your *own* adjusted gross income (about half the combined income, so you get to deduct more). It may also make sense for you to file your state return separately, so try filling it out both ways. And make sure to do this carefully. You may not be able to qualify for some tax breaks if you file separately.

4. **Check your withholding.** You filled out a W-4 when you started your job. Changes in your personal life, as well as changes in the tax law, may result in your having too little or too much tax withheld from your paycheck. If you get married, buy a home, have a baby, or experience any other major financial life change, you should reevaluate your withholding. Contact your human resources or employee benefits office to do this.

    If you receive a big refund from the IRS, you should probably increase the number of withholding allowances you claim. Although receiving a cash windfall from the IRS feels great, it isn't a smart financial move. It means you've been lending money to the IRS that could have been in an account earning interest for *you*. A refund occurs after you've given the IRS too much money during the year. The problem is, the IRS doesn't pay you interest for the additional money withheld from your paycheck during the year. And although some people say that over-withholding is a good "forced savings program," I don't agree. You're better off withholding the right amount and funneling small amounts of cash into an automatic savings program throughout the year. (See Chapter 2 for details.) That way you get forced savings plus earnings.

There are other ways that adjusting your withhold-ing can help you. If you just graduated from college, for instance, and you'll be working for less than 12 months this calendar year, request a special withholding method known as a part-year option. Then your employer will calculate your withholding based on the number of months you actually earn money this year, rather than basing the withholding on your annual salary. This will prevent overwithholding.

A warning: Don't claim more allowances than you deserve. This will result in your employer's withhold-ing too little tax during the year and you owing money at tax time. You're required to pay at least 90% of the tax you owe incrementally—as in over the course of the year. If you take too many allowances and pay less than 90%, you might be hit with a penalty and charged inter-est on the money you owe. Plus, of course, you'll need to come up with that IRS money when you file. At high income levels you may have to pay more than 100% of your previous year's payments. (Geez.)

5.   **Take advantage of state and local deductions.** Read your state's and your town's tax instructions carefully. Some states, including Alabama and Louisiana, allow you to deduct some of your federal income tax on your state return. For a full list, go to www.taxfoundation.org/tax data. Some states allow you to deduct the license fees for your car. And most states give a tax break to homeown-ers who paid local property taxes. (This is in addition to the federal tax break you get on property taxes.)

6. **Consider taxes when you invest.** If your tax rate is 25% or higher, look into investments that offer some tax advantages, such as tax-free money market funds. While it doesn't make sense to choose an investment solely for the tax break, it's a factor to consider. (See Chapter 5 for a simple formula that will help you determine whether tax-free investments are right for you.)

7. **Take advantage of tax-favored employee benefits.** If you work for a company that offers you the chance to use a Flexible Spending Account (FSA) to pay for child care or for medical expenses that aren't covered by your insurance, use it. Same thing with Health Savings Accounts (HSAs), which cover out-of-pocket medical expenses. (For details on both types of account, see Chapter 8). And, of course, contribute the maximum you can to your 401(k).

8. **If you're a self-employed performer, see if you're eligible for a special tax break.** Whether you itemize deductions or not, you may get your first big break on your tax form. That's because you're allowed to deduct business-related expenses (the cost of acting classes, headshots, costumes, etc.) if your AGI is $16,000 or less before this deduction. The rules about who can deduct these expenses are complex, so check the details at www.irs.gov; go to *Travel, Entertainment, Gift, and Car Expenses*, Publication 463.

9. **Consider refinancing high-rate credit card debt with a home equity loan.** The interest you pay on a home equity loan up to $100,000 is deductible. The interest you pay on credit cards is not. Keep in mind, though, that home equity loans come with risk—the collateral is your house. What's more, don't get into the trap of getting a home equity loan to live beyond your means. (For details, go to Chapter 3). If you are truly disciplined you can do this, but borrow only what you owe on your cards and pay it back as quickly as possible.

10. **You may want to consider taxes before you choose your wedding date.** Okay, call me unromantic. But if you both have fairly high incomes, the two of you might save hundreds of dollars if you marry in January rather than December. That's because you may owe more in taxes by filing a joint return than by filing two single returns. The general rule is that if you and your betrothed earn about the same income, you will probably save money by marrying after the first of the year. If one of you earns much more than the other, it's generally better to get married before the end of the year and file jointly.

The fact that married people sometimes pay more tax than singles is known as the "marriage penalty." Congress has been promising to abolish it for years. In fact, by the time you file your taxes this year the marriage penalty may no longer exist—in which case you should feel free to plan your wedding whenever you want!

DEDUCTIONS FOR THE SELF-EMPLOYED

If you work for yourself—that includes anyone who has his or her own company or who makes a living as a freelancer—you have certain responsibilities and are eligible for some special deductions.

If you're self-employed, the companies you do contract or freelance work for probably do not withhold taxes from their payments to you. But you can't simply wait until the end of the year to pay the IRS. Instead, you probably will have to pay income tax quarterly. Consult IRS Publication 505, *Tax Withholding and Estimated Tax*. You must also be sure to pay enough self-employment tax. For details, go to www.irs.gov and search for Self-Employment Tax, Topic 554. Even if you're desperately afraid of tax-related reading, get hold of these booklets and attempt to read them. After reviewing them, if you still find it difficult to determine your estimated quarterly tax or if you're unsure whether you need to pay self-employment tax at all, seek the help of a tax preparer. (For tips on finding one, see p. 296.)

As a self-employed person, you're eligible for many additional deductions. You can deduct half the Social Security and Medicare taxes you pay, for example. In 2009 you are also allowed to deduct all of your medical insurance premiums. You can deduct business travel expenses, whether or not they exceed 2% of your adjusted gross income. And you may be able to deduct the cost of office supplies and equipment. Get the *Tax Guide for Small Business,* Publication 334, from the IRS at www.irs.gov.

You might even be able to deduct your *home* office expenses. Keep in mind, though, that the IRS has very strict rules regarding home offices. You must use the space that you designate as your home office exclusively for business and on a regular basis. If your desk is in your living room, for example, you will have trouble proving that you use that portion of your home exclusively for work. Consult a tax guide or preparer. Also, get a copy of *Business Use of Your Home,* Publication 587, from the IRS.

As a self-employed person, one of your smartest tax (and savings) moves is to open an IRA. But the most you can contribute to an IRA is $5,000 each year. If you have more money to put aside, consider contributing to a special type of IRA known as a Simplified Employee Pension (SEP-IRA) plan. The rules are laid out on the IRS website (www.irs.gov) in Publication 590, *Individual Retirement Arrangements,* and Publication 560, *Retirement Plans for Small Business.* (For details on IRAs, SEPs, and SIMPLE IRAs, see Chapter 6.)

GETTING YOUR TAX LIFE IN ORDER

Probably the most daunting part of the tax process is getting your paperwork in order. This section offers a rundown of the various tax forms. It also includes a checklist to help you avoid drowning in paper.

FIGURE 9-2

WHAT, ME ITEMIZE?

A lot of young people think they don't earn enough to itemize. But consider the case of Jennifer, who recently left her job at a small architecture firm in Denver to work for a design company in New York City. (Moving costs: $1,400.) Her salary is $38,000, and she rents a studio apartment. She just bought a computer ($2,000) and a fax machine ($80) so she can do more work at home; her boss told her to buy them so that he could fax her work from his summer house, but he didn't pay for it. Jennifer uses the computer and fax exclusively for work. Before moving, she donated a couch, a dresser, and a bed to the Salvation Army. She also donated three shopping bags full of old clothes. (Total value of her donations: $2,000.) She paid out $2,000 in interest on her student loans in the past year. To see why it makes sense for her to itemize her deductions on the 1040 rather than take the standard deduction on the 1040A or EZ, take a look at the table below.

	1040EZ	1040A	1040
Total Income	$38,000	$38,000	$38,000
(minus) Student loan interest payments	0	2,000	2,000
(minus) Moving expenses	0	0	1,400
ADJUSTED GROSS INCOME (AGI)	38,000	36,000	34,600
Personal exemption	3,650	3,650	3,650
Charitable contributions	0	0	2,000
State and local taxes	0	0	3,129
Miscellaneous and business expenses*	0	0	1,388
Other itemized expenses	0	0	0
Total itemized deductions or standard deduction (whichever is greater)	5,700	5,700	6,517
EXEMPTION PLUS DEDUCTIONS	9,350	9,350	10,167
TAXABLE INCOME (AGI minus personal exemption and deductions)	28,650	26,650	24,433
FEDERAL TAX OWED	3,880	3,580	3,264

* Here's how you get $1,388 in miscellaneous and business expenses in the 1040 column. First, you calculate that 2% of Jennifer's AGI ($34,600) is $692. Then you subtract that amount from the $2,080 ($2,000 for the computer and $80 for the fax machine) in total miscellaneous and business expenses.

A Rundown of the Tax Forms

The easiest way to access tax forms is online, at www.irs.gov. Here are the basic forms you'll have to choose from:

- **1040EZ.** The IRS's 1040EZ is so named because it's the easiest to fill out. It's generally for single people, or couples filing jointly, with taxable income less than $100,000. To use this form, you must also earn less than $1,500 in taxable interest (from investments or savings accounts). You can't itemize your deductions on the EZ; it's meant for people who are best off with the standard deduction. Two good reasons *not* to use the EZ: You can't deduct your student loan interest payments or your contribution to a deductible IRA.

- **1040A.** This form is almost as simple as the EZ form. To use it, your total taxable income must be less than $100,000, but your taxable interest and dividends can be more than $1,500. This form does not allow you to itemize, but it does permit you to claim tax credits and take deductions for deductible IRA contributions and student loan interest payments.

- **1040.** This form is more complicated, but it's the one to use if you think the value of your itemized deductions is larger than the standard deduction. Also, if your income is $100,000 or more (or you receive certain types of income like rent or capital gains), you'll be *required* to fill out the 1040. In order to itemize on the 1040, you must fill out an additional form called Schedule A, which will help you figure out the value of your itemized deductions. (For an example of how filling out the 1040 and itemizing can work to your advantage, see Figure 9–2.)

Of course, you'll probably also need to file your state and local tax forms by April 15. You can download them from www.taxsites .com, which features links to all the state tax forms you may need.

Paperwork: What to Keep and What to Shred

Good record keeping is important when it comes to filing your taxes. If you use a tax preparer and he or she has to spend hours sifting through shoe boxes full of your receipts and documents, you may have to make more than one appointment, and you'll be charged extra. By keeping neat, accurate records, you will save time and money. Below are the names of tax-related file folders you should set up.

- **Tax Returns: 2009, 2010, 2011, etc.** Each year add a new folder to hold your most important tax documents, including income statements from your employers (W-2s) and a copy of your tax return (after it's filed, of course). Save each year's folder for at least at least three years; if you're audited, the IRS can request up to three years' worth of your tax records. (If you've underreported your income by 25% or more, the IRS can ask for returns from six years back. And if you've committed fraud, there's no time limit.) After three years, throw out your supporting paperwork, but hold on to a copy of the return (paper or electronic), your attached W-2s and 1099s, and any other IRS forms you filed. If you've sent money to the IRS, keep the canceled check (or a copy of it) or the bank statement showing a debit card payment. You want to be able to prove that payment down the line if there's ever a mixup and the IRS thinks you didn't file for a particular year.

- **Business-Related Expenses (Unreimbursed).** Save appropriate credit card receipts, entertainment and meal receipts, and receipts for tolls, taxis, parking, gas, car maintenance, tips, union dues, and subscriptions. (For more on what to save and how to save it, see Chapter 2.) If you plan to deduct the cost of a computer, BlackBerry, or cell phone, in addition to your receipts keep records that detail when you use the equipment for work and when you use it for leisure activity. If you're self-employed, save all receipts from business-related travel. Also, keep a detailed spending diary when you go on business trips, and file it in this folder.

- **Charitable Contributions.** Keep lists of property you've donated and receipts from organizations you contribute to. If you contribute money, save receipts from the charity as well and the canceled checks or the relevant pages from your bank or credit card statement.

- **Child Care/Dependent Care Expenses.** Hold on to documents indicating the dates and amounts of various fees you paid to an individual or a center to take care of your child or other dependent so you could work or look for work. (The money you pay to a sitter to watch your child so you can go to a movie is not deductible.) Also, jot down and save a list of the cost of meals and lodging expenses paid to a child care worker who lives in your home. To be able to claim the child care credit, you must make sure to pay the required employment taxes—Social Security, Medicare, and unemployment—for your employee. Keep strict records that prove these taxes were paid.

- **Home Improvements.** A home improvement, also known as a **capital improvement,** is a renovation that increases your home's value. These are not relevant for renters. But if you own a home, save all receipts related to home improvements. Although you can't deduct these expenses now, you can add them to the original purchase price of your home when you're ready to sell; this reduces the reported gain you get (selling price minus the amount you paid for the house) and therefore the amount of tax you pay on the sale. Routine repairs like painting don't count, but adding a room, putting on a new roof, installing a new toilet, paneling walls, or retiling a floor do.

  If you sell your home and make a profit, you currently don't have to pay tax on that profit if it's less than $250,000 if you're single or $500,000 if you're married and filing jointly. You can qualify for this tax break as long as the home has been your principal residence for at least two of the previous five years. Some people believe that these high exemptions mean you no longer have to keep a file on your home improvements, since few couples will see a profit of more than $500,000 on the sale of their homes. But since there's no telling how these laws will hold up in the future, I say keep the file. There's absolutely no downside to having a few extra documents in your financial folders, just in case. (For details go to www.irs.gov and consult Publication 530, *Tax Information for First-Time Homeowners*, or Publication 523, *Selling your Home*.)

- **Home (Purchase).** Keep the closing statement and any other paperwork related to the purchase of your home. You may need these documents for tax purposes when you sell your home.

- **Individual Retirement Accounts.** Keep papers that indicate when your IRA contributions were made, the amount you invested, the date you opened the IRA, and the source of any money you rolled over from an employer retirement plan into your IRA. This documentation will be useful when you withdraw the money upon retirement. It's especially important to hold on to copies of IRS Form 8606, which you'll need to file each year if you make nondeductible contributions to a traditional IRA. When you withdraw money from a nondeductible traditional IRA, you won't be taxed on the money you contributed but only on the earnings. Also, hold on to a copy of the special form (Form 5329) that you'll need to file if you make a penalty-free withdrawal from your IRA, as described in Chapter 6.

- **Medical Expenses (Unreimbursed).** If you pay any medical costs that your health insurance doesn't reimburse you for, keep the receipts. (For that matter, if you pay all or part of the premiums on your health insurance, keep track of those expenses as well.) If at the end of the year these expenses exceed 7.5% of your adjusted gross income, you can deduct the portion that's over this threshold.

- **Miscellaneous Deductions.** This catch-all folder should include receipts for all possible deductions, including financial publications, tax preparation, job search activities, and certain education expenses. Go through it at the end of the year to determine what is and what may not actually be deductible.

- **Mortgage Interest Payments.** If you own a home, keep your 1098 form in this folder. A 1098 is an annual statement from your lender indicating how much interest and principal you paid on your mortgage. It may also tell you how much property tax you paid. Co-op owners generally receive a 1098 indicating the portion of the interest they paid on the building's mortgage. Keep your private mortgage insurance (PMI) paperwork in this file as well. You may be able to deduct the premiums as though they were mortgage interest.

- **Mutual Funds.** Many funds provide a year-end statement that indicates how many shares you bought and sold that year (including purchases you made through a reinvestment plan) and the price of those shares. Hold on to these statements. You'll be taxed on any gain you made from selling shares, and you'll get a tax break on losses. You'll need the statements to figure out what your gain (or loss) was. There are several different methods you can use to calculate your gain—and some are more beneficial than others. For details that will help you figure out which method would be best for you, go to www.irs.gov and refer to Publication 564, *Mutual Fund Distributions*. If your fund doesn't send you a comprehensive statement of your transactions, call and request one.

- **Property and Real Estate Tax.** The monthly mortgage payment you make to your lender probably includes your property taxes. Lenders typically forward the tax to your local taxing authority. At the end of the year, you'll receive a statement from your lender about the amount of property tax you paid for the year. These payments are deductible, so hold on to these statements.

- **Police Reports, Insurance Claims.** With any luck, you won't need this file. But if you've been burglarized or had some identity theft problems (see p. 74), save these documents. If you suffered major losses, you may be able to deduct the value of uninsured items.

- **Stocks and Bonds.** If you own individual stocks and bonds, keep the statements you get from the brokerage firm or the company that issued them. Also hang on to any stock or bond certificates, preferably in a bank safety deposit box.

DO YOU NEED A TAX PREPARER?

One of the best ways to learn about your financial life is to prepare your own tax return. If you've had your taxes prepared professionally in the past, use the records from that year to help guide you. If you've never done your own taxes, you may be surprised to learn how easy it is—especially if you use a good tax book or software package. But if you're dead set against doing it yourself, at least take the time to find a decent preparer.

If You Don't Use a Preparer

The general instruction book that the IRS produces is well written and easy to understand. You can download Publication 17, *Your Federal Income Tax*, from the IRS website (www.irs.gov). But because it's also 300 pages and free in the mail, it's cheaper to call 800-TAX-FORM and ask for a printed copy.

If you intend to itemize deductions, you should also invest in one of the big fat tax guides available in any bookstore. Some good ones are *J.K. Lasser's Your Income Tax*, *Taxes for Dummies*, and

RAPID RIP-OFFS

When David, a teacher in New York City, walked into a local tax preparation office, he had a suspicion he might qualify for a refund that year. He was right: The IRS owed him almost $500. His tax preparer told him that he could file electronically and get his refund in a few weeks—or sign up for a special "rapid refund" program that would get his refund to him almost immediately. David jumped at the chance to get the money right away. But when his refund check arrived a few days later, he found that he had been charged $35 for the extra speed.

What David didn't understand is that he had actually signed up for a **refund anticipation loan**. Many tax preparers offer these products to customers who are eager to get their refunds as quickly as possible. Basically, the preparer lends the customer the amount of his or her refund, charging an outrageous fee for the service (the $35 that David paid works out to an annual interest rate of more than 200%) and then pocketing the actual refund when it arrives from the IRS.

Refund anticipation loans are even less beneficial now that electronic filing and direct deposit make it possible to get your refund in ten days. If you need money right away, just about any other way of getting it—even cash advances on your credit card—will be cheaper.

The Ernst & Young Tax Guide. Make sure you buy the correct book for the current year; you would use the 2011 guides to fill out your 2010 taxes. These books usually cost around $15 and are well worth the expense—even if you use computer software to file online, the books provide useful tax planning tips.

If you decide to file your own taxes online, go to the "Paper-Free Filing" box on p. 266.

If You Use a Preparer

The most obvious choices are either big-name chains such as H&R Block or the smaller mom-and-pop shops in your neighborhood. The advantage of these services is that they're usually inexpensive. If you're sure you aren't eligible for many deductions and that the standard deduction is for you, a storefront preparer is fine. Keep in mind that the level of knowledge can vary dramatically. Look for a tax preparation business that operates year-round rather than one that's open just a few months a year. Ask friends and family members to recommend specific preparers. Most chain preparers allow you to request a specific person.

If you have a somewhat more complicated return (for example, you're self-employed or you've received a large inheritance), you may want to find a preparer with more chops. One of the top credentials is **CPA**, which stands for **certified public accountant**. CPAs have to meet the toughest requirements to get licensed; they also can be expensive. Another, usually cheaper option, is an **enrolled agent**; the title refers to any preparer who has worked for the IRS as an auditor or in some similar job for five years or who has passed a difficult two-day exam. At the very least, find a preparer with a minimum of three years' experience filing returns. **Tax attorneys** are typically the most expensive alternative and are necessary only if you're in serious trouble with the IRS.

Be sure to ask what the preparer charges; there may be different rates for different preparers at the same company. You can often find an enrolled agent at a chain preparer like H&R Block; if possible, ask to work with one. Preparers usually file your return electronically, so if you're due a refund you will get it faster than you would if you mailed in your return.

Finally, no matter who you have fill out your forms, look over the forms carefully. *You* are responsible for making sure all the information on your return is true and correct. Take the time to really read it before you sign and submit it.

FINANCIAL CRAMMING

- Figure out your marginal tax bracket. This is important to know. See Figure 9–1.

- Fill out your tax forms as soon as possible, but not too soon. If you're owed a refund, file right away; the quicker you mail in your forms, the faster you'll get your check. If you owe money to the IRS, file in early April so you can hang on to your cash as long as possible.

- If you're expecting a refund, file electronically and sign up to have your refund deposited directly into your bank account. Your money will arrive within ten days rather than the six to eight weeks it takes if you file by mail.

- If you received a big refund from the IRS, fill out a new W-4 form to adjust your withholding. Since the IRS doesn't pay you interest on the money you overpay during the year, you're better off keeping this money in a bank account or money market fund.

- If you owe the IRS money but you can't afford to pay, send in your return along with whatever payment you can afford by April 15 anyway and set up an installment plan. You'll have to pay a penalty, but it won't be as stiff as the penalty for late filing.

- Take full advantage of the tax credits available to you if you have children or educational expenses, as described on pp. 279–81. They are money in your pocket.

- Look at the list of deductions beginning on p. 273. If you're eligible for some of them, fill out the 1040 form to see if itemizing saves you money. And be aware that you can take some deductions—like those for deductible IRA contributions or student loan interest payments—whether you itemize or not.

- If you're self-employed, you're not supposed to wait until the end of the year to pay Uncle Sam. You may be required to pay your taxes quarterly (every three months) or you could be penalized. For details, read Self-Employment Tax, Topic 554, available at www.irs.gov.

MAKING THE MOST OF MILITARY BENEFITS

Know What You Deserve
if You Serve

I F YOU ARE one of the millions of young people who have served in the military, National Guard, or reserves in the last few years, you've earned some benefits not available to most people. Below is a rundown, and when you're ready to get more details on the programs, go to the National Military Family Association (www.nmfa.org).

- **Student loan forgiveness.** If you went to an accredited college before enlisting, the military will pay off $1,500 of your unpaid federal student loans or a third of the amount you owe (whichever is greater) for every year of active duty, up to a maximum of $65,000 for the Army and Navy and a max of $10,000 for the Air Force. This includes all PLUS, Perkins, and Stafford loans. So if you owe $10,000 and served for two years, the military will cover $6,667. Make sure you take advantage of this if you're eligible. You may also qualify for loan forgiveness if you were in the National Guard or the Reserves. To get more information, go to www.finaid.org/military.

- **Financial help if you go back to school.** According to the
  G.I. Bill from 2008 (also known as the Post-9/11 G.I. Bill),
  the government is committed to paying some or all of your
  college costs for four academic years, including tuition and
  fees, housing, books, and even (possibly) a moving allowance. After 90 consecutive days of active post-2001 duty in
  the armed services, National Guard, or Reserves, the government will pick up 40% of the cost of the most expensive public undergraduate school in your state. The benefits
  scale up the longer you serve; after three years of active duty
  (or if you get a disability discharge), that same bachelor's
  degree is effectively *free*.

  There are limitations. The program won't pick up all the
  bills if you're getting an advanced degree or going to a school
  that is more expensive than any public college in your state.
  Some private schools will give you a discount to bring their
  tuition in line with what the government will pay, but you'll
  still probably have to pay out of pocket. Furthermore, this
  version of the G.I. Bill usually won't pay for correspondence
  courses, on-the-job training programs, flight school, appren-
  ticeships, or other nonacademic programs.

  One note: If you were in the service before 2009, you
  may have signed up for the previous version of the G.I. Bill
  (known as the **Montgomery G.I. Bill**), which operated more
  like a savings plan. If you've already started contributing, you
  have the option to either stay in this plan or convert to the
  new education benefits program described above. It may or
  may not be a better option for you, so check www.gibill2008
  .org for all the pros and cons of each version of the G.I. Bill.

- **Additional education dollars.** At enlistment, you may be offered additional money to pay for school down the road if
  your recruiter is especially impressed with your skills. This
  is known as a "college fund," a "kicker," or a "supplemen-
  tal benefit," but it boils down to a lump sum (the amount
  varies) that the government will add to your other G.I. Bill
  benefits for paying future education costs. Before you enlist
  (or reenlist), try to negotiate a better deal.

- **A no-down-payment mortgage.** If you've served 24 months of active duty and are now home (or you're currently on active duty and have been for at least 6 months), you can apply to have the Veterans Administration *guarantee* your home loan. You'll still have to apply for a normal mortgage with a bank or other lender, but because of the guarantee, your mortgage officer will waive all or part of the normal down payment requirement. (See p. 185 for details.) National Guard and Reservists qualify for this benefit after six years of service. Unfortunately, with no down payment you'll end up paying more interest, so unless you have a very specific reason to want to buy a home right away, you should probably wait and try to build up a down payment of at least 10%.

- **Help in preventing foreclosure.** Lenders are not allowed to foreclose on your home for nine months after you return from duty. If you've been injured and cannot work, they may also not be able to take your home from you if you haven't yet received your disability money and need it to pay your mortgage. For help, try the nonprofit Operation Homefront (www.operationhomefront.net).

- **Inexpensive health care.** Those currently in the military and their immediate families can get free medical treatment on the base, or can pay a small annual premium (up to $150 for individual coverage or $300 for families) for other health plans that allow visits to civilian doctors. Those who've left the military can enroll in the VA health care system (although noncombat injuries will have low priority).

- **Special sources of insurance.** Active duty and former military personnel and their immediate families can purchase home and auto insurance through USAA (www.usaa.com) or Armed Forces Insurance (www.afi.org).

- **Tax-favored retirement savings.** You can voluntarily contribute to the Thrift Savings Program, which basically works like a 401(k) for civilian and military federal employees—

there's a $16,500 maximum contribution per year. Unfortunately, the military doesn't offer any kind of matching program. (For that reason, you may be better off with a Roth IRA, so see Chapter 6.) Also, reservists called to active duty can take early distributions from their IRAs or 401(k)s without paying the 10% penalty everyone else must pay, although they do have to pay any tax owed.

- **Simpler bankruptcy rules.** National Guard members and reservists who served at least 90 days in Iraq or Afghanistan can declare bankruptcy even if they earn more than the average salary in their home state. This is a special exemption to the normal bankruptcy rules (see p. 80). Of course, bankruptcy is never a good option; it will wreck your credit report and make it harder for you to get low-rate auto loans and home loans in the future. Still, if it's your only option, it will be easier for you than someone who hasn't been in the military. (For more details on bankruptcy, see p. 80.)

- **Family leave.** If you have a serious duty-related injury, members of your immediate family can take up to 26 weeks off in a 12-month period to care for you. Unfortunately, they will not be paid for that time.

- **A pension, if you stay twenty years.** All military personnel who serve at least twenty years can draw **retirement pay**. This translates into a pension of 50% to 75% of your preretirement working income and is adjusted for inflation thereafter. (Unfortunately, if you leave before the twenty years is up, you don't get any pension at all.)

- **Provide for your heirs.** The sad but true reality of military life is that people die. The immediate family of active duty personnel killed in the line of duty receives $100,000 tax-free. If you're in active service, you're eligible to buy additional disability and life coverage at a relatively low cost through the government or USAA (www.usaa.com).

FURTHER READING

If you've read through this entire tome, congratulations! You have all the basic information you need to have a prosperous financial life. If you are a glutton for punishment, below are some very selective recommendations. These are the books I would tell my friends to read if they wanted to know more about various topics. I have also included magazines, web pages, and pamphlets that may interest you. Some of the publications listed here are mentioned in the individual chapters, while others are not.

BOOKS

Investing

Christopher L. Jones. *The Intelligent Portfolio: Practical Wisdom on Personal Investing from Financial Engines.* Hoboken: Wiley, 2008. Sound advice from a top portfolio guru.

Burton G. Malkiel. *A Random Walk Down Wall Street.* New York: W.W. Norton, 2007. This updated classic is a must-read for anyone who wants to lean more about investing.

———. *The Random Walk Guide to Investing.* New York: W.W. Norton, 2007. Provides the tools for individual investors to apply the "random walk" philosophy to their own portfolios.

David F. Swenson. *Unconventional Success: A Fundamental Approach to Personal Investment.* New York: Free Press, 2005. Yale University's chief investment officer set out to tell investors how they could beat the market, only to conclude that they can't. Heavy reading, but required if you really want to delve into this topic and get the inside scoop.

Andrew Tobias. *The Only Investment Guide You'll Ever Need*. San Diego: Harvest Books, 2005. An excellent (and witty) overview of key investment concepts.

Insurance

Jack Hungelmann. *Insurance for Dummies*. Hoboken: Wiley, 2001. A good one-stop guide to all the major areas of insurance, how to shop for them, and what to watch out for.

Lee and Carla Rowley. *Cheap Insurance for Your Home, Automobile, Health & Life: How to Save Thousands While Getting Good Coverage*. Ocala: Atlantic Publishing, 2008. Probably the best one-stop guide to all the major areas of insurance out there at the moment.

Taxes

The following three books are excellent tax guides. Make sure to get the most current edition!

Peter W. Bernstein, ed. *The Ernst & Young Tax Guide*. New York: Vanguard Press, 2007.

The J.K. Lasser Institute. *J.K. Lasser's Your Income Tax*. Hoboken: Wiley, 2007.

Eric Tyson, Margaret Munro, and David J. Silverman. *Taxes for Dummies*. Foster City: IDG Books, 2007.

General Personal Finance

Jane Bryant Quinn. *Making the Most of Your Money: Smart Ways to Create Wealth and Plan Your Finances in the '90s*. New York: Simon & Schuster, 1997. Although its 900-plus pages may be a bit overwhelming, and some of it will be irrelevant to people in their twenties and thirties, this encyclopedic guide is the best.

Miscellaneous

American Bar Association. *The American Bar Association Guide to Credit & Bankruptcy*. New York: Random House Reference, 2006.

Denis Clifford. *Nolo's Simple Will Book*. Berkeley: Nolo Press, 2007. A good resource if you're thinking of writing a will.

Kalman Chany with Geoff Martz. *Paying for College Without Going Broke*. New York: Random House/Princeton Review, 2008. A comprehensive primer on college financing issues.

PERSONAL FINANCE MAGAZINES

Kiplinger's
Money
SmartMoney

BLOGS AND MESSAGE BOARDS

Get Rich Slowly. Created by a self-described "average guy" who took control of his finances and worked his way out of debt, this site now provides smart coverage on a variety of money topics. (www.getrichslowly.org)

The Simple Dollar. Another motivational blog created by a young guy who dug himself out of debt and now wants to help other people do the same. (www.thesimpledollar.com)

I Will Teach You to Be Rich. A blog with tips about banking, saving, and investing. (www.iwillteachyoutoberich.com)

Wesabe.com. One of the biggest personal finance message boards out there, this site gives you a chance to share tips and information with over 100,000 other people.

FREE PAMPHLETS AND COMPANY PUBLICATIONS

All of these are available online; just search for the document's title on the relevant website.

Debt

Before You File for Personal Bankruptcy: Information About Credit Counseling and Debtor Education, available from the Bureau of Consumer Protection (www.ftc.gov).

Building a Better Credit Report, available from the Bureau of Consumer Protection (www.ftc.gov).

Choosing a Credit Card: The Deal Is in the Disclosures, available from the Bureau of Consumer Protection (www.ftc.gov).

Consumer Handbook to Credit Protection Laws, available from the Bureau of Consumer Protection (www.ftc.gov).

Credit Repair: Self-Help May Be Best, available from the Bureau of Consumer Protection (www.ftc.gov).

How to Dispute Credit Report Errors, available from the Bureau of Consumer Protection (www.ftc.gov).

Keys to Vehicle Leasing, available from the Federal Reserve (www.federalreserve.gov/pubs/leasing).

Understanding Credit Reports and Scores, available from Fair Isaac Corp. (www.myfico.com).

Insurance

Consumer's Guide to Auto Insurance, available from the National Association of Insurance Commissioners (www.naic.org).
Consumer's Guide to Home Insurance, available from the National Association of Insurance Commissioners (www.naic.org).
Guide to Individual Disability Insurance, available from America's Health Plans (www.ahip.org).
Questions and Answers about Health Insurance, available from America's Health Plans (www.ahip.org).

Investing

Mutual Fund Investing: What to Consider When Choosing Your Mutual Funds, available from WISER, the Women's Institute for a Secure Retirement (www.wiserwomen.org).

Mortgages

Buying a Home, available online from the Department of Housing and Urban Development (www.hud.gov/buying).
Mortgage Servicing, available from the Bureau of Consumer Protection (www.ftc.gov).
What's the Point of Points?, available from HSH Associates (www.hsh.com/pointofpoints.html).

Retirement

Maximizing Your Company Savings Plan, available from the Employee Benefit Research Institute (www.choosetosave.com).
Taking the Mystery Out of Retirement Planning and *What You Should Know About Your Retirement Plan*, both available from the Pension and Welfare Benefits Administration (www.dol.gov/dol/pwba).

Taxes

Guide to Free Tax Services, available from the Internal Revenue Service (www.irs.gov).
Your Federal Income Tax, Publication 17, available from the Internal Revenue Service (www.irs.gov).

SPECIAL ACKNOWLEDGMENTS

EVERY VERSION OF *Get a Financial Life* has been an enormous team effort. Beginning on p. 311, I've listed nearly 700 sources to whom I turned for expertise in both the original and current editions of the book. This special section, however, acknowledges those people who have made contributions above and beyond the call of duty.

First, the financial experts who have given generously of their time in helping me prepare all three versions of *Get a Financial Life*. Special thanks go to investment advisors Lew and Karen Altfest; student loan advisor and president of Campus Consultants Kalman Chany; fee-only insurance consultant Glenn Daily; professor of bank management at the University of Virginia Richard DeMong; Credit.com credit advisor Gerri Detweiler; communications consultant of the Consumer Bankers Association Fritz Elmendorf; vice president at HSH Associates Keith Gumbinger; executive director of the Women's Institute for a Secure Retirement Cindy Hounsell; life insurance actuary with the Consumer Federation of America James Hunt; director of consumer affairs at the Insurance Information Institute Jeanne Salvatore; and president of CNW Marketing Research Art Spinella.

I also owe a debt of gratitude to the following people, whose expertise was invaluable in putting together this new edition of the book: associate director for external relations at the Center for Retirement Research Andrew Eschtruth; consumer advocate buyer's agent of CarQ.com Linda Lee Goldberg; publisher of FinAid.org and director of advanced projects at FastWeb.com Mark Kantrowitz; senior financial analyst of Bankrate.com Greg McBride; senior public affairs specialist at the National Association of Realtors Walter Molony; loan officer at Stratis Financial Marty O'Malley; consumer services manager at Consumer Action Joseph Ridout; retirement expert and fellow of the Employee Benefit Research Institute Jack VanDerhei; public affairs manager of Fair Isaac Corp. Craig Watts; vice president of financial literacy at Money Management International Catherine Williams; financial planner Rolf Winch; and fee-only insurance advisor Scott Witt.

And I greatly appreciate the assistance given by these experts at various earlier stages of writing *Get a Financial Life*: Kent Allison, Camilla Altamura, Roy Assad, John Battaglia, David Berson, Jack Bonné, Raschelle Burton, Ed Chang, Karen Christie, Steven Enright, Wilson Fadely, Karen Ferguson of the Pension Rights Center, Martin Fleisher, Jerry Gattegno, Sheldon Jacobs, James Johnson, Stuart Kessler, L. Harold Levinson, Gail Liberman, Brian Mattes of Vanguard, Keith Maurer, Randall McCathren, credit card guru Robert McKinley, Michael Moebs, Bob Murray, Edward L. Neumann, Sharon Ridenour, Tom Ochsenschlager, Glenn Pape, Diane Rivers, Don Roberts, Martin M. Shenkman, Janice Shields, William Speciale, and Eric A. Wiening of the American Institute for Chartered Casualty Property Underwriters.

My former coworkers at *Money* were incredibly generous with their time and help when I was writing the first edition of *Get a Financial Life*. They included Caroline Donnelly, Richard Eisenberg, Judy Feldman, Carla Fried, Eric Gelman, Jordan Goodman, Kelly Smith, and Patti Straus. I would especially like to thank Gary Belsky and Walter Updegrade for their incredibly valuable feedback on the original edition. My gratitude also goes to Tyler Mathisen of CNBC and Frank Lalli, the former managing editor of *Money*, who has been a mentor to me. From *Glamour*, I'd like to thank Cindi Leive, Ellen Seidman, Noelle Howey, and Rebecca Webber.

Many friends and colleagues also offered valuable input at various stages. They include Rick Allen, Robin Alssid, Andrew Bradfield, Richard Burgheim, Larry Burke, Eileen Choi, Nicole Chong, Fran Claro, Joe Claro, Paul Cohen, Jon Cowan, Adam Feldman,

Elizabeth Fenner, Anne Fentress, James Gates, Lynn Goldner, Glenn Hodes, Jennifer Jaeck, Jonathan Karp, Sam Kerstein, Skye Ketron, John Kildahl, Maki Kitamura, Janet Klosklo, Michelle Kosch, Steve Kotsen, Kathy Landau, Michael Kantor, Harold Kobliner, Kenneth Kobliner, Miriam Diamond Kobliner, Perry Kobliner, Shirley Kobliner, Megan McCrudden, Carmen Morais, Vanessa O'Connell, Max Phillips, Melissa Phipps, Parker Reilly, Ruby Reilly, Mark Safire, William Safire, Rebecca Scott, Adam Benjamin Shaw, Jacob Samuel Shaw, Rebecca Belle Shaw, Jonah Sacks, Anne Morgan Spalter, Michael Spalter, Lisa Turvey, David Witt, and Dave Zinczenko.

I would also like to single out Jessica Ashbrook, Lisa Barron, Scott Martin, and Kerry Shaw, who have put in literally hundreds of hours helping me ensure that every data point in the new edition has been meticulously researched, checked, and rechecked. I am also especially indebted to Danielle Claro, whose insight, humor, and remarkable editing skills were, and continue to be, a godsend.

I owe gratitude to Simon & Schuster, notably to Sarah Pinckney Whitmire (my editor on the original version with Bob Asahina), Doris Cooper, the intrepid and talented Michelle Howry (my current editor), Christine Lloreda (who guided me through all three editions), Rachel Rader, Trish Todd, and Mark Gompertz. I would like to thank Gordon Kato, who believed in this book from the beginning, and Kate Lee of ICM as well as Suzanne Gluck of the William Morris Agency.

I want to thank Rebecca Belle, Adam Benjamin, and Jacob Samuel for being incredibly patient during late nights and worked weekends—and for making me laugh.

And most of all, I would like to thank my husband, David, who continues to offer complete, unwavering love and devotion. He is my inspiration.

ACKNOWLEDGMENTS

The following is a list of the hundreds of people who generously gave of their time and expertise over the years to make this book possible. If anyone has inadvertently been left out, I apologize.

INTRODUCTION

Larry Cohen, SRI International; Carmen Denavas, Census Bureau; Neal Fogg, Center for Labor Market Studies at Northeastern University; Steven Haugen, Bureau of Labor Statistics; Jeffrey Hackett, National Opinion Research Center; Stephanie Schlandt, Payment Systems; Andrew Sum, Center for Labor Market Studies at Northeastern University; David Tong, SRI International; Stephanie White, Bureau of Labor Statistics.

Chapter 2: Get a Grip on Your Financial Life

Durant Abernathy, National Foundation for Consumer Credit; Mari Adam, Adam Financial Associates, Inc.; Kent Allison, PriceWaterhouseCoopers; Mark Beal, CPA; David W. Bennett, FMC Financial Group; Debbie Bianucci, Bank Administration Institute; Kent Brunette, American Association of Retired Persons; Anthony Burke,

Internal Revenue Service; Gail Cunningham, National Foundation for Credit Counseling; Peg Downey, Money Plans; Ericka Ecker, The Spacialist; Steven Enright, Enright, Mollin, Cascio & Ramusevic; Wilson Fadely, Internal Revenue Service; Steven Haugen, Bureau of Labor Statistics; Pat Keefe, Credit Union National Association; Ross Levin, Accredited Investors; Greg McBride, Bankrate .com; Ed Mierzwinski, U.S. Public Interest Research Group (PIRG); Bill Moss, American Express Company; Glenn Pape, Ayco Company; John Pfister, Chicago Title and Trust Company; John Rogers, Bureau of Labor Statistics; Steve Sanders, Sanders Investment Advisors; Kyle Selberg, BankingMyWay.com; Ken Scott, Ken Scott Communications; William Speciale, David L. Babson & Company; Marilyn Steinmetz, Mutual Service Associates; Kristyn Stout, The Ryland Group; Jeannette Weiland, Bank Administration Institute; Stephanie White, Bureau of Labor Statistics.

Chapter 3: Dealing with Debt

John Abadie, NationsBank Corporation; Mari Adam, Adam Financial Associates; Fiona Adams, Student Loan Marketing Association (Sallie Mae); Jonathan Adkins, Debt Counselors of America; Deb Adler, New York State Credit Union League; Deborah Ankrom, Student Loan Marketing Association (Sallie Mae); Stephanie Babyak, Department of Education; Bill Banks, Chemical Bank; Sandra Baum, The College Board; Gary Beanblossom, Department of Education; Monica Beaupre, American Express Company; Ricky Beggs, Black Book; Ed Block, Automotive Lease Consultants; James A. Boyle, College Parents of America; Elaine Cafasso, Oak Brook Bank; Glenn Canner, Federal Reserve Board; Dennis Carroll, National Center for Education Statistics; Nancy Castleman, Good Advice Press; Kalman Chany, Campus Consultants; Tim Christensen, Department of Education; Karen Christie, Bankrate.com; Alex Cobos, Volkswagen of America; Larry Cohen, SRI International; Paul Combe, Knight College Resource Group; James Daly, Credit Card News; Linda Del Castillo, Student Loan Marketing Association (Sallie Mae); Dr. Richard F. DeMong, McIntire School of Commerce, University of Virginia; Gerri Detweiler, Credit.com;

Claire Diamond, AT&T Universal Card Services; Robyn Eckard, Kelley Blue Book; Rachel Edelstein, Department of Education; Liz Eischeid, TransUnion Corporation; Marc Eisenson, Good Advice Press; Fritz Elmendorf, Consumer Bankers Association; Brad Fay, Roper Organization; Susan Forman, Visa USA; Gerhard Fries, Federal Reserve Board; Jean Frohlicher, National Council of Higher Education Loan Programs; Luther Gatling, Budget & Credit Counseling Services; Jane Glickman, Department of Education; Linda Goldberg, CarQ.com; Edward Gonciarz, Goldberg, Gonciarz & Scudieri; David Graubard, Kera & Graubard; Jeffrey Green, Faulkner & Grey; Rod Griffin, Experian; Keith Gumbinger, HSH Associates; Robert Hall, Corestates Dealer Services Corporation; Charles Hart, Chart Software; Dayna Hart, General Motors Corporation; Ed Harting, Auto Lease Guide; Paul Havemann, HSH Associates; Robert Heady, Bank Rate Monitor; Evan Hendricks, Privacy Times; Stephen Henson, Kelley Blue Book; Stuart Himmelfarb, Roper Organization; Jeanne Hogarth, Federal Reserve Board; Martha Holler, Student Loan Marketing Association (Sallie Mae); Brenda Horner, Consolidated Credit Counseling Services; Wendy Huntington, Student Loan Marketing Association (Sallie Mae); Joseph Hurley, SavingforCollege.com; Edie Irons, The Project on Student Debt; Dr. Robert Johnson, Credit Research Center, Purdue University; Dr. Jim Jurinski, University of Portland; Mark Kantrowitz, FinAid.org; Mike Kidwell, Debt Counselors of America; Jacqueline King, The College Board; Dottie Kingsley, Department of Education; Ross Kleinman, Student Loan Marketing Association (Sallie Mae); Laura Knapp, The College Board; Paula Knepper, National Center for Education Statistics; Janis Lamar, TRW Information Systems & Services; Tony Langan, The Chase Manhattan Bank; Phyllis Laubacher, MasterCard International; Roberta Lazarz, Credit Union National Association; Anne Leider, Octameron Associates; Jean Lesher, American Bankers Association; Gail Liberman, Bank Rate Monitor; Lee Anne Linderman, Zions Bancorporation; Ronald S. Loshin, Bank Lease Consultants; Chris Lynn, Oak Brook Bank; John Maciarz, General Motors Corporation; Norm Magnuson, Associated Credit Bureaus; Drew Malizio, National Center for Education Statistics; Garry Marquiss, Bank One Corporation; John Marsh, Wachovia Bank of Georgia; Colleen Martin,

TransUnion; Nancy Mathis, Congressman Joseph Kennedy's Office; Randall McCathren, Bank Lease Consultants; Robert B. McKinley, RAM Research Corporation; David Melancon, Visa USA; Maria Mendler, Citibank; Ed Mierzwinski, U.S. Public Interest Research Group (PIRG); Scott Miller, Student Loan Marketing Association (Sallie Mae); Bob Murray, USA Group; Fatimah P. Nasra, Experian; Martin Neilson, Seafirst Bank; Jim Newell, Student Loan Marketing Association (Sallie Mae); Michael O'Brien, MasterCard International; Kit O'Kelly, European American Bank; Bussie Parker, Debt Counselors of America; Travis Plunkett, Consumer Federation of America; Mike Ramirez, CPA; William Redman, European American Bank; Ruth Lammert-Reeves, Georgetown University; Bruce Reid, AT&T Universal Card Services; Andrea Retsky, Congressman Joseph Kennedy's Office; Joseph Ridout, Consumer Action; Mark Rodgers, Citibank; Marcello Rojtman, Department of Education; Denise Rossitto, Student Loan Marketing Association (Sallie Mae); Stephanie Schlandt, Payment Systems; Dick Schliesmann, Wells Fargo Bank; Hans Schumann, AT&T Universal Card Services; Tom Sclafani, American Express Company; Ken Scott, Ken Scott Communications; Nick Sharkey, Ford Motor Credit Company; Tarry E. Shebesta, National Vehicle Leasing Association; Sheila Shekar, Visa USA; Lewis Siegel, Pirro, Collier, Cohen & Halpern; Jenny Smith, Oakbrook Bank; Henry Sommer, Miller, Frank & Miller; Art Spinella, CNW Marketing Research; Jennifer Spoerri, Nolo Press; Virginia Stafford, American Bankers Association; Amy Sudol, The Chase Manhattan Bank; Dr. Charlene Sullivan, Credit Research Center, Purdue University; Marcia Sullivan, Consumer Bankers Association; Terry Sullivan, General Motors Corporation; Ruth Susswein, Bankcard Holders of America; Laura Szabo-Kubitz, The Project on Student Debt; Greg Tarmin, American Express Company; David Tong, SRI International; Francine Van Nevel, Credit Union National Association; Jonathan Wahl, Edmunds, Inc.; Dr. Elizabeth Warren, Harvard Law School; Gail Wasserman, American Express Company; Craig Watts, Fair Isaac Corp.; Laura Weiss, Consumers Union; Sharlene Weldon, Bankrate.com; Dr. Jay Westbrook, University of Texas at Austin Law School; Lance Wilcox, J.D. Power & Associates; Catherine Williams, Money Management International; Lisa Williamson, Ward's Information Products;

Jeff Wischerth, European American Bank; Labat Yancey, Equifax; Anissa Yates, Experian; Steve Zeisel, Consumer Bankers Association; Steve Zwillinger, Department of Education.

Chapter 4: Basic Banking

Heatherun Allison, Federal Reserve Bank; Kent Allison, Price-WaterhouseCoopers; Karen Altfest, L.J. Altfest & Company; Lew Altfest, L.J. Altfest & Company; Caryl Austrian, Federal Deposit Insurance Corporation; Peter Bakstansky, Federal Reserve Bank of New York; Brad Ball, Citibank; Linda A. Barlow, financial planner; David Barr, Federal Deposit Insurance Corporation; Richard Beebe, Bank of America; Debbie Bianucci, Bank Administration Institute; Brian Black, Bank Administration Institute; Alexander Bove, law offices of Alexander Bove, Jr.; Dan Brennan, Federal Reserve Bank of St. Louis; Jim Bruene, Online Banking Report; Neal Chambliss, Furash & Company; Diane Coffey, The Dreyfus Corporation; Jeff Comerford, The Equitable; Troy B. Daum, Wealth Analytics, Inc.; Elda Di Re, Ernst & Young; Lorna Doubet, Wells Fargo Bank; Fritz Elmendorf, Consumer Bankers Association; Steven Enright, Enright Financial Advisors; Allan Fisher, California Reinvestment Coalition; Linda Foley, Identity Theft Resource Center; Linda Gladson, Varner & Brandt, LLP; Elizabeth Greak, Corner & Greak Financial Consultants; John Hall, American Bankers Association; Eric Halperin, Center for Responsible Lending; Jennifer Harlan, Society Bank; Kathlyn Hoekstra, Federal Deposit Insurance Corporation; Gunnar Hughes, Twentieth Century Services; Sheldon Jacobs, The No-Load Fund Investor, Inc.; Caroline Jervey, Bauer Communications; Jerry Karbon, Credit Union National Association; Cathy Keary, Merrill Lynch & Company; Pat Keefe, Credit Union National Association; Ken Kehrer, Kenneth Kehrer & Associates; David Klavitter, Credit Union National Association; Tom Klipstone, General Motors Corporation; Dina Lee, Ernst & Young; Stephen Ledford, Global Concepts; Ross Levin, Accredited Investors; Gail Liberman, Bank Rate Monitor; Scott MacDonald, Southwestern Graduate School of Banking at Southern Methodist University; Jane Mahoney, The Equitable; Joyce Manchester, Congressional Budget Office; Brian

Mattes, The Vanguard Group; Greg McBride, Bankrate.com; Diana Mehl, BanxQuote; Michael Moebs, Moebs Services; Anne Moore, Synergistics Research Corporation; Edward L. Neumann, Furash & Company; Steve Norwitz, T. Rowe Price Associates; Karen Oetzel, Credit Union National Association; Obrea Poindexter, Division of Consumer & Community Affairs; Barbara Raasch, Ernst & Young; Christopher Renyi, Forrester Research, Inc.; Ellen Ringel, Price Waterhouse; Kevin Roach, Price Waterhouse; Richard Robida, Speer & Associates; Mark Rodgers, Citibank; Jay Rosenstein, Federal Deposit Insurance Corporation; Mimi Rossetti, Payment Systems; James Royal, Informa plc; Dr. John Sabelhaus, The Urban Institute; Pam Sabin, Fiserv.com; Judith Saxe, Kronish, Lieb, Weiner & Hellman; Joel A. Schoenmeyer, attorney at law; Kyle Selberg, Banking MyWay.com; Dr. Janice Shields, Center of Study for Responsive Law; Robert Siciliano, IDTheftSecurity.com; Dr. Jonathan Skinner, University of Virginia; Barton Sotnick, Federal Reserve Bank of New York; Chrissy Snyder, Janus Capital Corporation; William Speciale, David L. Babson & Company; Virginia Stafford, American Bankers Association; Ellen Stuart, Chemical Bank; Michele Stuvin, Executive Enterprises; Jack Tatom, Federal Reserve Bank of St. Louis; Paul Thompson, Credit Union National Association; Joseph Votava, Nixon, Peabody Attorneys at Law; Chad Watkins, Informa plc; Sandra Weiksner, Cleary, Gottlieb, Steen & Hamilton.

Chapter 5: All You Really Need to Know About Investing

Camilla Altamura, Lipper, Inc.; Lew Altfest, L. J. Altfest & Company; Mark Beauchamp, North American Securities Administrators Association; Jennifer Bright, R.L. Polk & Company; Jim Cain, Lehman Brothers; Lisa Cholnoky, Smith Barney; Peter Cinquegrani, Investment Company Institute; Mark Coler, Mercer & Associates; John Collins, Investment Company Institute; Bob Connor, Smith Barney; Pete Crane, iMoneynet, Inc; Kim Crawley, Morgan Stanley & Company; Don Criniti, Fidelity Investments; Diane Cullen, Dalbar Financial Services; Jon M. Diat, Standard & Poor's; Courtney Goethals Dobrow, Morningstar, Inc.; Holly Duncan, Financial Engines, Inc.; Richard Erickson, USAA; Dominic Falaschetti, Ibbotson Associates; Georgina Fiordalisi, Duff & Phelps Credit Rating Company; Nick Gendron, Lehman Brothers; Lynne Goldman, Cerulli Associates; Trista Hannan, Morningstar, Inc.; Rowena Itchon, T. Rowe Price Associates; Sheldon Jacobs, The No-Load Fund Investor, Inc.; Paula Kahanek, Ibbotson Associates; Dawn Kahler, Wiesenberger/Thomson Financial; Charles Kassouf, Mercer & Associates; Teri Kilduff, Fidelity Investments; Russ Kinnel, Morningstar, Inc.; Patrice Kozlowski, The Dreyfus Corporation; Annette Larson, Morningstar, Inc.; Keith Lawson, Investment Company Institute; Marilyn Leiker, Lipper Analytical Services; Mark N. Lindblom, Morgan Stanley & Company; Stephanie Linkous, United Services Advisors; Pam Livingston, E*Trade; Jeanine Magill, Morningstar, Inc.; John Markese, American Association of Individual Investors; Brian Mattes, The Vanguard Group; Patrick McVeigh, Franklin Research & Development; Norman Mehl, BanxQuote; Bob Mescal, Institute for Econometric Research; Marilyn Morrison, Fidelity Investments; Chip Norton, IBC/Donoghue; Steve Norwitz, T. Rowe Price Associates; Roger Nyhus, Frank Russell Company; Glen King Parker, Institute of Econometric Research; Chris Phillips, Frank Russell Company; Teri Redinger, IBC/Donoghue; Matthew Scott, Domini Social Equity Funds; Mo Shafroth, Charles Schwab & Company; Ramy Shalaan, Wiesenberger/Thomson Financial; Kimberly Stamel, Morningstar, Inc.; Tom Taggart, Charles Schwab & Company; Thomas Tays, United Services Advisors; Jon Teall, Lipper Analytical Services; Lukasz Thieme, Lipper, Inc.; Robyn Tice, Fidelity Investments; Maurice Turner, Working Assets Capital Management; Julie Ann Urban, Ibbotson Associates; Michael Van Dam, Morningstar, Inc.; Andrea Vassallo, Financial Engines, Inc.; Ken Volpert, The Vanguard Group; Bob Waid, Wilshire Associates; John Worth, The Vanguard Group; Mark Wright, Morningstar, Inc.

Chapter 6: The Brave New World of 401(k)s

Kent Allison, PricewaterhouseCoopers; Ted Barna, PriceWaterhouseCoopers; Harvey Berger, Grant Thornton; Andrea Bierstein,

Western New England College School of Law; Joanna Bolden, American Association of Retired Persons; Jack Bonné, Gateway Asset Management; Kent Brunette, American Association of Retired Persons; Anthony Burke, Internal Revenue Service; Heather Chappel, PricewaterhouseCoopers; Steve Ciolino, Ernst & Young; Joe Conway, Towers Perrin; Gloria Della, Department of Labor; Asma Emneina, Financial Engines; Steven Enright, Enright Financial Advisors; Andrew Eschtruth, Center for Retirement Research; Wilson Fadely, Internal Revenue Service; Karen Ferguson, Pension Rights Center; Edward Ferrigno, Profit Sharing / 401(k) Council of America; Martin Fleisher, pension consultant; Phil Gambino, Social Security Administration; Jerry Gattegno, Deloitte & Touche; Hal Glassman, Department of Labor; Mary Ann Green, MBL Life Assurance Corporation; Tom Hakala, KPMG Peat Marwick; Ed Hansen, Mercer & Associates; Cindy Hounsell, Women's Institute for a Secure Retirement (WISER); Christopher L. Jones, Financial Engines; Richard Koski, Buck Consultants; Ross Levin, Accredited Investors; Tom Margenau, Social Security Administration; John Markese, American Association of Individual Investors; Doug Mollin, Enright, Mollin, Cascio & Ramusevic, Inc.; Mike Packard, Pension Benefits Guaranty Corporation; Glenn Pape, Ernst & Young; R. Michael Parry, American Planning Group; Carolyn Pemberton, Employee Benefit Research Institute; Stephanie Poe, Mercer & Associates; Mark Puccia, Standard & Poor's; Tangela Richardson, Social Security Administration; Robert Runde, American Planning Group; Rania Sedhom, Buck Consultants; Christine Seltz, Hewitt Associates; Greg Spencer, Bureau of the Census; Susan Stawick, Internal Revenue Service; David Strauss, Pension Benefits Guaranty Corporation; Jack Vanderhei, Employee Benefit Research Institute; James Velten, Coopers & Lybrand; Paul Westbrook, Westbrook Financial Advisors; David Wray, Profit Sharing / 401(k) Council of America; Caryn Zappone, Hewitt Associates.

Chapter 7: Oh, Give Me a Home

Gopal Ahluwalia, National Association of Home Builders; Rick Beebe, Bank of America; Mark Beal, CPA; David W. Bennett, FMC

Financial Group; Mark Berman, The Townsend Consulting Group; David Berson, Federal National Mortgage Association (Fannie Mae); Katherine Billings, Federal Home Loan Mortgage Corporation (Freddie Mac); Amy Bonitatibus, Federal Home Mortgage Corporation (Fannie Mae); Mary Burt, National Association of Mortgage Brokers; Raschelle Burton, Federal National Mortgage Corporation (Fannie Mae); Kevin Bussell, Rent.net; Mark Calabria, National Association of Realtors; Michael Carliner, National Association of Home Builders; Pam Carmichael, HOME Inc.; Andrew Carswell, National Association of Home Builders; Ed Chang; Brian Chapelle, Mortgage Bankers Association of America; Laura Clavier, Merrill Lynch & Company; Wayne Collett, Countrywide Funding Corporation; Nancy Condon, Federal Home Loan Mortgage Corporation (Freddie Mac); William A. Connelly, Department of Housing & Urban Development; Gail Cunningham, National Foundation for Credit Counseling; Josh Dare, Federal National Mortgage Association (Fannie Mae); Douglas Duncan, Mortgage Bankers Association; Michelle Elliott, National Association of Home Builders; Robert Engelstad, Federal National Mortgage Association (Fannie Mae); John Ferchen, Norwest; Mark Ferrulo, Florida Public Interest Research Group (PIRG); Lauren Francis, JPMorgan Chase; Monica Gallagher, Hewitt Associates; Joe Gilvary, Bureau of the Census; Vince Gisonti, Deloitte & Touche; Elizabeth Greak, Corner & Greak Financial Consultants; Ginna Green, Center for Responsible Lending; Keith Gumbinger, HSH Associates; Steven Haugen, Bureau of Labor Statistics; Kevin Hawkins, Federal National Mortgage Association (Fannie Mae); Mollie Hightower, National Association of Mortgage Brokers; Liz Johnson, National Association of Realtors; Ted Jones, Real Estate Research Center; Joel Kan, Mortgage Bankers Association; Cathy Keary, Merrill Lynch & Company; Carolyn Kemp, Mortgage Bankers Association; Sam Khater, National Association of Realtors; Alfred King, Federal National Mortgage Association (Fannie Mae); Andrew Kochera, National Association of Home Builders; Doug Krug, Norwest; Mindy La Branche, National Council of State Housing Agencies; Toni Langkau, New York State Housing Authority; Sandy Levy, Universal Lending; John Lewis, G.E. Capital; William Lloyd, Norwest Mortgage; Dick Manuel, Department of Housing & Urban Development; Howard Marder, New

York State Housing Authority; Greg Martin, Draper & Kramer, Inc.; Laura Maxwell, Deloitte & Touche; Daniel McCue, Joint Center for Housing Studies at Harvard University; Ken McKinnon, Department of Veterans Affairs; Jason Menke, Wells Fargo Bank; Ed Mierzwinski, U.S. Public Interest Research Group (PIRG); Walter Molony, National Association of Realtors; Paul Mondor, Mortgage Bankers Association of America; Katie Monfre, Mortgage Guaranty Insurance Corporation; Larry Montague, Deloitte & Touche; Trish Morris, National Association of Realtors; Eileen Neely, Federal National Mortgage Association (Fannie Mae); Bonnie O'Dell, Federal National Mortgage Association (Fannie Mae); Martin O'Malley, Stratis Financial Corporation; David Olson, Wholesale Access; Forest Pafenberg, National Association of Realtors; Wendy Peca, Chicago Title and Trust; Sharon Peters, Institute of Real Estate Management; Julie Reeves, National Council of State Housing Agencies; Cheryl Regan, Federal Home Loan Mortgage Corporation (Freddie Mac); Sharon Ridenour, Norwest Mortgage; Sam Rogers, Center for Responsible Lending; Douglas Robinson, Federal Home Loan Mortgage Corporation (Freddie Mac); Vicki Rydell, Mortgage Bankers Association; Michelle Sabolich, Atomic Public Relations; Connie St. John, Bank of America; Margot Saunders, National Consumer Law Center; Michael Schlerf, Mortgage Bankers Association of America; Christine Seltz, Hewitt Associates; Jay Shackford, National Association of Home Builders; Adrian Skiles, Atlanta Mortgage Group; Dave Totaro, Dime Savings Bank; Rick Trilsch, Florida Public Interest Research Group (PIRG); John Tuccillo, National Association of Realtors; Robert Van Order, Federal Home Loan Mortgage Corporation (Freddie Mac); Bob Visini, LoanPerformance LLC; John H. Vogel, Tuck School of Business Administration at Dartmouth College; Andrea Waas, National Association of Mortgage Brokers; Susan M. Wachter, The Wharton School, University of Pennsylvania; Margery Wasserman, National Association of Personal Financial Advisors; Sabrina White, Merrill Lynch & Company; William White, Department of Veterans Affairs; George Wilson, Department of Housing & Urban Development; Susan E. Woodward, mortgage market guru, Sand Hill Econometrics; Lemar C. Wooley, Department of Housing and Urban Development; Jean Wussow, National Association of Realtors; Kris Yamamoto, Countrywide Funding Corporation; Catherine Zimring, Countrywide Funding Corporation.

Chapter 8: Insurance: What You Need and What You Don't

Roy Assad, RBA Insurance Strategies; Rich Bailey, Unumprovident; Bob Barney, Compulife; Kathy Bell, Progressive Auto Insurance; Kip Biggs, State Farm Insurance Company; Birny Birnbaum, Consumers Union and the Center for Economic Justice; Bob Bland, Quotesmith; Phyllis Bonfield, American Society of Chartered Life Underwriters; Joseph Bosnack, Sr., Arthur Rothlein Agency; Ann H. Brockmeyer, Hartmann & Associates; Steve Brostoff, American Council of Life Insurers; Bruce Bruscia, InterWest Insurance Services; Karen Burger, American Institute for Chartered Property & Casualty Underwriters; Anthony Burke, Internal Revenue Service; John Calagna, New York State Department of Insurance; Brenda Cargile, Federal Crime Insurance Program; Dee Caruso, Illinois Department of Insurance; Paul Cholette, Blue Cross & Blue Shield Association; Diane Coffey, American Council on Life Insurance; Mark Connor, Department of Labor; Richard Coorsh, Health Insurance Association of America; Sam Cunningham, Anderson & Anderson Benefits Insurance Brokers; Glenn Daily, fee-only insurance consultant; Gloria Della, Employee Benefits Security Administration; Dan Devine, Employee Benefit Research Institute; Jack Dolan, American Council of Life Insurers; Bill Dommasch, Geico; Henry Dowdle, Provident Life & Accident Insurance Company; Pam Drellow, Blue Cross & Blue Shield Association; Rob Eddy, National Association of Insurance and Financial Advisors; Andrew Ede, MassMutual Life Insurance Company; Susan Farmer, American Society of Chartered Life Underwriters; Terrence Fergus, KPMG Peat Marwick; Mary Fortune, UNUM; LaToya Gardner, Allstate Insurance Company; Scott Garland, State Farm Insurance Company; Anne Getz, Moody's Investors Services; Terrence Gordon, Avis Rent-a-Car System; Ed Graves, The American College; Gene Grebowski, American Council on Life Insurance; Paul Gribbons, Massachusetts Mutual Life Insurance Company; Don Haas, Haas Financial Services; Karen Hamilton, American Institute for Chartered Property Casualty Underwriters; Ed Hansen, Mercer; Judith Hill, The American College; Rick Hill, 20th Century Insurance Company; Katherine Hoffman, National Association of Professional Insurance Agents; Dr. Erin Holve, AcademyHealth; Charles Horne, Amica Mutual Insurance Company; James Hunt, Consumer Federation of America; Robert Hunter, Consumer Federation of America; Ted Huntington, Professional Insurance Agents of California & Nevada; Amy Ingram, Termquote; Kenneth Ingram, Termquote; Matthew J. Jachelski, Financial Solutions Group, Inc.; Linda Jackson, Department of Labor; Donald Jayne, Executive Financial Systems; James Johnson, UNUM; Chuck Jones, ChoicePoint Asset Company; Peter Katt, independent life insurance advisor; Susan Keller, Golden Eagle Insurance Company; Dr. Peter Kensicki, East Kentucky University; Chris Ketchum, American Institute for Chartered Property Casualty Underwriters; Rick Koski, Buck Consultants; Amy Kraus, Mutual of Omaha Insurance Company; Randy Lamm, Allstate Insurance Company; Arlene Lilly, American Council of Life Insurance; Eliot Lipson, independent insurance consultant; Dick Luedke, State Farm Insurance Company; Jim Marks, Society of Chartered Property Casualty Underwriters; Greg Marsh, Geico; Brandi Marth, Fireman's Fund Insurance Company; Robert Marvin, Internal Revenue Service; Judith Maurer, Low Load Insurance Services, Inc.; Keith Maurer, Low Load Insurance Services, Inc.; Mike Mayers, Beall, Garner, Screen & Geare Company; Larry Mayewski, A.M. Best Company; Ken McDonnell, Employee Benefit Research Institute; Wayne McHargue, American United Life Insurance Company; Jennifer McInnis, Amica Mutual Insurance Company; Annalise McKean-Marcus, Hertz Corporation; Robert Miller, New York Life Insurance Company; Al Minor, Health Insurance Association of America; Tom Monson, State Farm Insurance Company; Rhonda Moritz, A.M. Best Company; Todd Muller, Independent Insurance Agents of America; Tim Murphy, Northwestern Mutual Life Insurance Company; Nan Nases, Illinois Department of Insurance; Haig Neville, Haig Neville Associates; Eric Nordman, National Association of Insurance Commissioners; Mike Norton, UNUM; Donald Oakes, Society of Chartered Property Casualty

Underwriters; Mike Odom, Blue Shield of California; Bill O'Neill, Standard & Poor's; Kendall-Leigh O'Neill, Time Warner; John Paganelli, First Transamerica Life Insurance Company; Jerry Parsons, State Farm Insurance Company; Carolyn Pemberton, Employee Benefit Research Institute; Nancy Peskin, Metropolitan Life Insurance Company; Chris Petrocelli, Petrocelli Group; Irving Pfeffer, insurance consultant; Tim Pfeifer, consulting actuary; Jerome Phillip, Mutual of Omaha Insurance Company; Stephanie Poe, Mercer; Mark Prindle, Risk Management Solutions; Diana Reace, Hewitt Associates; Donna Reichle, National Automobile Dealers Association; John Roman, American Association of Preferred Provider Organizations; Fred Rumack, Buck Consultants; Walter Runkle, Consumer Credit Insurance Association; Jeanne Salvatore, Insurance Information Institute; Bob Sasser, State Farm Insurance Company; Paul Schattenberg, USAA; Tracy Schauer, IDEA; Iris Shaffer, Blue Cross & Blue Shield of Illinois; David Seldin, Blue Shield of California; Craig P. Shanley, Amica Mutual Insurance Company; Tracy Sherman, UNUM; Dr. Harold Skipper, Department of Risk Management & Insurance Research, Georgia State University; Judy Snelson, Allied Insurance Agencies of America; Camille Sorosiak, American Hospital Association; Steve Stark, Selectquote; Dale Stephenson, National Conference of Insurance Guarantee Funds; Morey Stettner, insurance consultant; Mark Stevens, Federal Emergency Management Agency; Dottye Stewart, Wholesale Insurance Network; Jennie Storey, Provident Life & Accident Insurance Company; Ron Sunderman, Skogman Carlson Insurance; Phil Supple, State Farm Insurance Company; Doug Tillett, National Association of Life Underwriters; Julie Vokracka, American Express Company; Billy Watson, Anderson & Watson; Lisa Wetherby, Society of Financial Service Professionals; Don White, The Group Health Association of America; Eric Wiening, American Institute for Chartered Property & Casualty Underwriters; Rolf Winch, Lifetime Financial Partners LLC; Scott Witt, Witt Actuarial Services; Jim Woods, lowestpremium.com; Loretta Worters, Insurance Information Institute; Gay Yellen, Ameritas Life Insurance Company; Mark Zagaroli, State Farm Insurance Company; John Zarubnicky, First Transamerica Life Insurance Company; Robert Zirkelbach, America's Health Insurance Plans.

Chapter 9: How to Make Your Life Less Taxing

Nancy Anderson, H&R Block; John Battaglia, Deloitte & Touche; Henri Bersoux, Ernst & Young; Andrea Bierstein, Kirby, McInerney & Squire; Robert Blodgett, TurboTax; Anthony Burke, Internal Revenue Service; Joan Carroll, Coopers & Lybrand; William Church, Ernst & Young; John Collins, Investment Company Institute; Gary DuBoff, Ernst & Young; Ed Emerman, A. Foster Higgins & Company; Wilson Fadely, Internal Revenue Service; David Fridling, Towers Perrin, Jerry Gattegno, Deloitte Tax LLP; Stephen Gold, Tax Foundation; Steven Gold, Center for the Study of the States; Jeffrey Gotlinger, Ernst & Young; Nadine Habousha, Arthur Andersen; Tom Hakala, KPMG Peat Marwick; David Hochstim, Bear Stearns; Ken Hubenak, Internal Revenue Service; Malin Jennings, Investment Company Institute; Judy Keisling, H&R Block; Sidney Kess, CPA; Stuart Kessler, Goldstein Golub Kessler & Company; Roger Kirby, Kirby, McInerney & Squire; John Koegel, Grant Thornton; Dina Lee, Ernst & Young; Terry Lemons, Internal Revenue Service; L. Harold Levinson, Vanderbilt University; Glenn Liebman, Ernst & Young; Norm Magnuson, Associated Credit Bureaus; Tom Margenau, Social Security Administration; Brian Mattes, The Vanguard Group; Daniel D. Morris, Morris + D'Angelo; Marilyn Morrison, Fidelity Investments; Colette Murphy, Ernst & Young; Tom Ochsenschlager, Grant Thornton; Maggie O'Donovan-Bolton, Coopers & Lybrand; Glenn Pape, Ayco Company; Jodi Patterson, Internal Revenue Service; Sylvia Pozarnsky, Ernst & Young; Todd Ransom, H&R Block; Ellen Ringel, PriceWaterhouseCoopers; Diane Rivers, tax attorney; Don Roberts, Internal Revenue Service; Jeff Saccacio, Coopers & Lybrand; Sheri Sankner, BDO Seidman; Bertram Schaeffer, Ernst & Young; Martin Shenkman, tax attorney; Susan Stawick, Internal Revenue Service; Ronald Stone, Stone & Associates; Richard Stricof, BDO Seidman; Peter L. Tashman, CPA; Susan Van Alstyne, H&R Block; James E. Velten, Coopers & Lybrand; Mary Vogel, H&R Block; Sidney Weinman, Research Institute of America; Craig Wolman, Ernst & Young; Paul Yurachek, Gurtz & Associates; John Ziegelbauer, Grant Thornton.

INDEX

ABOUT THE AUTHOR

Beth Kobliner has been writing and speaking on personal finance for more than fifteen years. She was a staff writer at *Money* magazine for eight years, wrote the money column for *Glamour* magazine for six, and has also contributed numerous articles to the *New York Times*. A regular on television and radio, she has appeared several times on *Oprah* to talk about personal finance and has been a repeat commentator on CNN, MSNBC, NBC's *Today* show, CBS, ABC, and various PBS and NPR programs, including public radio's *Marketplace*. She began her career researching and writing more than one hundred columns for the personal finance pioneer Sylvia Porter, whose syndicated column appeared in over 150 newspapers nationwide.

Kobliner has also been an active spokesperson for the financial concerns of Americans in their twenties and thirties; she frequently speaks to college and corporate audiences, addressing a range of topics including credit card debt, student loan policy, investing, and long-term savings. She sits on the board of the Women's Institute for a Secure Retirement (WISER) and has testified before a U.S. Senate policy committee on young people's attitudes toward Social Security. She is an honorary advisor to the National Academy of Social Insurance and was a member of the Center for Strategic and International Studies' National Commission on Retirement Policy.

Kobliner graduated from Brown University and lives with her husband and three children in New York City.